When the United States
Invaded Russia

When the United States Invaded Russia

Woodrow Wilson's Siberian Disaster

Carl J. Richard

ROWMAN & LITTLEFIELD PUBLISHERS, INC.
Lanham • Boulder • New York • Toronto • Plymouth, UK

Published by Rowman & Littlefield Publishers, Inc.
A wholly owned subsidiary of The Rowman & Littlefield Publishing Group, Inc.
4501 Forbes Boulevard, Suite 200, Lanham, Maryland 20706
www.rowman.com

10 Thornbury Road, Plymouth PL6 7PP, United Kingdom

British Library Cataloguing in Publication Information Available

Library of Congress Cataloging-in-Publication Data
Richard, Carl J.
  When the United States invaded Russia : Woodrow Wilson's Siberian disaster / Carl J. Richard.
      pages cm
  Includes bibliographical references and index.
  ISBN 978-1-4422-1989-2 (cloth : alkaline paper)—ISBN 978-1-4422-1990-8 (electronic) 1. Soviet Union—History—Allied intervention, 1918–1920. 2. Siberia (Russia)—History—Revolution, 1917–1921. 3. Wilson, Woodrow, 1856–1924.
4. United States. Army. American Expeditionary Forces. 5. Counterinsurgency—Soviet Union—History. 6. United States—Military relations—Soviet Union.
7. Soviet Union—Military relations—United States. 8. United States—Foreign relations—1913–1921. I. Title.
  DK265.42.U5R53 2013
  947.084'1—dc23
                                                                    2012030731

Printed in the United States of America

For Reinhart Kondert and Matthew Schott,
beloved mentors, colleagues, and friends

~

Contents

~

Preface

In 1987 I received a telephone call from *ABC News with Peter Jennings*. The Soviet government was protesting an ABC miniseries called *Amerika*, which depicted a fictional Soviet occupation of the United States. The Soviet complaint did not concern the miniseries' inane dialogue and wretched acting; rather, the essence of the Russian protest was, "We've never invaded you, but you once invaded us." This was news to the producers of *ABC News*, who had never heard of the American intervention in Siberia. After doing some quick research, they contacted me because I had published an article about the subject the previous year. Unfortunately, I was unable to assist them in achieving their primary objective, the location of a surviving American veteran of the campaign, then almost seventy years in the past.[1]

Despite the brief piece that aired on *ABC News* soon after, most Americans remain unaware of the Siberian intervention, which still receives little or no attention in most textbooks. This is unfortunate because of the light that the intervention sheds on the survival of the Soviet regime and on subsequent Soviet-American relations and because of its pertinence to the numerous issues raised by counterinsurgency campaigns, a subject that has become crucial to the United States in recent years in the wake of the Afghanistan and Iraq interventions. One of the earliest U.S. counterinsurgency campaigns outside the Western Hemisphere, the Siberian intervention was a harbinger of things to come.

By contrast with their American counterparts, Soviet historians devoted tremendous attention to the Siberian intervention during the Cold War.

These historians contended that the United States was the instigator of the intervention, bullying its allies in a single-minded crusade to overthrow the Soviet government. They claimed that the United States attempted to partition Russia into a number of small states in order to restrict its power. They insisted that the Red Army smashed the gigantic Allied forces, already weakened by communist sentiment in their own ranks, compelling them to flee Russia. Even the most radical New Left historians in the United States did not defend these assertions, all of which postdated World War II and were flatly contradicted by the available evidence.[2]

Yet the Soviets had legitimate reasons for the bitterness they felt towards the United States, and knowledge of the Siberian intervention is essential to understanding their persistent fear and distrust of American officials. To a Russian child, the Soviet version of the intervention became as familiar as the story of George Washington and the cherry tree to an American child. While both stories were fictions, both contained elements of truth. George Washington never cut down the cherry tree, and the Red Army never defeated the small Allied forces in Russia. But Washington was an honest man by all accounts, and also by all accounts, the Allies ended their intervention in Siberia because they knew that they could not muster sufficient forces from their war-weary populaces to defeat the Red Army.

The United States government dispatched approximately 5,500 troops to northern Russia around the same time that it sent 8,500 soldiers to Siberia. I have chosen to deal exclusively with the Siberian intervention because American troops in North Russia served under British command and, thus, had far less control over operations there. As Christopher Lasch has noted, the North Russian intervention was "plainly directed at Germany" in its initial stage and was originally approved by the Bolsheviks. On March 5, 1918, Leon Trotsky, Soviet Commissar for Foreign Affairs, sent a telegram to the Murmansk Soviet, ordering it to cooperate with the Allied forces in the region against the Germans. Much like the Siberian intervention, however, the North Russian intervention soon became an overtly anti-Bolshevik operation. The United States removed its forces from northern Russia in the spring of 1919, almost a full year before American soldiers departed from Siberia.[3]

It should also be noted that there were Allied invasions of Russian soil in which the United States did not participate. The British sent an expedition into Transcaucasia with the intent of protecting oil fields from Turkish invaders, though these soldiers remained for a year after the armistice with the Central Powers ended the Turkish threat to the region. In the winter of 1918–1919, the French landed a small force along the northern coast of the

Black Sea. It accomplished nothing and withdrew quickly. Both the Finns and the Poles, recent subjects of the czars, took advantage of the Russian Civil War to invade western Russia. Finally, the Germans often failed to adhere even to the severe Treaty of Brest-Litovsk they had imposed on the Bolsheviks, invading Soviet areas continually until their own troubles on the Western Front made further incursions impossible.[4]

I have returned to the Siberian intervention after more than two decades spent in an unrelated field partly because I believe it is an interesting and important story that still remains largely unknown to the American public, but also because I believe it can teach us valuable lessons about the extreme difficulties inherent in counterinsurgency campaigns and thus the general inadvisability of interventions, and about the absolute need to secure the widespread support of natives if such a campaign is to achieve success, lessons that American policymakers tragically ignored later in Vietnam.

In the following chapters I will discuss the disasters suffered by the Allies during World War I that caused them to pressure the United States to intervene, demonstrate that President Woodrow Wilson decided to send American soldiers to Siberia in July 1918 in order to assist Czechs and anti-Bolshevik Russians in re-creating the Eastern Front against the Central Powers, show that Wilson decided to continue the intervention after the armistice in order to overthrow the Soviet government and to prevent the Japanese from absorbing eastern Siberia, identify the various Allied proposals for dealing with Russia at the Paris Peace Conference, and chronicle the hardships suffered by the American Expeditionary Force in Siberia. It will become clear that the intervention failed to meet any of its objectives, either before or after the armistice. Indeed, Allied support for the corrupt, autocratic, and oppressive regime of Alexander Kolchak backfired completely, causing many Russians who were not previously Bolshevik to rally around the red banner in order to defend their homeland against what they regarded as a czarist clique backed by foreign imperialists.

Notes

1. Carl J. Richard, "The Shadow of a Plan: The Rationale behind Wilson's 1918 Siberian Intervention," *The Historian* 49 (November 1986): 64–84.

2. George F. Kennan, "Soviet Historiography and America's Role in the Intervention," *American Historical Review* 65 (January 1960): 302–3, 307; George F. Kennan, *Russia and the West under Lenin and Stalin* (Boston: Little, Brown, 1960), 118. For reference to Soviet historian A. E. Kunina's false contention in 1951 that the United States had been "the initiator" of the intervention, see Nikolai V. Sivachev, *Russia*

and the United States, trans. Olga Adler Titelbaum (Chicago: University of Chicago Press, 1979), 43, 274n10. Although Sivachev corrected this error and a few others made by previous Soviet historians, he continued to insist, against all available evidence, that American intervention occurred at the behest of investment banks, and placed the sum of American aid to White forces at a preposterous $4 billion. See p. 54.

3. Christopher Lasch, "American Intervention in Siberia: Reinterpretation," *Political Science Quarterly* 77 (June 1962): 205; Kennan, *Russia and the West under Lenin and Stalin*, 69.

4. Kennan, *Russia and the West under Lenin and Stalin*, 116–17.

Acknowledgments

I would like to thank James Dormon, Reinhart Kondert, Matthew Schott, and Amos Simpson, all of whom gave me sound advice and encouragement when I first undertook this subject in the 1980s. I would also like to express my gratitude to my colleagues Chad Parker, Chester Rzadkiewicz, and Eran Shalev, who read a more recent version of the manuscript and provided valuable insights. Additionally, I would like to thank my editor, Susan McEachern, for her unfailing enthusiasm and wisdom. As always, I would like to thank my precious wife, Debbie, my other half, for her unceasing prayers and support.

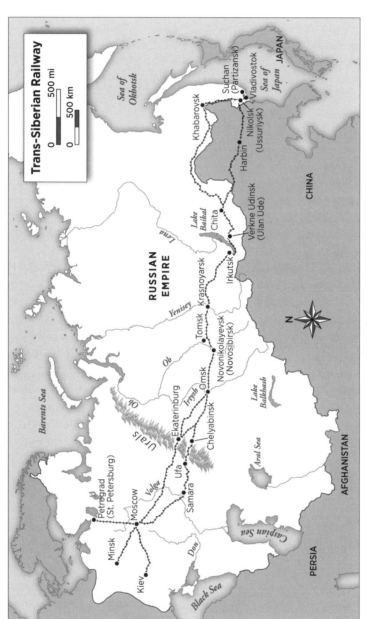

The Trans-Siberian Railway

CHAPTER ONE

~

The War to End All Wars

Only the dead have seen the end of war.

—George Santayana[1]

From 1914 to 1918 the nations of Europe focused their intelligence and energy on the perfection of the science of killing. Nations that had taken immense pride in calling themselves civilized were engaged in a campaign of slaughter on a scale that was unprecedented in the history of humankind. The number of young lives snuffed out in the struggle that was called "The Great War," before people began numbering their world conflicts, easily surpassed that of all previous wars.

To understand almost any twentieth- or twenty-first-century subject without understanding what occurred in World War I is difficult, if not impossible. It is like trying to comprehend the late medieval period while ig-noring the Great Plague. In addition to inaugurating modern warfare (tanks, machine guns, airplanes, and submarines all made their first appearance on a large scale in this war), the Great War had enduring political effects. The unprecedented carnage of the war led the Allies to impose the harsh Treaty of Versailles on Germany, which led, in turn, to the rise of Adolf Hitler and World War II. The war also led to the Bolshevik Revolution in Russia, which led, in turn, to a Cold War that lasted nearly half a century.

Like these other developments, the Siberian intervention finds its origin in the events of World War I. The disasters of that war eventually led to the departure of American soldiers for the distant land of Siberia.

Causes of World War I

Numerous volumes have been written to dispute the causes of World War I. Suffice it to say that there were many causes. Several powerful ideologies of the nineteenth century, such as nationalism, imperialism, militarism (increased by ignorance of the lethal nature of modern warfare since Europe had not suffered a general war in a century and its generals refused to learn the lessons of the U.S. Civil War, the Boer War, and the Russo-Japanese War), and fatalism about the inevitability of war spawned by Social Darwinism all played key roles, as did poor leadership and the development of alliance systems. By the start of the war in 1914 the Allies, which included Great Britain, France, and Russia (joined by Italy in 1915), were arrayed against the Central Powers of Germany, Austria-Hungary, and Turkey. Far from fostering peace, as expected in traditional balance of power theory, this balance actually encouraged war because each side became confident in its ability to win. Finally, the military strategies of both sides called for preemptive strikes, thereby making war more likely than peace after the onset of a crisis, as each side rushed to implement its strategy ahead of its opponent. For instance, Germany's Schlieffen Plan centered on knocking France out of the war in the West before turning to face Russia in the East. Thus, the assassination of Franz Ferdinand, the heir to the Austro-Hungarian throne, by a Bosnian nationalist, with the connivance of some members of the Serbian government, set in train a cascade of events that led inexorably to war. When the Austrians moved to invade Serbia, Russia mobilized its massive forces to help its traditional ally, prompting Germany to mobilize its own forces and initiate the Schlieffen Plan out of the fear that a Russian invasion of Germany would end all hope of averting a two-front war. The German invasion of Belgium in preparation for the invasion of France, in turn, led both France and Britain to declare war against Germany.[2]

Trench Warfare and Its Consequences

Ten million men were killed in World War I. France lost 17 percent of its soldiers, 1.7 million out of a little over nine million. Russia also lost 1.7 million men, Britain one million, Germany two million, and Austria-Hungary 1.5 million. The bodies of more than half of those killed in the West, and an even higher percentage in the East, were never recovered. Many survivors were badly mutilated.[3]

One reason that the casualties were so numerous is that the trench warfare that characterized the Western Front heavily favored the defensive, so that it was extremely difficult for an attacker to make any progress. When the Germans were stopped short of Paris on the Marne River, they retreated and entrenched themselves on favorable ground. Within a brief time, both sides possessed a line of trenches that extended 475 miles from the North Sea to neutral Switzerland, a line that changed little for almost three years. The ten-foot-deep trenches were fronted by massive entanglements of barbed wire and backed by an increasingly elaborate system of reserve trenches connected by communications trenches that extended for miles, a system so complicated it soon required guides and street signs. Whenever one side attacked, its massive artillery barrage generally accomplished little except to ruin any chance of achieving surprise. (Since telephone and telegraph wires were almost always immediately destroyed in the opening bombardment, and primitive radios, which could not yet transmit voices, only Morse code, and relied on massive batteries, were too slow to be useful and too unwieldy to be carried into battle, armies were forced to use such primitive means as flags, runners, and carrier pigeons to transmit the information necessary to target and retarget their artillery barrages accurately.) Attacking infantrymen crawled out of their own trenches, carrying sixty to eighty-five pounds of equipment on their backs (at a time when the average recruit weighed only 132 pounds), and marched across the "no man's land" of a few hundred yards that normally rested between the trenches to almost certain death, mowed down by rifle fire and machine guns while attempting to cut through dense tangles of barbed wire that were sometimes over a hundred yards deep. Even when the attackers managed to take the opposing trenches, they were almost immediately set upon by fresh, lethal reserves.[4]

Nevertheless, the military cultures on both sides were painfully slow to abandon their semi-mystical, Napoleonic faith in "the spirit of the offensive," which taught that a determination to continue attacking despite heavy casualties would bring victory. This stubbornness was exacerbated by the rareness with which top-ranking generals visited the front lines and their obliviousness when they did so. A British soldier wrote: "A fortnight after some exploit, a field-marshal or a divisional general comes down to a battalion to thank it for its gallant conduct, and fancies for a moment, perchance, that he is looking at the men who did the deed of valour, and not a large draft that has just been brought up from England and the base to fill the gap. He should ask the services of the chaplain and make his congratulations in the grave-yard or go to the hospital and make them there."[5]

In the Trenches at Verdun, 1916. Snark/Art Resource, NY.

Verdun

Although there were 850,000 European casualties of war in 1914, and two and a half million in 1915, the level of carnage reached new heights in 1916. At Verdun, General Erich von Falkenhayn, commander of German forces on the Western Front, hoped to draw French units into his "mincing machine" of heavy artillery. Falkenhayn knew that French pride would demand that Verdun be defended, though it jutted out of the French line as an awkward salient. He also knew that the French Chief of Staff, General Joseph Joffre, had neglected the defense of the old fortress. Thus, on February 21, 1916, the Germans rained 80,000 artillery shells on a fifteen-mile segment of the French line, the first of 20 million that would be fired by both sides in the battle zone by June 23 and would reduce forests to splinters and villages to rubble. The Germans easily broke through the line, so that Verdun appeared lost. Only one light railway and one road remained to supply it. Had the Germans destroyed these, they probably would have not only captured Verdun but also the entire French army stationed there, since Joffre had threatened court-martial for any officer who ordered a retreat.[6]

The French sent General Henri-Philippe Petain to command Verdun at this point. Besides inspiring confidence in his soldiers, Petain also widened the supply lanes to Verdun, so that it could be supplied and reinforced safely. The French also benefited from the willingness of the British to assume more of the Western Front, thus freeing more French soldiers to reinforce the fort, as well as from an Italian offensive on the Isonzo River in northern Italy and a Russian offensive at Lake Narocz in Lithuania, both of which distracted the Germans.[7]

Although the French managed to hold the old fortress in the Battle of Verdun, over 200,000 men were killed on each side. A Frenchman who participated in that campaign wrote, "The bread we ate, the stagnant water we drank, everything we touched had a rotten smell, owing to the fact that the earth around us was literally stuffed with corpses." It was the only prolonged offensive on the Western Front in which the attacking side did not lose more troops than the defending party. This anomaly was the result of the German practice of sending "advance groups," guinea pigs whose sole function was to draw enemy fire, in order to ascertain the location of least resistance along the front before the main force was committed to battle.[8]

The Somme

Douglas Haig, who had become Commander of the British Expeditionary Force in France in December 1915, was not disturbed by the extent of the French losses at Verdun. Believing that his own troops would succeed where the French had failed, Haig planned a summer offensive along the Somme that would be dominated by British soldiers.[9]

Everything went wrong. Haig was "overruled by his commanders" when he suggested using advance groups as the Germans had at Verdun. In the Allies' opening bombardment, 1500 guns fired one million shells, but only 450 of these guns were heavy artillery, the type necessary for destroying the concrete machine gun nests of the Germans. Also, Haig's field commander made matters worse by selecting an area of bombardment that was too wide, so that some machine gun nests were completely untouched when Allied troops advanced towards them on July 1, 1916. Furthermore, the French overruled British proposals that the attack be made at or before dawn, contending that their artillerymen required "good observation" for firing. The result, of course, was good observation for the many German machine gunners who had been largely unaffected by the preliminary bombardment. In addition, the British infantrymen were ordered to attack in close formation—in the words of military historian B. H. Liddell Hart, "symmetrically aligned, like rows of nine-pins ready to be knocked over." Each soldier carried sixty-six pounds of equipment on his back. It was "difficult to get out of a trench, impossible to move much quicker than a slow walk." Although the gaps that the British had cut in their own wire in preparation for the attack facilitated German targeting of their troops, aiming was largely unnecessary. A German machine gunner recalled, "When we started firing, we just had to load and reload. They went down in their hundreds. You didn't have to aim, we just fired into them."[10]

On the first day alone the British lost nearly 60,000 men. The Allies corrected only some of their tactical errors and continued the offensive. By the time November mud ended the Somme offensive, the British had experienced the greatest military catastrophe in their history, suffering 420,000 casualties, the French 194,000, and the Germans over 600,000. The German total would not have been so high had not a German general, emulating the Allies, ordered that every yard lost be taken by counterattack.[11]

The French Mutiny

Both the French and the British failed to learn the lessons of 1916. In 1917 French General Robert Nivelle launched a new offensive on the Western Front that was equally disastrous. The Germans shrewdly adopted a tactic of "defense in depth" that left the front line almost empty, while an intermediate zone behind was held by machine gunners stationed in shell holes and other strong positions, and the real strength of the defense lay in reserves deployed outside artillery range 10,000–20,000 yards behind the front. The resulting casualties were so demoralizing that French soldiers launched a mutiny, a sort of military strike in which they pledged to defend their own trenches but refused to continue attacking the enemy's.[12]

The Flanders Offensive

Nevertheless, the imperturbable Haig persuaded the reluctant British War Cabinet to approve a new offensive in Flanders for 1917. Liddell Hart later charged that Haig was able to secure permission by promising not to engage in an all-out assault on German positions but rather to take a gradual approach that he had already categorically ruled out in conversations with his own generals. British Prime Minister David Lloyd George opposed the offensive, saying, "We shall be attacking the strongest army in the world, entrenched in the most formidable positions with an actual inferiority of numbers. I do not pretend to know anything about the rules of strategy, but curious indeed must be the military conscience which could justify an attack under such conditions." Yet the War Cabinet approved the offensive, due partly to the desire to capture German submarine bases in Belgium.[13]

According to Liddell Hart, Haig's second deception occurred after the offensive began. In order to gain a continuation of the offensive, which was obviously failing miserably, Haig grossly exaggerated the number of enemy casualties in his reports to the War Cabinet. Before Haig guided Lloyd George on a tour of his "prisoner cages," he replaced healthy German prisoners with gaunt ones in order to demonstrate the success of the offensive in demoralizing and debilitating the Germans.[14]

Perhaps most importantly, Liddell Hart claimed, Haig failed to inform the War Cabinet about reports he had received from General Headquarters to the effect that the Ypres area, where he planned to make his primary assault, was a reclaimed marshland that would revert to its original state if its drainage system were destroyed by a prolonged bombardment. In fact, the commander of Haig's Intelligence Staff had also informed him that records for the last eighty years indicated that heavy rains broke over Flanders in early August "with the regularity of Indian monsoons." Haig did not inform his superiors of this report, either. While there is no reason to doubt Liddell Hart's account, its flattering portrayal of Lloyd George steadfastly ignores the fact that he could have used his own authority as prime minister to suspend the campaign at any time he wished. Although Haig deserves most of the criticism he has received, Lloyd George's timidity was certainly no profile in courage, and his subsequent, largely successful efforts to pin all of the blame on Haig, whom he failed to replace even after the Flanders campaign, were unseemly at best.[15]

The Flanders offensive began on July 31, 1917. The bare plain would have made British plans obvious to the Germans, even if their two-week bombardment had not. Though over four million shells poured forth from 3,000 artillery guns, the British failed to destroy the German machine gun nests on the right, which were situated on high ground. Thus, the bombardment succeeded only in eliminating any chance of surprising the enemy and in making the battlefield a quagmire, a situation worsened by steady torrential downpours. The bombardment churned up the ground to a depth of ten feet, exposing corpses buried after earlier fighting. When a British officer was ordered to consolidate his position, he replied, "It is impossible to consolidate porridge." Although the British achieved some success on the left, only death awaited those unfortunates who were sent to the right. The Germans had strengthened this position, already one of the strongest German positions on the Western Front, both geographically and militarily, by constructing nine layers of defenses, including a line of listening posts in shell holes, three lines of trenches, machine gun posts and pillboxes, and counterattack units in concrete bunkers. In September Lloyd George again opposed continuation of the offensive but again deferred to the expertise of the same general he would later vilify. In October, some minor successes were achieved due to the sheer volume of artillery expended, causing Haig to tell war correspondents absurdly, "We are practically through the enemy's defenses." Soon after, the mud became so deep, and the assaults so costly, that even Haig felt obliged to discontinue the offensive.[16]

As the price for gaining a few hundred yards to the former village of Pass-chendaele, 70,000 British soldiers were killed, another 170,000 wounded, in a sea of mud. Liddell Hart described the field conditions faced by British soldiers during the Flanders offensive:

> The broken earth became a fluid clay; the little brooks and tiny canals became formidable obstacles, and every shell-hole a dismal pond; hills and valleys were but waves and troughs of a sea of mud. Still the guns churned the treacherous slime. Every day conditions grew worse. What had once been difficult now became impossible. The surplus water poured into the trenches as its natural outlet, and they became impassible for troops; nor was it possible to walk over the open field—men staggered wanly over duckboard tracks. Wounded men falling headlong into the shell-holes were in danger of drowning. Mules slipped from the tracks and were often drowned in the giant shell-holes alongside. Guns sank till they became useless; rifles caked and would not fire; even food was tainted with the inevitable mud. No battle in history was ever fought under such conditions.

When Haig's adjutant general finally visited the battlefield, he was overcome by the impossibility of what he and Haig had been ordering the men to do, and his eyes filled with tears. "Good God," he cried, "did we really send men to fight in that?" Haig himself never visited the front until 1918, the last year of the war.[17]

Even that experience apparently taught Haig very little. As late as 1926 he was still writing: "I believe that the value of the horse and the opportunity for the horse in the future are likely to be as great as ever. . . . Aeroplanes and tanks . . . are only accessories to the man and the horse, and I feel sure that as time goes by you will find as much use for the horse—the well-bred horse—as you have ever done in the past."[18]

The Flanders offensive devastated the Allies. First, it dealt a heavy blow to British morale, which had previously impressed the Germans. British soldiers surrendered in large numbers during the offensive, speaking bitterly against the officers who had sent them into the mud. Second, the heavy losses of the British early in the offensive convinced General Paul von Hindenburg and his underling General Erich Ludendorff, the chief planners of the German war effort, that they could afford to send several more divisions against the Italians and Russians. The additional divisions contributed to a major breakthrough against the Italians, nearly destroying the Italian army in the process, and proved fatal to the Russian Army. Finally, after the Flanders offensive it became apparent that the British and French needed more help to defeat the Central Powers. Having lost hundreds of thousands of their best soldiers in mad offensives, they could not hope to defeat the Central Powers alone.[19]

American Intervention in the War

The British and French looked partly to the United States for aid. The first step to receiving that aid had already come before the Flanders offensive on April 6, 1917, when the United States declared war on Germany. There were two causes of American intervention in World War I. The primary reason was that in January 1917 the Germans declared that they would renew their practice of unrestricted submarine warfare. Henceforth, any ship sighted in a specified zone around Great Britain would be sunk. The first such German campaign to destroy the British economy and force Britain's exit from the war had ended when President Woodrow Wilson had issued an ultimatum to the German government threatening war in April 1916. But the following January the Germans decided to renew the unrestricted submarine campaign based on the calculation that Germany could starve the British into submission in six months' time, as well as deprive France and Italy of vital British coal. If so, Germany would be able to win the war before the unprepared United States, with its small professional army of 108,000 soldiers, could make its power felt in Europe. In 1919 Ludendorff recalled concerning the German decision:

> The Chief of the Naval Staff, a friend of the Chancellor, but at the same time a warm partisan of the unrestricted submarine war, was confident that the campaign would have decisive results within six months. The loss of freight space and the reduction of overseas imports would produce economic difficulties in England that would render a continuance of the war impossible. In forming this view he did not rely merely on his own professional judgment, but was also supported by the opinions of the distinguished economists. The shortage of shipping would cut down the transport of munitions, and in particular the huge transport of war material from England to France, which could also be attacked directly.

The experts were wrong, of course. But the success of the German generals in overruling the civilian authorities in this crucial decision was indicative of the power they had come to wield.[20]

The second cause of the United States' declaration of war against Germany was the Zimmerman telegram, which had been intercepted by both the British and the U.S. State Department. In this telegram the German foreign minister instructed the German minister to Mexico to offer the Mexican government the restoration of Texas, New Mexico, and Arizona in exchange for help against the United States should war erupt between the nations. When Congress hesitated to give Wilson the authority to do whatever was necessary to protect American shipping, Wilson released the telegram. Shortly thereafter, the Germans sank three American ships, leading to a congressional declaration of war.[21]

The United States gave the Allies immediate financial and naval aid. When the United States entered the war, the Allies were on the verge of economic collapse. Great Britain was spending seven million pounds per day, part of which was expended in the form of loans to the other Allies. Against the objections of many Americans, the U.S. Treasury began advancing $500,000 per month to the Allies. The United States, which had spent the first few years of the war protesting vehemently against both sides' encroachments on the rights of neutrals at sea, began to enforce the blockade of Germany with a ruthlessness that put the British to shame. As Assistant Secretary of State Frank L. Polk told British Foreign Secretary Arthur Balfour, only half in jest: "It took Great Britain three years to reach a point where it was prepared to violate all the laws of blockade. You will find that it will take us only two months to become as great criminals as you are." Also, the light craft and listening devices of the U.S. Navy were particularly helpful to the British against German submarines, which sank 860,334 tons of British shipping in April 1917 alone, before convoys, mine barriers, destroyers, patrol boats, and aircraft succeeded in largely neutralizing them.[22]

The Eastern Front

But although the Allies were delighted to receive American financial and naval aid, what they really believed they needed most were more soldiers facing the Central Powers. It was obvious to everyone that it would be at least a year before a sizable American army could be organized, trained, and transported to France. Thus, the Allies had to turn elsewhere for the kind of help for which they were most desperate.[23]

The second logical place to look for aid—or, rather, more aid—was Russia. The Allies hoped that heavy Russian pressure on the Central Powers in the East would save them in the West. But the Russians had been faring even worse than the British and French. In 1914 the Russians had invaded eastern Prussia, only to have 92,000 of their 200,000 soldiers captured, and another 50,000 killed or wounded, at the Battle of Tannenberg. This defeat was caused by infighting between the Russian generals and by their practice of exchanging uncoded radio messages that signaled to the enemy their movements and intentions. In 1915 the Germans and Austrians captured over a million Russian soldiers in two separate campaigns in the Carpathian Mountains and Galicia in Poland. In 1916 the Russians' ill-organized campaign in Galicia cost them another 100,000 soldiers.[24]

Incompetent Russian generals concocted a legend to justify these stupendous defeats, suffered by armies that outnumbered their German and Austrian enemies, a legend that Lloyd George later repeated most vividly in his memoirs. According to this tall tale, the Russian army had virtually no rifles, much less heavy artillery or machine guns. Only one out of every four Russian soldiers received a rifle, and he was not given much ammunition with it. Very often, it was difficult to retrieve these rifles from the grasp of the dead, killed in large numbers by German artillery and machine guns, so that the supply soon dwindled even further. The Russians possessed few artillery guns with which to answer this murderous fire, and they were always quickly silenced by German barrages aimed at them or by lack of ammunition. Under such conditions the Russian soldiers could only remain at their posts, holding the picks and shovels with which they fought and waiting to be "killed like partridges," retreat, or surrender.[25]

This legend makes for compelling reading, but there is virtually no truth to it. The Russians did experience a shell shortage in 1915 as the result of the czarist government's failure to plan for a long war and of its officials' excessive reliance on foreign suppliers, a shortage that Russian generals learned to exaggerate and employ as justification for all of their debacles. But there was no shell shortage in 1914, and even in 1915 the Germans' artillery advantage in the East was less than the Allies' superiority in the West, an advantage that did the Allies no good there. Furthermore, by 1916, Russia was producing 4.5 million shells per month as opposed to Germany's 7 million, which was divided between the Western, Italian, and Eastern fronts, so that it was the Russians who actually possessed the material advantage on the Eastern Front in 1916 and 1917. Indeed, when the Russians ended their involvement in the war, they possessed a reserve of 18 million shells. Between 1914 and

1917, there was a 2,000 percent increase in Russian production of shells, a 1,000 percent increase in production of artillery guns, and a 1,000 percent increase in production of rifles. By February 1916 nearly all of the two million Russian soldiers possessed a rifle. The legend of unarmed Russian peasants charging German machine guns is largely fictitious. Large numbers of Russians were captured not because they lacked weapons but for the same reason that many Austrians were captured by the Russians: the scarcity of roads and railroads on the Eastern Front meant that whenever there was a breakthrough, reinforcements could not arrive soon enough to save defenders and defenders could not retreat fast enough to avoid encirclement. The poor infrastructure of the Eastern Front, coupled with its vast size, meant that trench warfare and the immense advantages it conferred on the defensive side in the West did not prevail in the East.[26]

The Russians suffered military disasters in World War I not because of material shortages but because of incompetence, poor organization, and disunity. Most Russian campaigns were poorly planned. The deep division between aristocratic officers on the one hand and middle-class officers and poor enlisted men on the other was compounded by the absence of a clear chain of command. Russian forces were often virtually independent of one another and sometimes refused to share resources or cooperate in other ways. Too much of Russia's limited railway space was devoted to cavalry, a preserve of the aristocracy that the prodigious firepower of the modern rifle and the machine gun had rendered virtually worthless. The aristocrats who dominated the artillery department insisted that vast sums of money be spent on outdated fortresses that were destroyed or captured by the Germans in a short time and on fortress artillery that could not be used in the field. Far from working closely together as in nearly all other contemporary armies, cooperation essential to success, Russian infantrymen and artillerymen were often at odds. Aristocratic artillerymen had so much contempt for the poorly trained infantrymen, who were generally of the peasant class, that they sometimes declined to "waste" shells in their support. In one particularly appalling instance, artillerymen failed to bombard the enemy prior to an infantry assault, so that large numbers of soldiers were mowed down by German machine guns; when survivors clinging to shell holes hoisted the white flag of surrender, the artillerymen then fired on their own infantrymen in anger. The Russian railway system was primitive and possessed too few skilled railway men. Finally, officers' cruel beatings of their enlisted men discouraged loyalty.[27]

The First Russian Revolution

Thus, in March 1917 (February in the less accurate Julian calendar still employed in Russia at the time), the czarist regime was overthrown. A Provisional Government was established, pending the election of a constituent assembly. While the March Revolution was partly the result of hunger in the cities caused by a transportation breakdown, it was also the result of the disasters suffered by Russian troops, which were attributed to the incompetence and corruption of the czarist government. Angered by the brutal repression of the people by the czar's more loyal Cossacks, many Russian soldiers not only refused to aid in the repression but joined the revolutionary soviets, committees that formed spontaneously in military units and workshops.[28]

Unfortunately, the Allies did not understand the causes of the March Revolution. They seemed to regard it as a manifestation of the "true democratic spirit" of the Russian people rather than as a result of war exhaustion. Thus, when Wilson addressed Congress to call for a declaration of war against Germany the following month, he cited the "wonderful and heartening" events in Russia and called the Allied effort a war to make the world "safe for democracy," now that the sole autocratic regime among the Allies had been replaced by a democratic government. Remarkably, he further asserted that the Romanov dynasty "was not in fact Russian in origin, character, or purpose" and proclaimed that "Russia was . . . always in fact democratic at heart." Now that the alien despotism had been shaken off, the Russian people would add their might to the forces that were fighting for freedom in the world. Because the Allies did not appreciate the extent of Russian war weariness and because they desperately needed help against the Central Powers, they pressured the Provisional Government into continuing the war. Misconstruing Russian military problems, they redoubled their effort to ship unnecessary weapons and supplies to the Russians. Thus, during the short life of the Provisional Government, mountains of Allied supplies lay on the docks at Archangel and Vladivostok, where bureaucratic inefficiency and an overloaded railway system conspired to keep them.[29]

After the new "Kerensky Offensive," so named for the Provisional Government's prime minister and war minister Alexander Kerensky, failed in Galicia within a matter of days in July and a German counteroffensive took eastern Galicia in August and Riga in September, the authority of the Provisional Government collapsed. Desertions from the army soared and violent mutinies ensued, as soldiers were reduced to a diet of rotten herring. Many Russians now felt the same bitter resentment toward the Provisional

Government that they had felt toward the czarist regime. As the historian H. Stuart Hughes has written concerning the failure of the Kerensky Government, "The explanation of this failure is simple—the provisional government had not done the two things for which the people were clamoring: it had not taken Russia out of the war, and it had not satisfied the land hunger of the peasantry." He might have added that it had not solved the railway crisis that produced famine in the cities and rampant inflation throughout the nation. The overburdening of the primitive railway system by the massive increase in demand produced by the war generated an inflationary spiral that, in turn, led to a strike by the low-paid railway workers that only exacerbated the crisis. On the evening of his arrival at the Finland station in Petrograd on April 16, Bolshevik leader Vladimir Ilyich Lenin explained his three-part program to a cheering crowd. The program called for an immediate peace with the Central Powers, the nationalization of land, and an increase in power for the local soviets. By far, the most pressing of the needs addressed by Lenin's program was the need for peace.[30]

The Bolshevik Revolution

On November 7, 1917, the Bolsheviks seized power. In December the new Soviet Government signed an armistice, and the following March a peace treaty, with the Central Powers. The Treaty of Brest-Litovsk granted huge concessions, including nearly half a million square miles, an area three times the size of Germany, to the Central Powers, in exchange for the desperately needed peace. The land surrendered included the Ukraine, Finland, and Transcaucasia, as well as territory in Poland and the Baltic States that Russia had occupied for a century and a half.[31]

The Allies' failure to comprehend the extent of Russian war exhaustion, when combined with the Allies' own desperate need for aid against the Central Powers, led them to the policy of intervention in Russia. The same exhaustion would help lead to the utter failure of that policy.

Notes

1. George Santayana, *Soliloquies in England* (New York: Charles Scribner's Sons, 1924), 102.

2. For brief but competent discussions of the origins of World War I, see John Keegan, *The First World War* (New York: Alfred A. Knopf, 1999), 30, 52–69; H. Stuart Hughes, *Contemporary Europe: A History* (Englewood Cliffs, N.J.: Prentice Hall, 1961), 24–34.

3. Keegan, *First World War*, 3, 5–7, 421–23.

4. Ibid., 22, 137, 162, 176–78, 183, 316; John Ellis, *Eye-Deep in Hell: Trench Warfare in World War I* (New York: Pantheon, 1976), 10, 12, 16, 24–25, 33, 83, 85–91.

5. Ellis, *Eye-Deep in Hell*, 91, 197.

6. Keegan, *First World War*, 278–85; B. H. Liddell Hart, *The War in Outline, 1914–1918* (New York: Random House, 1936), 124–27; Hughes, *Contemporary Europe*, 61–62.

7. Liddell Hart, *War in Outline*, 127; Hughes, *Contemporary Europe*, 62.

8. Liddell Hart, *War in Outline*, 125; Hughes, *Contemporary Europe*, 63; Keegan, *First World War*, 285; Ellis, *Eye-Deep in Hell*, 59.

9. Liddell Hart, *War in Outline*, 113; Keegan, *First World War*, 289.

10. Liddell Hart, *War in Outline*, 130–35; Hughes, *Contemporary Europe*, 63; Keegan, *First World War*, 291–96.

11. Liddell Hart, *War in Outline*, 138; Hughes, *Contemporary Europe*, 63; Keegan, *First World War*, 295, 299.

12. Keegan, *First World War*, 322, 330.

13. Liddell Hart, *War in Outline*, 184–85, 189, 191.

14. Ibid., 195–96.

15. Ibid., 189; Keegan, *First World War*, 357–58.

16. Liddell Hart, *War in Outline*, 192–93, 197; Keegan, *First World War*, 358, 361, 367; Ellis, *Eye-Deep in Hell*, 45.

17. Liddell Hart, *War in Outline*, 197–99; Keegan, *First World War*, 368.

18. Ellis, *Eye-Deep in Hell*, 84.

19. Liddell Hart, *War in Outline*, 194–95, 200–207; Hughes, *Contemporary Europe*, 72.

20. Liddell Hart, *War in Outline*, 177–78; Hughes, *Contemporary Europe*, 69; Erich Ludendorff, *My War Memories* (London: Hutchinson, 1919), vol. 1, 315; Keegan, *First World War*, 351–52.

21. Edward M. Coffman, *The War to End All Wars: The American Military Experience in World War I* (Oxford: Oxford University Press, 1968), 7–8; Keegan, *First World War*, 351–52.

22. Liddell Hart, *War in Outline*, 179–80; Keegan, *First World War*, 353–54; Coffman, *War to End All Wars*, 96–101, 197.

23. Liddell Hart, *War in Outline*, 178–79; Hughes, *Contemporary Europe*, 69; Coffman, *War to End All Wars*, 18–19, 187–88.

24. Liddell Hart, *War in Outline*, 56–58, 102–4, 139–41; Keegan, *First World War*, 147–49, 306; Hughes, *Contemporary Europe*, 51–52; Norman Stone, *The Eastern Front, 1914–1917* (New York: Charles Scribner's Sons, 1975), 51, 58, 63–66, 165, 231.

25. David Lloyd George, *War Memoirs of David Lloyd George* (Boston: Little, Brown, 1935–1937), vol. 1, 383–94.

26. Stone, *Eastern Front*, 12–13, 49, 133, 147, 151–52, 163, 210–12, 226, 254.

27. Ibid., 12–13, 25, 28, 32, 35–36, 49–50, 66, 94, 131, 134, 157, 168–69, 171, 229.

28. Keegan, *First World War*, 333–35.

29. George F. Kennan, *Russia and the West under Lenin and Stalin* (Boston: Little, Brown, 1960), 68, 93; Stone, *Eastern Front*, 157; David S. Foglesong, *America's Secret War against Bolshevism: U.S. Intervention in the Russian Civil War, 1917–1920* (Chapel Hill: University of North Carolina Press, 1995), 50–51.

30. Stone, *Eastern Front*, 282, 284, 288, 295, 299–301; Hughes, *Contemporary Europe*, 69, 89; Keegan, *First World War*, 338–39.

31. Keegan, *First World War*, 342.

CHAPTER TWO

~

The Shadow of a Plan

I have been sweating blood over the question what is right and feasible
to do in Russia. It goes to pieces like quicksilver under my touch.

—President Woodrow Wilson, July 8, 1918,
two days after his decision to intervene in Siberia[1]

Historians have proposed at least six theories to explain U.S. intervention
in Siberia in 1918. In this chapter I will evaluate each of these hypotheses in
order to shed some light on the chaotic situation into which President Wilson dispatched thousands of American soldiers. I will demonstrate that each
of these theories is incorrect except the last, the hypothesis that Wilson sent
American forces to Siberia to help the Czechs and Russian anti-Bolsheviks
overthrow the Soviet Government as the first step in re-creating the Eastern
Front against the Central Powers with Russian troops.

Siberia

Siberia is a vast land of almost five million square miles. It extends nearly
4,000 miles between Chelyabinsk just east of the Ural Mountains and Vladivostok on the Pacific Ocean and approximately 1,750 miles between the
Arctic Ocean and the borders of China and central Asian nations. While
western Siberia is flat and marshy, eastern Siberia is hilly, rough, and thickly
forested. Eastern Siberia boasts Lake Baikal, the largest freshwater lake in
the world, 5700 feet at its deepest, fed by over 300 rivers. Siberia is frost free

only about half the time of European Russia. Russian colonization of Siberia dates only from 1581–1582, but the Russian population began to outstrip that of the various Asiatic native groups long before the construction of the Trans-Siberian Railway (1891–1905) cemented the region's connection to European Russia. At the time of the intervention Siberia was still a frontier area partly populated by recent immigrants fleeing war and searching for opportunity. It was a region largely unhampered by the tradition of serfdom that characterized European Russia and possessed a much larger percentage of small landowners.[2]

The German War Prisoners Theory

The first theory regarding the Siberian intervention, advanced by Christopher Lasch, maintains that Wilson decided to intervene because he was frightened by persistent rumors that armed war prisoners working for the Central Powers were securing control of Siberia. There were approximately 800,000 German and Austro-Hungarian prisoners of war in Siberia when the Bolsheviks signed an armistice with the Central Powers in December 1917, just one month after overthrowing the Provisional Government. Less than one-tenth of these prisoners were German, though the Allies referred to them repeatedly as "German prisoners." The Bolsheviks managed to convert a few thousand prisoners, virtually none of whom were German, to their communist ideology and to utilize them in the Red Army.[3]

The Bolshevik practice of arming these prisoners created problems when the State Department began receiving a growing number of erroneous reports claiming that prisoners were being armed on a far greater scale than was in fact the case. These prisoners, it was alleged, were being led by German officers and were acting for Germany. They might attempt either to seize strategic points in Siberia or to capture the 700 tons of Allied supplies, worth an estimated $750 million to $1 billion, located at the Pacific port of Vladivostok. These supplies, a monument to the inefficiency of the czarist and provisional governments that had never paid for them, lay strewn along the docks and stacked in open fields, exposed alike to environmental and criminal elements. The quantities of these supplies staggered the imagination: a mountain of cotton bales, millions of rounds of ammunition, 37,000 train wheels, enough steel rails to build a third track from Vladivostok to Petrograd, and enough barbed wire to fence Siberia. Not to mention one lonely and rather mysterious submarine.[4]

Lasch's contention that Wilson believed these war prisoner stories ignores the two key factors that caused the president to doubt their accuracy. First, many knowledgeable officials flatly contradicted the rumors. On March 2, 1918, the State Department asked Willing Spencer, U.S. chargé d'affaires in China, to order Lieutenant Colonel William S. Drysdale to "proceed westward towards Irkutsk if he considers it safe to do so and report facts as to situations verifying or correcting rumors of the arming of German prisoners." On March 16, Spencer transmitted Drysdale's report that the prisoners were properly guarded. "Little probability of prisoners being armed," he declared.[5]

Further evidence of the falsehood of the war prisoner rumors arrived in the form of the Webster-Hicks reports. In March, Colonel Raymond Robins, head of the American Red Cross Commission in Russia, and British envoy R. H. Bruce Lockhart sent an American and a Briton, Captains William B. Webster and W. L. Hicks, to investigate the war prisoner allegations. Important aspects of the Webster-Hicks reports were then transmitted to the State Department by U.S. Ambassador to Russia David R. Francis in a series of reports the following month. Webster and Hicks, who traversed the western part of Siberia unvisited by Drysdale, concluded in the most unequivocal terms that there was no cause for alarm. The few thousand armed prisoners were ardent socialists operating under Bolshevik officers and were despised by their former officers, who were compiling lists of these "traitors." The Soviet Government even offered to limit the arming of war prisoners to 1,500 men and to allow Allied consuls to investigate periodically to ensure the enforcement of the limit. Webster and Hicks concluded that "if there is an arming of prisoners of war on a large scale it is a mystery where the arming is taking place and where the prisoners are being kept." Thus, General William S. Graves, Commander of the American Expeditionary Force in Siberia, wrote in his memoirs, "It is difficult to understand why the United States sent representatives to get certain specific information about war prisoners, and then decided to send troops to Siberia to frustrate any action taken by organizations of German and Austrian war prisoners which United States representatives said did not exist." The answer to this question, of course, is that the United States did not send troops to Siberia because of war prisoner rumors.[6]

At least three other highly trusted men corroborated the reports of Drysdale, Webster, and Hicks. U.S. Ambassador to Japan Roland S. Morris reported on March 7, 1918, concerning one wild story about the prisoners, "I have traced this rumor to French sources, and therefore doubt its accuracy, as most of the alarming rumors in reference to Siberia during the last two months have [the] same origin." The source for many of these stories was the French Consul-General at Irkutsk, an anti-Bolshevik with the ironic name of Gaston Bourgeois. Other sources included the French embassy in Russia and an anti-Bolshevik general. On April 10, U.S. Minister to China Paul S. Reinsch added, "There is no evidence of a concerted plan on the part of the Germans to control Siberia through the prisoners of war nor could such an attempt succeed. Earlier reports about armed war prisoners were exaggerated; most of these reports came from one source in Irkutsk." Perhaps even more influential was Morris's April 13 account regarding Czech leader Thomas G. Masaryk, who had just traveled the length of Siberia and knew the conditions there. Masaryk found no evidence of the existence of a substantial number of armed German or Austrian prisoners in Siberia.[7]

Second, Lasch's theory ignores the fact that Wilson knew that the armed war prisoners could not be acting under the direction of Germany because the Germans were clearly upset with the Bolsheviks for arming them. On April 17, Ambassador Francis reported that Germany was disturbed by war prisoner activity in Siberia. On April 22, Francis's assertion was supported by the U.S. Consul-General in Moscow, Maddin Summers, who wrote that the Germans were demanding that the Soviet government halt the arming of war prisoners immediately. Since both Francis and Summers made no secret of the fact that they were ardent anti-Bolsheviks, their reports could not be discounted easily. On April 25, Reinsch concurred with them, saying that the Germans were "apparently alarmed at the spread of Bolshevik allegiance among prisoners." In fact, U.S. Consul in Vladivostok John K. Caldwell referred to the armed war prisoners as "internationalists" and U.S. Consul in Irkutsk Ernest L. Harris referred to them as "revolutionists." Both Caldwell and Harris were also passionate anti-Bolsheviks.[8]

These factors had already convinced Secretary of State Robert Lansing that there was no need for alarm. It is true that, on March 24, Lansing was upset enough to write to the president, "If the reports, which persist, that the military prisoners in Siberia are organized under German officers and have succeeded in occupying Irkutsk are confirmed, we will have a new situation in Siberia which may cause a revision of our policy." But the fact that the secretary of state envisioned the potential validation of these reports as creating a "new situation" indicates that he doubted their accuracy, and the wild rumor concerning the occupation of Irkutsk by German prisoners was soon proved false. Even more instructive is the notation that Lansing's memorandum bears: "This was returned to me 3/26/18 by the Prest. who said that he quite agreed but did not think the situation yet warranted a change of policy." Indeed, there was no change of policy for several months, despite the persistence of the rumors. On April 22, Lansing submitted to Wilson a state department memorandum that declared, "There is no indication . . . that the arming of prisoners is extensive." Regarding the prisoners, the memorandum mentioned reports of "numerous instances of disaffection among the Austro-Hungarians—both of officers and of men—towards their own government." On April 30, Lansing told Japanese Ambassador Ishii Kikujiro that the prisoners had even "conspired with the Bolsheviks to arrest and kill their own superiors, the German officers."[9]

Wilson's actions reveal his doubts concerning the war prisoner allegations. Lansing's memorandum regarding the July 6 White House meeting in which Wilson announced his decision to intervene is important in this regard. Wilson's only mention of the war prisoners at the meeting was his declaration that public announcements regarding intervention should focus on the need to prevent the war prisoners from controlling Siberia. In Wilson's July 17 *aide memoire*, his formal statement announcing his decision to intervene, intended for distribution to the Allied embassies, there is no mention of war prisoners. But in the August 3 paraphrase of the *aide memoire*, intended for distribution to the press, the war prisoners reemerge, and, in fact, are presented as the primary motive for intervention. In short, it is clear that Wilson, having decided on intervention for other reasons, seized on the war prisoner rumors as justification to the press for his decision to intervene. Wilson's political instincts told him that he could deflate the inevitable opposition to Siberian intervention by utilizing public war hysteria.[10]

It should be noted here that Lasch also contended, as a subordinate part of his theory, that a contributing factor to Wilson's decision to intervene was his belief in the authenticity of the Sisson Documents. Edgar Sisson was the former city editor of the *Chicago Tribune* who had been sent to Russia in the winter of 1917–1918 to aid the Committee on Public Information's Russian Bureau in its efforts to restore Russian enthusiasm for the Allied war cause. Throughout the month of February 1918 Sisson purchased from an anti-Bolshevik journalist photographs of documents purporting to demonstrate that top Bolshevik leaders, including Vladimir Lenin and Leon Trotsky, were acting as paid agents of the German General Staff. These photographs had allegedly been stolen from Bolshevik party files. The photographs bought by Sisson were different from those previously purchased by Ambassador Francis in that the new ones indicated that the Bolsheviks were still acting as paid agents of the German government after the Bolshevik Revolution. (The Germans had indeed transported Lenin from his place of exile in Zurich to Petrograd after the March Revolution and had given him some financial support, an excellent investment given his subsequent withdrawal of Russia from the war. As Lenin himself put it, in a letter to a Bolshevik representative in Sweden in August 1918: "Nobody ever asked the Germans for help, but we had an understanding. . . . There was a coincidence of interests. We would have been idiots not to have taken advantage of it.") When Sisson pressed for additional evidence, he was sold fourteen "originals." All but one of the fourteen documents were alleged to have been stolen from the "secret offices" of the German General Staff in Russia. Sisson arrived in Washington in May 1918 with the fourteen "originals" and fifty-five photographs of documents.[11]

Leaving aside the lack of evidence that Wilson and Lansing believed in the authenticity of the Sisson Documents, one wonders at the credulity of anyone who so believed. To believe in their authenticity was to believe that Bolshevik leaders were completely subservient to the Germans at the same time that the Red Army was resisting German advances into Soviet Russia; that the Brest-Litovsk negotiations were completely fraudulent; that Bolshevik leaders had managed to keep their complete subservience to Germany a secret from other Bolshevik officials and from the Russian public for a long period of time; that the German General Staff maintained two secret offices in Russia for an equally long time without leaving a hint of their existence; that German officials would casually list the names of Germany's agents in routine dispatches in the middle of a war, including the names of those Bolsheviks whom they desired to be elected to the Soviet Central Committee; that these sensitive documents would be kept in Bolshevik party files where anyone might see them; that German officials would write with impeccable grammar in the Russian language yet use archaic words when writing in German, when, as State Department officials well knew, even the Soviet government seldom wrote diplomatic communications in Russian; that German officials would sign their names in Cyrillic characters rather than in the modern Latin alphabet standard in Germany and the rest of the Western world; and that German officials would date their documents according to the Julian calendar used in Russia rather than the Gregorian calendar used in Germany and the rest of the West, though such a practice would cause confusion in German files. In short, nearly everyone who scrutinized the Sisson Documents regarded them as laughable forgeries. Lockhart, the British envoy to the Bolsheviks, later wrote that they were "so palpably forged that even our own secret service would have nothing to do with them." He added that within months of the surfacing of the documents, it had been ascertained that letters supposedly written by different individuals in various European cities had actually been written on the same typewriter.[12]

Indeed, the State Department enraged Sisson by showing little interest in his documents. Department officials knew that documents of dubious authenticity concerning the Bolsheviks had been floated by anti-Bolsheviks even before the November Revolution. Thus, the State Department declined to have the documents published, though many department officials despised the Bolsheviks. Although some of their reluctance to publish stemmed from apprehensions about Bolshevik reprisals against Americans in Russia, State Department officials also knew that the documents were such obvious forgeries that their publication would prove more harmful than helpful to the administration. Secretary of State Lansing told Wilson's closest adviser, Colonel Edward House, that he did not accept their authenticity, and House agreed. Even Ambassador Francis, who first transmitted their text to the State Department, declared that he did not believe they were authentic. He believed that while the Bolsheviks were willing to accept financial aid from the Germans, or anyone else for that matter, they used such aid to promote their own goal of global revolution. He noted that the Bolsheviks were resisting German incursions in the Ukraine, Finland, and the Baltic States at the time.[13]

Once again, the president's attitude was clear. Wilson abided by the State Department's decision not to publish the documents until September 15, 1918, soon after the landing of American forces in Siberia, a time when Wilson needed to deflate the critics of his Russian policy. The documents were published in pamphlet form by the Committee on Public Information. The originals were not shown to the press, but historian Samuel Harper was called in to verify their authenticity. Harper, who concluded that there was no reason to doubt their authenticity, later implied in his memoirs that he had been pressured to so conclude.[14]

Wilson rebuffed requests by State Department officials that he turn over the Sisson Documents to them for analysis, saying that "he did not have time to lay hands on documents." In 1921, when Wilson left office, the new White House secretary found no trace of them. They were discovered in a White House safe in December 1952, and further evidence has revealed them to be forgeries.[15]

The evidence available in 1918 was more than sufficient to cast deep suspicion on the authenticity of the Sisson Documents. The actions of the State Department and President Wilson reveal clearly that the documents, like the war prisoner rumors, were not considered a genuine cause for concern. Having made a reluctant decision to intervene in Siberia on other grounds, Wilson was determined to use all of the weapons at his disposal to place his critics on the defensive.

The Japanese Theory

The second intervention theory, first advanced by John Albert White and later supported by Betty M. Unterberger, maintains that Wilson decided to intervene in Siberia in order to prevent the Japanese from invading the region unilaterally and exerting sole control over it. This theory holds that as the summer of 1918 approached, it became obvious to Wilson that the Japanese were prepared to invade Siberia. This realization led Wilson to support Allied action because he reasoned that if the Japanese invaded Siberia alone, it would be much more difficult to force them to withdraw at a later time than if they invaded as part of an Allied force understood to be invading and withdrawing in unison. Unterberger added that Wilson considered a unilateral Japanese invasion of Siberia particularly dangerous because it might threaten free trade in China.[16]

White and Unterberger used different methods to deal with the lack of documentation supporting their theory. White's method was to imply that American diplomats of the day did not write about their suspicions concerning the Japanese because they feared offending Japan, a nation officially allied with the United States in World War I. The problem with this hypothesis is that it does not explain why American diplomats did not write secretly to one another concerning these suspicions if they were powerful enough to necessitate sending an American army to Siberia. By contrast, Unterberger's method was to cite the suspicions that Wilson expressed concerning the Japanese *after* he had decided to intervene. But Wilson's suspicions of the Japanese in August 1918, suspicions created by their actions in that month, cannot be used to explain his decision to intervene in July. Wilson would have been foolish not to be suspicious of the Japanese after they began dispatching to Siberia numbers of troops vastly exceeding the 12,000 they initially agreed to send.[17]

Although some American policymakers were indeed suspicious of Japan before August 1918, Japan was hardly the United States' only trade rival in the Far East, and Wilson was no more suspicious of the Japanese than he was of the British and French. In fact, the first report to the State Department sent by Ambassador Francis from Russia on May 2, 1916, blamed the British for the sudden decision of the czarist government not to sign a commercial treaty with the United States. British Prime Minister David Lloyd George wrote in his memoirs that Wilson was apprehensive about intervening in Russia partly because he feared that the British desired to replace the Soviet Government with a friendly czarist regime. Indeed, by January 3, 1918, Wilson had received a report claiming that a British military attaché in Russia, Lieutenant Colonel Alfred Knox, had actually worked to oust the Provisional Government in the hope of obtaining a stronger government in Russia. On May 28, Wilson read a report by the U.S. representative to the Supreme War Council, General Tasker H. Bliss, that stated regarding the proposed Siberian intervention, "I distrust everything I hear on this subject here. . . . [The British and French] would like to see something like the old regime restored." Bliss's remark must have struck a nerve because Wilson replied to his war council representative the same day through U.S. Chief of Staff Peyton C. March that the Allies "should not have as their ultimate object any restoration of the ancient regime."[18]

Nor had the Bolshevik publication of the secret treaties concocted by the British and French, treaties that divided the spoils of war while the war was still in progress, lessened Wilson's suspicion of them. Indeed, it is largely due to these revelations that Wilson stressed the need for "open covenants" in his Fourteen Points Speech. Also, it was not the Japanese, but the British and French, who were constantly pressuring Wilson to agree to Japanese intervention.[19]

But perhaps the greatest evidence that Wilson was suspicious of the British and French lies in the fact that he excluded them from his intervention plan. The plan called for the United States and Japan to send 7,000 troops each to Siberia but made no mention of any British or French forces accompanying these. In fact, Wilson did not make haste to inform the British and French of his decision to intervene. Learning of the decision from the Japanese, British Ambassador to the United States Lord Reading must have been especially distressed, given that, on July 3, only three days before the president's decision to intervene, Wilson had promised not to make any such decision without first consulting the Allies. Reading's notes of that meeting alleged: "I then said to the President that I presumed that he would also consult the three allied Governments [of Britain, France, and Italy] before publicly announcing a policy or even arriving at a conclusion. He said that he certainly would not act without having communicated with our three Governments." On July 8 Lansing urged Wilson to notify the British and French of his decision before they learned of it from the Japanese, on the grounds that failure to do so would "deeply offend" them, but Wilson made no reply. In fact, when Wilson met Lord Reading that same day, he told him falsely that he had not yet made a decision on the matter. Thus, shocked to learn on July 9 that the decision had already been made to exclude British and French troops from the intervention, Reading, joined by the French and Italian ambassadors, held a meeting with Lansing the same day, in which Reading warned Lansing that "he was sure his Government would not understand action which did not include all parties." By his own account, Lansing angered the ambassador further: "I repeated that I thought . . . if expediency was opposed to British participation that, to my mind, ended it." Lansing recorded, "The British Ambassador was manifestly disturbed." While the

French and Italians were happy just to have Wilson finally approve intervention after pressuring him relentlessly for six months to do so, Reading was upset "because he felt that Great Britain had been ignored." Against Wilson's
policy, the British immediately sent a battalion from Hong Kong to Siberia,
and later dispatched some Canadian forces, and the French and Italians sent
small detachments as well. The participation of the British and French upset
Lansing, who wrote on August 3, "The participation of these two Governments will give the enterprise the character of interference with the domestic
affairs of Russia and will create the impression that the underlying purpose is
to set up a new pro-Ally Government in Siberia if not in Russia." Evidently,
Lansing did not believe that limited intervention by Japanese and American
troops alone carried such a connotation.[20]

The few American policymakers who were more suspicious of Japan than
of Britain and France opposed American intervention based on these very
suspicions. For instance, much has been made of Secretary of War Newton
D. Baker's subtle implication, in the introduction to General William S.
Graves's memoirs, published in 1931, that American intervention was designed to block Japanese absorption of Siberia. But Baker never supported
intervention on this or any other ground prior to Wilson's decision, and
Baker's letter of November 27, 1918, written a few months after the start
of the intervention, complained that American intervention was counter-
productive precisely because it was providing a "cloak" behind which Japan
could carry out its schemes to dominate the Far East. It seems clear that
Baker's views at the time of the intervention were better expressed in his
contemporary message to the president than in a statement written thirteen
years later, after Japan had just invaded Manchuria.[21]

Like the secretary of war, both the U.S. representative to the Supreme
War Council and the U.S. Army chief of staff opposed the Siberian intervention based on their suspicion of the Japanese. Tasker Bliss even went
so far as to suggest that if the Japanese occupied the whole Trans-Siberian
Railway, rather than coming into conflict with the Germans, they might
forge an agreement to divide Russia between them. Bliss declared that
Japanese intervention in Siberia presented "a grave danger" and, despite
tremendous pressure from other members of the council, he would consent
to approve only the occupation of Vladivostok and even that with great
reluctance. March held a similar view. After Wilson announced his decision to intervene in Siberia at a White House meeting on July 6, 1918,
March shook his head. Wilson evaluated the gesture correctly, saying,
"You are opposed to this because you do not think Japan will limit herself
to 7,000 men and that this decision will further her schemes for territorial

aggrandizement." When March responded affirmatively, Wilson replied, "Well, we will have to take that chance." Two conclusions emerge from this exchange. The first is that had Wilson's suspicion of the Japanese been as great as March's, he would, like March, have opposed American intervention. The second is that Wilson was not sufficiently suspicious of the Japanese to let it affect his decision to intervene, a decision based on other considerations.[22]

Secretary of State Lansing was not obsessed with fears of the Japanese, either. In fact, during the brief period when Lansing was disturbed by the war prisoner rumors, he suggested to the president that the Japanese might be sent into Siberia as a "mandatory" of the Allies, in order to deal with the problem. When it became clear that the problem did not exist, the matter was dropped. But this incident reveals that Lansing had no great qualms about calling for Japanese intervention if it became necessary.[23]

Although it has been argued that Wilson was more fearful of Japanese intentions than Lansing, such was not the case. In fact, Japanese Ambassador Ishii wrote in his memoirs that, when negotiating with Lansing, he always found him to be much milder when Lansing had just come from a meeting with the president. Ishii concluded that Wilson was more "objective" about Japan than Lansing.[24]

Although Wilson was not unduly suspicious of the Japanese, he opposed intervention by Japan alone because he feared a violent reaction by the Russian people. On February 4, 1918, one day after meeting with the president, British envoy Sir William Wiseman wrote that Wilson was opposed to Japanese intervention for two reasons: because he doubted, having conversed with Ambassador Ishii, that Japan would consent to it, and because he believed that Japanese intervention would drive Russia into the arms of Germany. On February 15, British Ambassador Lord Reading, having met with Wilson the same day, cited the same two reasons for Wilson's opposition to Japanese intervention. In a second meeting with the ambassador on February 27, Wilson argued again that Japanese intervention would alienate the Russian populace. On March 2, the president made the same point at a cabinet meeting. On March 4, after meeting with Wilson, Colonel House wrote British Foreign Secretary Arthur Balfour, reiterating the same point: Japanese intervention would cause a massive uprising by the Russian people against the Allies, a development that Germany would dearly love. House had made the same argument directly to the president on February 2 and continued to reiterate it to the British throughout March. Secretary of State Lansing agreed, citing a statement of the former Russian ambassador to France to the same effect.[25]

On May 30, at another meeting with Wilson, Wiseman argued that the Russian situation could not be worse. Wilson strongly disagreed. Wiseman recorded the president's observations: "We could make it much worse by putting the Germans in a position where they could organize Russia in a national movement against Japan. If that was done he would not be surprised to see Russian soldiers fighting with the Germans on the Western Front." Wilson knew that he was not the only one who worried that Japanese intervention would drive Russia into the arms of Germany: so did prominent anti-Bolsheviks, who advocated a multinational Allied intervention instead, and so did some of the Japanese themselves. This widespread belief was understandable, given the racial and cultural animosity between the Russians and the Japanese and given the fact that Japan had inflicted a humiliating defeat on Russia in the Russo-Japanese War only fourteen years earlier.[26]

Furthermore, beginning in March 1918, Wilson received assurances from the Japanese that convinced him that they would not invade Siberia without his consent. On March 7, Wilson learned that Japanese Foreign Minister Motono Ichiro had just intimated to the British that Japan would find it very difficult to intervene in Siberia without American materials and financial aid. On March 19, Motono handed Ambassador Morris a memorandum that Morris forwarded to the president. The memo assured Wilson that Japan would "refrain from taking any action on which due understanding has not been reached between the United States and the other great powers of the Entente." On April 29, Lansing reported concerning his meeting with Ambassador Ishii: "My interview with the Ambassador was in every way satisfactory. He is most frank and evidently desirous to do only what is entirely acceptable to this Government, and he assured me that is the wish and purpose of his Government." Ishii had also remarked that Japan did not want a "Germanized Russia," the likely result of a unilateral Japanese intervention in Siberia. On May 16, Ambassador Morris reported that the Japanese cabinet did not wish to intervene unilaterally, although the French were pressuring Japan to do so. On June 22, Morris reported that, despite alarm in Japan over the "growing disorder in Siberia," the Japanese still did not wish to incur American disapproval by intervening alone.[27]

But the most pleasing news came on June 26, when Ishii wrote to Lansing that despite intense British and French pressure, the Japanese government had just announced that its officials "could not feel at liberty to express their decision before a complete and satisfactory understanding on the question was reached between the three powers and the United States." Lansing showed this telegram to the president on the following day, and on June 28, Wilson replied, "I have read this communication with genuine pleasure." Indeed, after the May 30 meeting with Wilson, Wiseman had written regarding the president: "He realized that the U.S. Government held the key to the situation in that the Japanese Government would not intervene without their sanction; but it would be odious for him to use such power except [as] the best interests of the common cause demanded it." The fact that the Japanese had not already intervened in Siberia in the absence of American approval, despite many months of British and French pressure to do so, must have reinforced Wilson's belief that the Japanese would follow his lead, whatever he decided. If he intervened in Siberia, it would have to be for reasons other than any anxiety over what the Japanese might do.[28]

The Allied Pressure Theory

The third intervention theory, advanced by Eugene P. Trani, maintains that Wilson decided to intervene in Siberia as a result of a tremendous campaign, launched by the British and French, to pressure him to do so. Trani claims that a flood of Allied pressure, reaching its height in the summer of 1918, forced Wilson to swallow his misgivings and submit to intervention. This decision, suggests Trani, was made easier by Wilson's preoccupation with the enormous enterprise of mobilizing two million men for the Western Front.[29]

Perhaps the only point on which all historians of the Siberian intervention agree is that Allied pressure on Wilson to intervene was strong and continuous. Japan had demonstrated that it would not intervene without American support, and the British and French felt that only Japan, the sole ally whose forces were not committed to the Western Front, could supply enough troops for a new Eastern Front against the Central Powers, their ardent dream. Thus, it was absolutely necessary to obtain Wilson's approval of intervention.

The Allies attempted to gain that approval through the dual methods of isolation and direct pressure. First, William Wiseman attempted to isolate Wilson on the Siberian question. Wiseman proposed to do so by obtaining the consent of Wilson's chief military advisers, Tasker Bliss and Newton Baker, and of his chief political adviser, Colonel Edward House, for intervention. In the first two instances they failed. On June 4, 1918, Bliss complained to Secretary of War Baker:

> British and French general staff bureaus and their ministries of foreign affairs give out nothing but that which is favorable to the idea of this intervention. . . . Then I make myself a sort of an *advocatus diaboli* and suggest conceivable disadvantages, merely for the purpose of assuring that the question will be fairly

considered in all of its phases. I note a feeling of irritation. In other words, I have never seen or heard the question rationally discussed here, as though the parties to the discussion really wanted to get at all of the "ins and outs" of it. I do not believe that the question can be considered in this unbiased light anywhere except in Washington.

He was preaching to the choir. Baker made a similar nuisance of himself by pointing out to the British and French that Japanese intervention could accomplish nothing since the Japanese were adamant in their refusal to proceed west of Irkutsk: "I mentioned to Lord Reading that Irkutsk was too many thousand miles from the eastern front to be of any help. He replied, 'It is nearer than Vladivostok,' to which I replied that that sounded to me like saying that a man was nearer the moon when he was standing on top of his house, in view of the fact that he would still be too far away to have any chance of getting there."[30]

Wiseman eventually succeeded in converting House, however. On June 21, House reluctantly reversed his previous, vociferous stance against Allied intervention in Siberia, writing Wilson to support it, though even then House referred to Balfour's letter in support of the policy as "a panicky document in the main" and scoffed at his declaration that the Allies could not win the war without reviving the Eastern Front. Indeed, Balfour's conclusion was disproved by subsequent events.[31]

As part of his campaign to secure American support for intervention, Wiseman also urged the British Foreign Office to stop referring to the security of India in every dispatch to America concerning the issue. Some British diplomats were so obsessed with the security of India that they justified intervention in Siberia on the incredibly dubious ground that the Germans would otherwise not only control thousands of miles of Siberian territory but invade the Indian subcontinent as well. Leaving aside the fantastic nature of this scenario, which was on a par with the fear that the Germans would transform Vladivostok into a submarine base, some American officials were understandably disturbed by the thought of intervention merely as a means of protecting British interests in India. The practice of referring to India in dispatches to America died hard, however, because it had become a subconscious part of the act of writing for so many British diplomats.[32]

The British and French also applied a torrent of direct pressure on Wilson. As early as December 24, 1917, only two weeks after the Bolsheviks signed an armistice with the Central Powers, the Supreme War Council recommended intervention. On January 8, 1918, the French Ambassador to the United States, Jean Jusserand, began an unceasing campaign to secure

Wilson's approval for it. On January 28, the British embassy in Washington began its own campaign. Dispatches from the Allied embassies and the Supreme War Council, continuing throughout the spring, attempted to create fears in Wilson's mind regarding the war prisoners. They failed. In late June, Lloyd George sent Wilson a memorandum written by Balfour that assured him that any fears he had of a British attempt to establish a czarist regime in Russia were completely groundless. At midnight on July 2, the Supreme War Council, which had been pressing its American representative and the U.S. War Department to support intervention, wired Wilson, strongly urging Allied intervention as vital to victory in the war against the Central Powers. This message was approved by the new Supreme Commander of Allied Forces, General Ferdinand Foch, on whose advice Wilson had already decided to send troops to northern Russia.[33]

Nevertheless, there are two flaws in Trani's theory. The first is that Trani greatly underestimated Wilson's level of concern about Russian affairs. Although the situation on the Western Front certainly took precedence over all else in Wilson's thoughts, he was by no means apathetic about Russia. In fact, he was only slightly exaggerating when he wrote that he was "sweating blood" over the question of what he should do with regard to Russia, or when he wrote, "I do not know that I have ever had a more tiresome struggle with quicksand than I am having in trying to do the right thing in respect of our dealings with Russia."[34]

Second, whether or not Allied pressure played a role in Wilson's decision to intervene in Siberia, it was clearly not the decisive factor. In fact, Wilson's advisers considered Allied thinking regarding the subject irrational. Colonel House wrote to Wilson on March 3, 1918: "The French have come to hate the Russians and do not care what befalls them and for reasons which are obvious. The English that are in power have such intense hatred for Germany that they have lost their perspective."[35]

Far from intervening merely to please the British and French, Wilson was becoming exasperated with them. On June 8, Tasker Bliss wired Secretary of War Baker. In this message, shown to Wilson on June 21, Bliss wrote that he had told the other members of the Supreme War Council that "it was doing no good to fire Joint Note after Joint Note to the President, simply reiterating what they said before." Three days later Colonel House warned a French envoy carrying a note for the president from French Prime Minister Georges Clemenceau that urged intervention not to "go into the subject in detail," assuring him that when it came to "the old story of Japanese intervention," the president "knew it in its every phase." Three days later House cut off another French envoy in the midst of trying to sell intervention by telling him "that I knew every argument for and against so perfectly that I had no difficulty in repeating them in my sleep." Since the president was in the same boat, House warned the second envoy as he had the first to keep his talk with the president regarding the subject brief. Wilson obviously appreciated these efforts by his advisers to spare him endless reiterations of the same sales pitch. On March 22, after reading a stack of British memoranda given him by Lansing, all of which advocated intervention, Wilson fired this note back at the secretary of state: "They still do not answer the question I have put to Lord Reading and to all others who argue in favor of intervention by Japan, namely, What is it to effect and how will it be efficacious in effecting it? The condition of Siberia furnishes no answer." Until that answer came in June 1918 more than six months of persistent, intense Allied pressure accomplished nothing.[36]

The Bolshevik Theory

A fourth theory, advanced by William Appleman Williams, maintains that Wilson decided to intervene in Siberia solely in order to overthrow the Soviet government. According to Williams, "Intervention as a consciously anti-Bolshevik operation was decided upon by American leaders within five weeks of the day Lenin and Trotsky took power." Like the North Russian intervention, the Siberian intervention "was a long-debated and long-delayed tactical move in support of the basic anti-Bolshevik strategy that had been established in December 1917." Williams's reference to that month was an allusion to Wilson's short-lived proposal to offer financial aid to anti-Bolshevik general Alexey Kaledin, a plan the president quickly withdrew, Williams noted, because he feared a backlash against the Allies by the Russian people. According to Williams, Wilson considered the Bolsheviks dangerous because of their radical socialist doctrines and because the closed economic system they favored presented a threat to trade in the region. Thus, even after relinquishing his proposal to aid Kaledin, Wilson looked for ways to overthrow the Bolsheviks, finally settling on a policy of armed intervention on behalf of anti-Bolshevik forces in July 1918. Williams contended that Wilson viewed the need to overthrow the Soviet government as greater than the necessity of defeating the Central Powers. This is why, Williams maintained, Wilson declined the opportunity he was offered to cooperate with the Bolsheviks against the Germans, and it is why he deflected troops from the Western Front, at the height of the German offensive there, to destroy the Soviet government.[37]

It is true that Wilson established an early aversion to the Bolsheviks, but this was as much a product of circumstances as of ideological differences. The first major action taken by the Soviet government on assuming power was its call for a general armistice between the Allies and the Central Powers, something the Allies could not support while the Central Powers occupied most of Europe. This Bolshevik declaration came at a particularly inopportune time for Wilson, who was engaged in an intense struggle with domestic pacifists for popular support. Indeed, in his first speech after the Bolshevik Revolution with any reference to Russia, Wilson warned against those "as fatuous as the dreamers of Russia" who advocated a premature peace that would leave Germany in a threatening position. Wilson's Fourteen Points Speech of January 1918 was largely an attempt to counter the Bolshevik call for a general armistice. In that speech Wilson praised the Bolsheviks' peace terms so that he might criticize the Germans for rejecting them. The following month Wilson found "an unusual amount of truth" in a memorandum written by Samuel Gompers, the leader of the American Federation of Labor, and pro-war socialist William English Walling that warned of a combination of "war weariness" and "Utopian dreams fanned into new life by the Russian revolution" that might lead to crippling strikes not only in Europe but even among immigrant workers in the United States. Coming at the height of World War I, such strikes might very well cost the Allies the war. Secretary of State Lansing agreed with this assessment. Indeed, the Wilson administration was so alarmed by the potential effects of opposition to the war that its officials began rigorously enforcing the Espionage Act of 1917, a law that essentially criminalized such opposition, after the Bolshevik Revolution.[38]

But the public relations problem that the Bolsheviks had caused Wilson was only the tip of the iceberg. In Wilson's mind, the principal effect of the Bolshevik Revolution was that there would no longer be a large Russian army tying down German divisions in the East. While it is true that the collapse of the Russian army began before the Bolsheviks seized power, it is also true that as long as the Provisional Government remained in power and at war, there had at least been some hope of the revival of Russian armed forces, which is why the Germans were unwilling to transfer their eastern divisions to the Western Front until Russia formally withdrew from the war. Lansing estimated that the Bolshevik withdrawal of Russia from the war would add two or three years to it and cost the United States alone hundreds of thousands of lives and billions of dollars. The withdrawal of Russia from the war inevitably caused great bitterness toward the Bolsheviks among the Allies. Lloyd George described the Allied feeling toward the Bolsheviks well when he wrote, "It was not merely their atrocities that excited resentment, but their abandonment of the Allied cause at a critical stage in the struggle. This betrayal very nearly precipitated an irreparable disaster in the spring and summer of 1918. As France had gone into the war to back up Russia when she was attacked, French statesmen regarded the Treaty of Brest-Litovsk as an act of perfidy." Leaving aside the highly dubious nature of this interpretation of the war's origin, the feeling of betrayal Lloyd George described was certainly real. Lansing wrote: "Those who today claim to represent the [Russian] nation threaten to violate treaties made with other free peoples, to make friends with the most inveterate enemy of Russian aspirations, and to abandon the faithful friends of Russia in the great struggle against the Prussian autocracy. In light of this program, so contrary to democratic ideas of honor and duty, it cannot be that the Bolshevik leaders represent the Russian people or express their true will." Added to this bitterness was the concern felt at the time that, whatever the Bolsheviks' intentions, the chief result of the Bolshevik Revolution might be to open up Russia for German exploitation. As Lloyd George recalled, "It was apprehended that the destructive working of Bolshevism might in fact prove merely to have broken up and ploughed a field in readiness for planting with Prussianism." In addition to the other troubling ramifications of the treaty, the Allies feared that German control of the Ukraine, which had long been the breadbasket of Europe, might in itself be sufficient to negate the crucial effects of the Allied blockade of Germany.[39]

If, then, the Bolsheviks made a very poor impression on Wilson early in his experience with them, they did not improve matters on February 10, 1918, when they repudiated all debts to the Allies incurred by previous Russian governments. As in the case of their withdrawal from the war, this action was understandable from the Bolshevik point of view. Given the economic state of Russia at the time, it would have been extremely difficult for any government to have repaid Russia's war debt. But this repudiation of debt cost the United States $187,729,750 (the portion of the $350 million in American aid allotted to the Provisional Government that had already been disbursed) and cost the other Allied governments, already struggling to finance the war, millions more. Wilson wrote that fidelity to debts should be considered a requisite for recognizing any Russian government.[40]

Neither was Wilson delighted with the Bolsheviks' constant appeals to the world's masses for the overthrow of all capitalist governments. Rather, Wilson was startled by "the impudence" of Trotsky's proposal to send Bolsheviks to the United States and other countries "to propose the overturning of all governments not dominated by the working people." Nor could Wilson have been pleased when Trotsky declared in a speech that the United States had entered the war at the behest of Wall Street and the munitions makers (oddly enough, a charge later repeated by conservative American isolationists during the 1930s).[41]

But Wilson's greatest complaint against the Bolsheviks concerned their dissolution of the Constituent Assembly of Russia. On January 19, 1918, the Bolsheviks forcibly dispersed the popularly elected Constituent Assembly, in which they had won less than a quarter of the seats. As a result, on January 21, Secretary of State Lansing argued that all question of recognizing the Soviet government should be dropped "as being hostile to [the] Constituent Assembly." The same day Wilson wrote, in anger and frustration, that "the reckless Bolsheviki have already broken it up because they could not control it. It is distressing to see things so repeatedly go to pieces there." To Wilson, it seemed clear that the Bolsheviks' poor performance in the elections and their use of force to dissolve the Constituent Assembly invalidated their claim to represent the Russian people.[42]

But while it is true that Wilson disliked the Bolsheviks, Williams was incorrect in stating that Wilson considered them a greater threat than the Germans in the first half of 1918. There were two reasons why Wilson did not accept extremely tentative offers from the Bolsheviks for cooperation against the Germans. First, Wilson doubted that he could count on the Bolsheviks to mount a sustained war effort against the Central Powers. Among the Bolsheviks, the Trotskyite faction held that the Soviet government ought to adopt a "no war, no peace" policy toward the Germans, resisting their incursions while avoiding a full-scale war against them. This policy, proposed by Trotsky on February 10, 1918, led him to request, on March 19, that the United States dispatch army officers to aid him in organizing, drilling, and equipping the embryonic Red Army, and that the United States provide railway experts and equipment to help the Soviet government solve serious transportation problems. But the same "no war, no peace" policy precluded any Bolshevik invitation to the Allies to send troops to Russia. Indeed, on June 14, Sir William Wiseman reported that Wilson did not expect to receive such an invitation and, on June 25, Wilson learned that "the most important official of [the] Soviet in Easter[n] Siberia stated . . . that [the] Soviets will never ask [for] intervention." Indeed, they never did. The only "cooperation" Trotsky desired was American aid in building up the Red Army and Soviet transportation. The most Wilson could hope for was that the Red Army would then be used to resist German incursions into Russia. Trotsky's policy did not propose carrying resistance to Germany any further. One reason Trotsky was reluctant to invite the Allies to intervene was that he feared that by the time they arrived in Russia in force, the

Germans, angered by their impending intervention, would capture Moscow and Petrograd, the most important cities in Russia and the most vital centers of Soviet power.[43]

The Leninites, on the other hand, demanded complete peace. Vladimir Lenin, the undisputed leader of the Bolsheviks, stated repeatedly in each of his speeches the need for a "breathing spell" from war in Russia if the Soviet government were to survive. Lenin believed that if Russia would only concentrate on solving its internal problems and allow the capitalist governments to destroy one another, a worldwide workers' revolution would spring to its aid. Thus, while Lenin supported Trotsky's efforts to secure Allied aid for the Red Army, he was absolutely opposed to any Soviet invitation to Allied troops to intervene in Russia for any purpose, and he made this position abundantly and repeatedly clear both to Trotsky and to the Allies. Highly suspicious of Allied motives, he also doubted that any new Allied support could revive the Russian will to fight any more than massive Allied aid had under the Provisional Government. When he quietly dispatched questionnaires to the army, which was now at only one-fifth its pre-Revolutionary size, the results were not encouraging: a solid majority of soldiers responded that the army could mount no serious resistance to the German army and that Petrograd was bound to fall if the Soviet government returned Russia to the war. The cry of the soldiers was still, "Peace at any price!" To make the same mistake that the Provisional Government had made in continuing the war would be to invite the same result, the fall of the government. It would be far wiser to stay out of the war and allow the two capitalist alliances to destroy one another, thereby paving the way for the international socialist revolution Lenin anticipated.[44]

The Russian Congress of Soviets almost always supported Lenin's positions. Its March 8 resolution to maintain the peace was little more than a paraphrase of Lenin's speech of the previous day. In fact, it was Lenin's threat of resignation from the party that caused the Bolsheviks to accept the harsh German ultimatum of late February 1918 that eventuated in the equally harsh Treaty of Brest-Litovsk, which the Soviet Congress ratified by a huge majority. While Trotsky's fame might have been equal to Lenin's in the West, their power and influence in Soviet Russia were hardly comparable by the spring of 1918; while rival commissars often challenged Trotsky's proposals at cabinet meetings, a mere sentence from Lenin decided nearly every issue. Thus, in late April, when Lockhart, who was close to Trotsky, declared disappointedly that Trotsky's already limited influence was declining even further, it raised serious doubts as to the desire of the Bolsheviks to engage in even minimal resistance to the Germans. Wilson himself stated that Trotsky's view did not represent that of the majority of Bolsheviks.[45]

But even if Wilson had not possessed grave doubts regarding the willingness of the Bolsheviks to engage in a sustained war effort against Germany, there was another reason he felt he could not aid the Bolsheviks. Wilson knew that once strengthened by American aid, the Red Army was, in the words of U.S. Consul in Petrograd Roger C. Tredwell, "more likely to be used for internal than external warfare." In other words, the Red Army would be used to crush the anti-Bolsheviks, whom Wilson considered to be the vast majority of Russians. Thus, the vast majority of Russians, in sheer desperation, would turn to Germany for aid against the Bolsheviks. Wilson was warned against this occurrence by a prominent anti-Bolshevik, Ariadna Tyrkova-Williams, a leader of the Constitutional Democrat Party, on April 26, by the anti-Bolshevik League for the Regeneration of Russia on May 28, by Russian exiles in Switzerland on June 11, by the U.S. Ambassador to France on June 12, and by the U.S. Ambassador to Russia on June 22. Tyrkova-Williams expressed the general feeling: "Russians belonging to all classes are ready to practice with the devil himself to get rid of the bolsheviks [and] their anarchy. . . . If the Allied governments come to an agreement with Trotsky, all the vital forces of the country would really turn towards Germany." She added, as did the others, that even the failure of Wilson to support the anti-Bolsheviks actively would force them to turn to the Germans for help. Thus, as early as May 16, Lansing warned British Ambassador Lord Reading that even if Trotsky made a request for intervention, the Allies should approach it with caution since its acceptance would array them against "the elements antagonistic to the Soviets."[46]

Finally, Williams's argument that Wilson demonstrated his greater fear of the Bolsheviks by diverting soldiers from the Western Front in order to destroy them may be disposed of quickly. First, 8,500 troops (counting the support personnel) could hardly have made much difference on the Western Front, particularly in light of the military tactics that prevailed there at the time. Indeed, when writing to Wilson in support of intervention, Supreme Commander of Allied Forces Ferdinand Foch wrote, "In my opinion the sending by you of American troops to Russia is justified, for no appreciable diminution of the number of troops to be sent to France will result therefrom." Second, approximately 3,500 of the 8,500 soldiers Wilson sent to Siberia were transported from the Philippines. These 3,500 men had never been intended for the Western Front; their sole function was to garrison the Philippines. Third, the American troops in Siberia were supplied from the ships that normally supplied the Philippines garrisons, so that not a single ship was diverted from the Western Front for the Siberian intervention.

Even if one adds the 5,500 troops sent to North Russia, the impact of the Russian interventions on American operations in France was negligible. In the words of the military historian Edward M. Coffman, "The demands of the Russian expedition on manpower and resources were too small to affect the AEF program." The American Expeditionary Force to which Coffman referred was the massive U.S. army stationed on the Western Front, which numbered over one million troops at the time Wilson decided to send a few thousand soldiers to Siberia.[47]

Thus, the question that Wilson had to ask himself was not, as Williams would have it, should I divert American forces from the Western Front to destroy the Bolshevik menace, but rather, with which of the Russian factions should we ally ourselves against Germany? Based on Wilson's dislike of the Bolsheviks, on his doubts as to their willingness to carry on a prolonged war against Germany, and on his belief that the anti-Bolsheviks constituted the vast majority of Russians, Wilson had little doubt that he must ally himself with the anti-Bolsheviks. But because intervention might well be viewed as an act of imperialism by the Russian people, particularly if the intervening force were largely Japanese, Wilson was reluctant to intervene.

On the other hand, time was running out. The Germans' spring offensive had been successful, and they were now standing on the doorstep of Paris. Wilson desperately needed a large but acceptable intervention force. And then startling news came.

The Czech Theories

The final two theories are so similar that they will be considered together. The fifth theory, advanced by George F. Kennan, maintains that Wilson decided to intervene in Siberia in order to rescue the Czech Corps, so that it could be transported to the Western Front. The sixth theory, advanced by Robert J. Maddox, maintains that Wilson decided to intervene in order to help the Czechs and anti-Bolsheviks overthrow the Soviet government as the first step in re-creating the Eastern Front. According to Maddox, Wilson hoped that American forces would help the Czechs and their anti-Bolshevik Russian supporters "defeat the Soviet regime and bring Russia back into the Allied camp." Maddox continued, "Indirectly, therefore, Wilson hoped to re-constitute the eastern front, as did Great Britain and France, but he thought it could be done only by the Russians themselves, not by foreigners." It is this final theory that best explains Wilson's motive for approving the Siberian intervention.[48]

The startling news that caused Wilson to reconsider intervention concerned the Czech Corps. Made part of the Russian Army by the Provisional Government in 1917, the corps consisted of approximately 70,000 Czechoslovakians, most of whom were prisoners of war and deserters from the Austro-Hungarian Army. They joined the Russian Army in order to fight for the creation of an independent Czechoslovakia, which was then a subject of the Austro-Hungarian Empire. The corps, which had served superbly during the Galician Campaign of 1917, was placed in a difficult situation when the Soviet government signed an armistice with the Central Powers.[49]

On February 7, 1918, Czech leader Thomas Masaryk proclaimed that the corps was now under French command. On March 26, Soviet Commissar of Nationalities Joseph Stalin authorized free passage for the Czechs to Vladivostok via the extensive Trans-Siberian Railway. From there, they could be transported to the Western Front by sea. On April 26, however, French Prime Minister Clemenceau informed his foreign minister that he wanted the Czech Corps transferred to the Western Front "by the swiftest means," referring to either the Archangel route through the White Sea or the Murmansk route via the Arctic Ocean. The following day the Supreme War Council decided to ask the Soviet government to dispatch those Czech units that had not yet passed east of Omsk to Archangel and Murmansk. Thus, on May 8, the officers of the Czech Corps learned that the western part of their force was to be diverted to Archangel and Murmansk, by agreement between the Supreme War Council and the Bolsheviks. The eastern portion of the corps would continue to Vladivostok.[50]

This agreement greatly displeased the Czechs, who feared that the Bolsheviks were attempting to divide the corps in order to hand part of it over to the Central Powers. In such a case the Austro-Hungarians would deal very harshly with the Czech deserters; their German allies had already executed Czechs captured in the Ukraine. Czech suspicions of Bolshevik intentions were exacerbated by the coincidence that the Bolshevik general who signed the order stopping the Czech trains possessed a German name. Nor did the Bolsheviks endear themselves to the Czechs by purposely delaying some trains in order to give Czech communists in their employ a chance to recruit members of the corps into the Red Army.[51]

But the real trouble began on May 17, when the Czechs briefly occupied the Siberian town of Chelyabinsk just east of the Urals. This action was the result of an incident three days earlier, in which a Hungarian prisoner, part of a group being repatriated, hurled a large lump of cast iron from a broken stove from the back of a train that had just begun pulling out of the station at a group of Czech soldiers below him. The iron struck a soldier in the head, mortally wounding him. Before the train could gather steam the soldier's enraged comrades then climbed onto it and forced the driver to stop. The Czechs bludgeoned the Hungarian to death. Local Soviet officials then arrived with a detachment of Red Guards and subpoenaed and removed a number of legionnaires involved in the incident to the town, which was about three miles from the station. When a Czech officer and a delegation went to the town to demand the release of the legionnaires, the Bolsheviks arrested and imprisoned them as well. Two Czech battalions then marched into town, secured the release of all of the prisoners, seized more arms and ammunition for themselves from Soviet stocks, and then withdrew.[52]

Far from mollified by the Czech withdrawal from the town and their renewed pledge not to oppose Soviet authority, on May 21 an angry deputy of Trotsky ordered that all Czech units along the Trans-Siberian Railway be detrained and that the Czechs be organized into labor groups or drafted into the Red Army. On the previous day, the Bolsheviks also arrested leading members of the Russian branch of the Czech National Council in Moscow. These leaders then ordered Czech officers to surrender the corps' weapons to the Bolsheviks. The Czech officers ignored the disarmament orders, reasoning that their jailed leaders had been pressured into issuing them. On May 25, Trotsky ordered, "Every armed Czechoslovak found on the railway is to be shot on the spot." Furthermore, any Soviet official failing to enforce the disarmament order would be charged with treason. As a result of this order, fighting between the Bolsheviks and the Czechs erupted all along the western portion of the Trans-Siberian Railway. By early June, the Czechs had captured much of western Siberia and were protecting anti-Bolshevik governments springing up there. By overreacting to the brief occupation of Chelyabinsk, Trotsky had provoked the very Czech uprising he feared.[53]

The startling news of the Czechs' sudden control of western Siberia, achieved in a matter of weeks, swept like a shock wave through the United States. By the end of May 1918, the Czechs had gone from complete obscurity to being idealized heroes in the imagination of the American public. The reports of their victories were crucial to Wilson's decision to intervene in Siberia.[54]

Wilson's previous fear that Allied intervention would alienate the Russian people, who would view it as an imperialist enterprise, was now overridden simultaneously by two considerations. The first was the alarming military success of the Central Powers in the late spring and early summer of 1918. Even Great Britain and the United States were now unsafe from German attacks. Great Britain was struck continually by German air raids. In early

June two German submarines terrorized the U.S. Atlantic coast. Due to these attacks, the port of New York was closed completely, while the U.S. Senate debated the question of whether American coasts and shipping were properly protected from the German menace. Incredibly, the streets of Fifth Avenue and Broadway were dimmed in order to hinder German air raids. It remains a mystery from what base it was expected that the Germans would launch their biplanes. Perhaps the far-sighted officials of Manhattan anticipated the development of the aircraft carrier.[55]

The news on the Western Front was even bleaker. The chief development there was the great success of General Erich Ludendorff's spring offensive. On May 27, after the French ignored the warnings of an American intelligence officer that the Germans would attack them at the Chemin des Dames Ridge, the Germans broke through and advanced twelve miles, a penetration so sudden and deep that it amazed even Ludendorff. Three days later, the German Army was again on the Marne River, the outskirts of Paris. Barrages from long-range German artillery, combined with air raids, pounded the city. From March to July 1918 the German Army inflicted over one million casualties on the Allies.[56]

Meanwhile, the commander of the American Expeditionary Force in Europe, John J. Pershing, was painfully slow in committing American troops to battle. Pershing was firmly opposed to sending U.S. soldiers into combat before they had been organized into American divisions and had Wilson's full backing for this position. Understandably, Pershing did not like the idea of Americans fighting under foreign commanders, and British and French generals had not exactly covered themselves with glory in the war. But the process of organizing American divisions was time consuming. Furthermore, Pershing made matters worse by insisting that valuable shipping space be reserved for cavalry units, whose value on the Western Front had long been called into question. As Supreme Commander Foch told Pershing in frustration, "The American Army may arrive to find the British pushed into the sea and the French driven back behind the Loire, while it tries in vain to organize on lost battlefields over the graves of Allied soldiers."[57]

In fact, despite Pershing's unwillingness to let his troops fight under foreign command, he agreed with Foch's bleak assessment of the situation on the Western Front. On June 17, he wrote to Secretary of War Baker, "If further serious reverses come to us this year it is going to be very difficult to hold France in the war." Morale among the Allies was so low that Pershing worried that their despair would rub off on his own men. Pershing urged that as many American soldiers as possible be sent to France in the next few months. Stricken with fear at the prospect of the fall of Paris, the Allies made

the transportation of American troops to France the greatest naval priority of
1918. U.S. Army Chief of Staff Peyton March promised, "We'll pack them in
like sardines," even keeping his promise at the expense of vital supplies, and
the British so escalated their transportation of American doughboys (allegedly so called by the Allies because the large buttons on their uniforms made
them look like gingerbread men) that they soon surpassed the American
navy in this endeavor.[58]

The rapid transportation of large numbers of American soldiers to France
was also the request of the prime ministers of Great Britain, France, and Italy.
On June 2, they drafted a joint message to Wilson, in which they stated:

> General Foch has presented to us a statement of the utmost gravity, which
> points out that the numerical superiority of the enemy in France, where 162
> Allied divisions are now opposed by 200 German divisions, is very heavy, and
> that there is no possibility of the British and French increasing the number
> of their divisions (on the contrary, they are put to extreme straits to keep
> them up); there is a great danger of the war being lost unless the numerical
> inferiority of the Allies can be remedied as rapidly as possible by the advent
> of American troops.

The prime ministers urged that large numbers of American soldiers and
machine gunners be sent to France immediately and estimated that another
100 American divisions would be needed to achieve victory over the Central
Powers. Meanwhile, officials of the French government were packing their
papers, preparing to evacuate Paris for Bordeaux, while Clemenceau toyed
with the idea of giving up the city without a fight. By July 6, the day Wilson
decided to intervene in Siberia, the situation had not improved. On that day
the assistant secretary to the U.S. ambassador to France, Jefferson Caffery,
wrote to his family in Lafayette, Louisiana, that the two plagues of Paris,
inflation and German air raids, were doing more damage than ever.[59]

According to Arthur Balfour and William Wiseman, the Allies believed
that they needed a new Eastern Front in order to prevent Germany from
redirecting approximately forty divisions (around one million men) to the
Western Front, in order to prevent Germany from utilizing Russian resources, and in order to negate the morale boost that the end of the war in
the East had given the Austro-Hungarians. These old arguments began to
impress themselves with new force on Wilson's mind as the Germans closed
in on Paris.[60]

The second consideration that led Wilson to choose intervention was the
startling success of the Czechs in Siberia. On June 13, 1918, U.S. Minister
to China Paul Reinsch wrote:

It is the general opinion of Allied representatives here in which I concur that it would be a serious mistake to remove Czecho-Slovak troops from Siberia. With only slight countenance and support they could control all of Siberia against the Germans. They are sympathetic to the Russian population, eager to be accessories to the Allied cause, the most serious means [menace] to extension of German influence in Russia. Their removal would greatly benefit Germany and further discourage Russia. If they were not in Siberia it would be worth while to bring them there from a distance.

Four days later, after reading this dispatch, Wilson wrote to Lansing: "There seems to emerge from this suggestion the shadow of a plan that might be worked, with Japanese and other assistance. These people are cousins of the Russians." The significance of Wilson's last sentence cannot be overemphasized. As if by a miracle, he had now found an intervention force that he felt certain would be viewed sympathetically by the Russian people.[61]

On the same day Wilson met with a French diplomat. The diplomat told Wilson that Clemenceau considered intervention "imperative not only because he believes it will be effective but he believes it will stimulate the morale of the French people more than anything else, and that they need stimulating in this hour of trial." Wilson answered that he would consider the whole Siberian situation again and that he would reply soon. Wilson added that he was expecting to see Masaryk soon and that the Czech leader "would furnish information and thus aid him in forming [an] opinion." On June 19, Wilson wrote regarding the assurances of the All-Russian Union of Cooperative Societies, a union of pro-democratic, anti-Bolshevik groups, that they would support intervention: "This dispatch has interested me very much. These associations may be of very great service as instruments for what we are planning to do in Siberia. By the way, I saw Professor Masaryk yesterday and he seemed to think well of the plan." The plan was to help the Czechs and anti-Bolsheviks overthrow the Soviet government as a prelude to re-creating the Eastern Front.[62]

On June 25, a former cabinet member of the Provisional Government assured the State Department that the Russian people would support Allied intervention against both the Bolsheviks and the Germans. He added, "It is hardly necessary to emphasize how fortunate is the presence of Czecho-Slovak troops in Siberia and how highly desirable is their participation in inter-allied action in Siberia." On the same day a report from U.S. Consul in Vladivostok John K. Caldwell observed regarding the Czech Corps: "This force is a splendidly adequate nucleus for a new Siberian army. With Allied support an army of [a] minimum 200,000 can be organized against [the]

Germans in European Russia. This may well result in bringing Russia also back in[to the] war."[63]

On the next day Wilson wrote to Thomas Dixon, an advocate of intervention, "The creation of an Eastern Front is a more colossal undertaking than I think anyone can have an idea of who is not dealing directly with questions of creating and supplying an army overseas, but that aspect of the matter and every other is having our daily study." On June 27, General Foch wrote to Wilson, "In the interest of military success in Europe, I consider the expedition to Siberia as a very important factor in victory."[64]

The Supreme War Council's July 2 memorandum to Wilson also stressed the importance of the Czechs. It declared: "The recent action of the Czecho-Slovak troops has transformed the Siberian situation. . . . Provided intervention takes place in time, there will be a Slav army in western Siberia on which Russian patriots can rally, which eliminates the risk of Russian public opinion being thrown into the arms of Germany, as might have been the case if intervention were effected by forces almost entirely Japanese." On July 6, Secretary of the Navy Josephus Daniels replied to Admiral Austin M. Knight's June 26 query concerning U.S. policy regarding the Czechs. Daniels replied only that Knight should use his small force in Vladivostok to secure the city in conjunction with other Allied forces. Vladivostok, Daniels wrote, would be used "as a base for the safety of Czechs and as a means of egress for them should the necessity arise." It is clear from this dispatch that Wilson intended to maintain the Czechs in Siberia in order to help the anti-Bolsheviks overthrow the Soviet government and re-create the Eastern Front. Only if it became necessary would the Czechs leave Russia.[65]

In fact, on July 8, Secretary of State Lansing received a message from representatives of the Czech National Council in Russia that stated: "The only object, and the most ardent desire of the Czecho-Slovak troops, is to arrive as soon as possible upon the French front, but, should the Allies, together and unanimously, esteem that the final result of the war would be best attained, under present circumstances, by the return of our troops to the Russian front to be created, then our army would obey the order of its supreme political leader, Professor Masaryk." On the same day Lansing met with Japanese Ambassador Ishii to tell him of the president's decision to intervene in Siberia. Regarding this discussion with the ambassador, Lansing wrote:

> We also considered the possibility of a friendly attitude by the Russians towards the Czecho-Slovaks thus aided and also the possible consequence of their forming a nucleus about which the Russians might rally even to the extent of becoming again a military factor in the war. . . .

We both agreed, however, that while we had these possibilities in mind, no plans could be predicated upon them, and that the objective for the present should be limited to furnishing facilities for the Czecho-Slovaks at Vladivostok to form a juncture with those near Irkutsk by obtaining control of the Amur branch of the Trans-Siberian Railway.

In discussing the foregoing, Ishii said: "The possibilities of extending the program will depend very much upon the way the Siberian people view the present plan (if it is adopted) and how other Russians will look upon it. This we cannot tell until our forces are actually landed at Vladivostok. That will test the question. If they are friendly, we can revise our program." Lansing replied that he agreed entirely. Thus, the plan was to wait and see how the Russian people reacted to the intervention forces, but the ultimate hope was that they would rally around the Czechs and help them overthrow the Soviet government and establish a new Eastern Front against the Central Powers. Indeed, two days later, Lansing reassured the British ambassador that the Siberian expedition "may well be the means eventually of creating a Russian front." Finally, on August 21, Lansing, following the policy on which he and Ishii had agreed, answered a June 10 request from the British embassy for information concerning transportation of the Czechs to the Western Front, writing, "The delay in acknowledging the Embassy's memorandum was unavoidable on account of the uncertainty of the Siberian situation. . . . The Department will reserve judgment in the matter until the situation has become more clarified." The fact that a year later the U.S. government had still neither prepared a single transport for the evacuation of the Czechs nor made any effort to have them transported by any of the other Allies is as telling regarding its real Siberian policy as the patent absurdity of sending 14,000 soldiers (counting the Japanese, under Wilson's plan) to "rescue" 70,000.[66]

The French, who had official responsibility for the Czechs, canceled all of their own efforts to arrange transports for them on July 5, 1918. The British had falsely promised the French that they would provide the transports but never made any effort to do so because their actual plan was similar to Wilson's, to use the Czechs to restore the Eastern Front, the major difference being that the British initially wanted to post half of the Czechs in northern Russia to achieve that objective, a plan made impossible by the Czech Corps' unwillingness to be divided and by the Czech uprising against the Bolsheviks, which closed off any possibility of the Bolsheviks allowing the Czechs transit to Archangel through their European territory. When Clemenceau first discovered that the British had misled him, he reacted angrily, since he still hoped to use the Czechs on the Western Front, but he quickly fell in line with the British plan. Indeed, given the severe shortage of Allied transports caused by the United States' virtual monopolization of Allied shipping in order to dispatch its desperately needed soldiers to France, it is unlikely that the Allies could have mustered enough transports for the 70,000 Czechs in 1918 even if they had so desired.[67]

One objection that has been raised to Maddox's theory is that Wilson, in his July 6 White House meeting, declared that it was impossible to resurrect the Eastern Front. According to Lansing, Wilson concluded "[t]hat the establishment of an eastern front through a military expedition, even if it was wise to employ a large Japanese force, is physically impossible." But it is clear from Wilson's reference to "a large Japanese force" that it was not the re-creation of the Eastern Front that he considered impossible but its restoration by foreign forces. The re-creation of the Eastern Front by Russians was not only possible in Wilson's mind but was the ultimate goal of intervention.[68]

In fact, in his July 17 *aide memoire*, Wilson wrote, "Military action is admissible in Russia, as the Government of the United States sees the circumstances, only to help the Czecho-Slovaks consolidate their forces and get into successful cooperation with their Slavic kinsmen and to steady any efforts at self-government or self-defense in which the Russians themselves may be willing to accept assistance." Within this clever sentence, denying interference in Russian internal affairs while holding out hope to the anti-Bolsheviks, lies the heart of Wilson's policy of Siberian intervention. American and Japanese troops would maintain a low profile while guarding the Trans-Siberian Railway. This would free the Czechs to "consolidate their forces," thus offering protection to the anti-Bolshevik armies and governments then organizing. The anti-Bolsheviks were the "Slavic kinsmen" to whom Wilson referred, while "self-government" referred to democratic institutions absent from the Bolshevik regime, and "self-defense" referred to resistance against the Germans. In Wilson's mind, the re-creation of an Eastern Front by Russian forces, even on a relatively modest scale, not only would revive Allied morale, then sorely strained by the German assault on Paris, but would compel the Germans to retain crucial divisions in the East, which might well be the difference between victory and defeat in the war. Even if the intervention failed to accomplish these goals, the sole cost would be the diversion of a few thousand soldiers who would hardly have made much difference among the millions stationed on the Western Front.[69]

At this time Wilson considered the overthrow of the Soviet government only one step toward the greater goal of overthrowing the German government. The Eastern Front against the Central Powers could be reestablished only by first overthrowing the Soviet government, which was committed to peace with them. With German soldiers seemingly on the verge of taking Paris and German artillery shells exploding in the city, Wilson clearly feared the German menace more than the Bolshevik menace. Only after it became apparent that the downfall of the German government was imminent could the Bolshevik menace assume any large position in his thoughts. Had there been no war, it is highly unlikely that Wilson would ever have sent troops to Siberia. But having sent them, it became easier to justify their presence there, even after the armistice.

Notes

1. Charles Seymour, ed., *The Intimate Papers of Colonel House Arranged as a Narrative* (Boston: Houghton-Mifflin, 1926–1928), vol. 3, 415.

2. N. G. O. Pereira, *White Siberia: The Politics of Civil War* (Montreal: McGill-Queen's University Press, 1996), 11–15; Carol Willcox Melton, *Between War and Peace: Woodrow Wilson and the American Expeditionary Force in Siberia, 1918–1921* (Macon, Ga.: Mercer University Press, 2001), 34.

3. Christopher Lasch, "American Intervention in Siberia: Reinterpretation," *Political Science Quarterly* 77 (June 1962): 219–20; George F. Kennan, *Russia and the West under Lenin and Stalin* (Boston: Little, Brown, 1960), 95–96.

4. Carl W. Ackerman, *Trailing the Bolsheviki: Twelve Thousand Miles with the Allies in Siberia* (New York: Charles Scribner's Sons, 1919), 42; Kennan, *Russia and the West under Lenin and Stalin*, 93; Arthur S. Link, ed., *The Papers of Woodrow Wilson* (Princeton, N.J.: Princeton University Press, 1966–1994), Lord Arthur Balfour to Lord Reading, February 26, 1918, vol. 46, 472; Memorandum of Breckinridge Long, March 2, 1918, vol. 46, 514; Frank L. Polk to Wilson, March 6, 1918, vol. 46, 554–55; James William Morley, *The Japanese Thrust into Siberia, 1918* (New York: Columbia University Press, 1957), 38.

5. U.S. Department of State, *Papers Relating to the Foreign Relations of the United States, Russia, 1918* (Washington, D.C.: Government Printing Office, 1931–1932; reprint, New York: Kraus, 1969), Frank L. Polk to Willing Spencer, March 2, vol. 2, 63–64; Willing Spencer to Robert Lansing, March 16, vol. 2, 80.

6. Ibid., David R. Francis to Robert Lansing, April 2, vol. 2, 96; April 13, vol. 2, 123; April 18, vol. 2, 125; April 22, vol. 2, 131; C. K. Cumming and Walter W. Pettit, eds., *Russian-American Relations: March 1917–March 1920: Documents and Papers* (New York: Harcourt Brace, 1920; reprint, Westport, Conn.: Hyperion, 1977), 124, 166–68, 177, 179–82; R. H. Bruce Lockhart, *British Agent* (New York: G. P. Putnam's Sons, 1933), 248–49; William S. Graves, *America's Siberian Adventure, 1918–1920* (New York: Cape and Smith, 1931), 26.

7. U.S. Department of State, *Foreign Relations, Russia, 1918*, Roland S. Morris to Robert Lansing, March 7, vol. 2, 71; April 13, vol. 2, 122; Paul S. Reinsch to Robert Lansing, April 10, vol. 2, 117. For reference to the sources of the rumors, see Willing

Spencer to Robert Lansing, March 6, vol. 2, 70; John F. Stevens to Robert Lansing, May 30, vol. 2, 181–82; David R. Francis to Robert Lansing, June 14, vol. 2, 211.

8. Ibid., David R. Francis to Robert Lansing, April 17, vol. 2, 125; Maddin Summers to Robert Lansing, April 22, vol. 2, 129–30; Paul S. Reinsch to Robert Lansing, April 25, vol. 2, 137; John K. Caldwell to Robert Lansing, June 14, vol. 2, 210; Ernest L. Harris to Robert Lansing, June 20, vol. 2, 217.

9. U.S. Department of State, *Papers Relating to the Foreign Relations of the United States: The Lansing Papers, 1914–1920* (Washington, D.C.: Government Printing Office, 1939–1940), Lansing to Woodrow Wilson, March 24, 1918, vol. 2, 357n47; Link, *Papers of Woodrow Wilson*, Robert Lansing to Wilson, April 22, 1918, vol. 47, 399; Ishii Kikujiro to Shinpei Goto, April 30, 1918, vol. 47, 473.

10. U.S. Department of State, *Foreign Relations, Russia, 1918*, July 6 Lansing memo, vol. 2, 262–63; July 17 *aide memoire*, vol. 2, 287–90; August 3 paraphrase, vol. 2, 328–29.

11. George F. Kennan, "The Sisson Documents," *Journal of Modern History* 28 (June 1956): 130–31; John Keegan, *The First World War* (New York: Alfred A. Knopf, 1999), 338–39; Ilya Somin, *Stillborn Crusade: The Tragic Failure of Western Intervention in the Russian Civil War, 1918–1920* (New Brunswick, N.J.: Transaction, 1996), 13.

12. Kennan, "Sisson Documents," 134, 138–40; Lockhart, *British Agent*, 219, 229.

13. Kennan, "Sisson Documents," 131; Link, *Papers of Woodrow Wilson*, David R. Francis to Robert Lansing, February 13, 1918, vol. 46, 341; Robert Lansing to David R. Francis, February 18, 1918, vol. 46, 373n5; Diary of Colonel Edward House, September 24, 1918, vol. 51, 104.

14. Kennan, "Sisson Documents," 131–32.

15. Ibid., 133; Link, *Papers of Woodrow Wilson*, Joseph P. Tumulty to Edith Wilson, March 26, 1920, vol. 65, 134–35.

16. John Albert White, *The Siberian Intervention* (Princeton, N.J.: Princeton University Press, 1950), 261–62; Betty M. Unterberger, *America's Siberian Expedition, 1918–1920* (Durham, N.C.: Duke University Press, 1956; reprint, New York: Greenwood, 1969), 87–88. See also Betty M. Unterberger, *The United States, Revolutionary Russia, and the Rise of Czechoslovakia*, 2nd ed. (College Station: Texas A & M University Press, 2000), 263–64.

17. White, *Siberian Intervention*, 262; Unterberger, *America's Siberian Expedition*, 84. It is true that Wilson was briefly suspicious of the Japanese in January 1918 when they rather tactlessly informed U.S. Ambassador Roland Morris that they wished to be left alone to handle any emergencies in Siberia, but the strongly worded messages Wilson ordered in reply silenced the Japanese. See Link, *Papers of Woodrow Wilson*, Wilson to Robert Lansing, January 20, 1918, vol. 46, 46–47; Wilson to Frank L. Polk, January 28, 1918, vol. 46, 117–18. Unterberger's assertion that Wilson was pushed into intervention when, in May 1918, he learned that the Japanese were prepared to invade Siberia with Chinese approval is also fallacious. The State Department had learned of Japanese-Chinese cooperation from the Chinese themselves as early

as February and was far from frantic about it. See U.S. Department of State, *Foreign Relations, Russia, 1918*, Paul S. Reinsch to Robert Lansing, February 23, vol. 2, 55; Robert Lansing to Walter Hines Page, February 27, vol. 2, 58. For the Japanese agreement to send only 12,000 soldiers to Siberia as late as August 3, see Link, *Papers of Woodrow Wilson*, Frank L. Polk to Woodrow Wilson, August 3, 1918, vol. 49, 175.

18. U.S. Department of State, *Lansing Papers, 1914–1920*, David R. Francis to Lansing, May 2, 1916, vol. 2, 310–12; David Lloyd George, *War Memoirs of David Lloyd George* (Boston: Little, Brown, 1935–1937), vol. 6, 171; Link, *Papers of Woodrow Wilson*, William Boyce Thompson Memo, January 3, 1918, vol. 45, 444; Newton D. Baker to Wilson, May 28, 1918, vol. 48, 181; Peyton C. March to Tasker H. Bliss, May 28, 1918, vol. 48, 182.

19. Seymour, *Intimate Papers of Colonel House*, vol. 3, 323–24.

20. U.S. Department of State, *Foreign Relations, Russia, 1918*, July 6 Robert Lansing Memo, vol. 2, 263; Robert Lansing to Woodrow Wilson, July 9, vol. 2, 270; Link, *Papers of Woodrow Wilson*, Lord Reading to Lord Arthur Balfour, July 3, 1918, vol. 48, 513; July 8, 1918, vol. 48, 566; Robert Lansing to Woodrow Wilson, July 8, 1918, vol. 48, 561; Lord Arthur Balfour to Lord Reading, July 10, 1918, vol. 48, 622; Kennan, *Russia and the West under Lenin and Stalin*, 113, 115; Roy MacLaren, *Canadians in Russia, 1918–1919* (Toronto: Macmillan of Canada, 1976), 145–46; Norman E. Saul, *War and Revolution: The United States and Russia, 1914–1921* (Lawrence: University Press of Kansas, 2001), 293.

21. Graves, *America's Siberian Adventure*, xi–xii; Link, *Papers of Woodrow Wilson*, Newton D. Baker to Wilson, November 27, 1918, vol. 53, 227.

22. Link, *Papers of Woodrow Wilson*, Tasker H. Bliss to Henry P. McCain, February 19, 1918, vol. 46, 392; Peyton C. March, *The Nation at War* (Garden City, N.Y.: Doubleday, 1932), 126.

23. U.S. Department of State, *Lansing Papers, 1914–1920*, Lansing to Woodrow Wilson, February 27, 1918, 355; March 24, 1918, 358.

24. Ishii Kikujiro, *Diplomatic Commentaries*, trans. and ed. William R. Langdon (Baltimore: Johns Hopkins University Press, 1936), 123.

25. Link, *Papers of Woodrow Wilson*, Colonel Edward House to Wilson, February 2, 1918, vol. 46, 214–15; Robert Lansing to Tasker H. Bliss, February 2, 1918, vol. 46, 219; Sir William Wiseman to Sir Eric Drummond, February 4, 1918, vol. 46, 250; Robert Lansing to Wilson, February 9, 1918, vol. 46, 302; Robert Lansing to Walter Hines Page, February 13, 1918, vol. 46, 340; Lord Reading to the Foreign Office, February 15, 1918, vol. 46, 355; Lord Reading to Lord Arthur Balfour, February 27, 1918, vol. 46, 482; Memorandum by Frank K. Lane, March 2, 1918, vol. 46, 515; Colonel Edward House to Lord Arthur Balfour, March 4, 1918, vol. 46, 530–31; Lord Reading to Sir Eric Drummond, March 27, 1918, vol. 47, 171.

26. W. B. Fowler, *British-American Relations, 1917–1918: The Role of Sir William Wiseman* (Princeton, N.J.: Princeton University Press, 1969), 180; U.S. Department of State, *Foreign Relations, Russia, 1918*, Roland S. Morris to Robert Lansing, December 16, 1917, vol. 2, 9; Memorandum of Breckinridge Long, March 2, 1918, vol.

2, 62; Woodrow Wilson to Robert Lansing, April 29, 1918, vol. 2, 144; Link, *Papers of Woodrow Wilson*, Sir Cecil Rice to the Foreign Office, December 27, 1917, vol. 45, 370; December 29, 1917, vol. 45, 393; Lord Robert Cecil to the British Embassy, January 1, 1918, vol. 45, 420; Sir William C. Greene to the Foreign Office, March 7, 1918, vol. 46, 571.

27. Link, *Papers of Woodrow Wilson*, Sir William C. Greene to the Foreign Office, March 7, 1918, vol. 46, 571; Roland S. Morris to Robert Lansing, March 19, 1918, vol. 47, 77; U.S. Department of State, *Foreign Relations, Russia, 1918*, Robert Lansing to Woodrow Wilson, April 29, 1918, vol. 2, 144; Roland S. Morris to Robert Lansing, May 16, 1918, vol. 2, 162–63; June 22, 1918, vol. 2, 219.

28. Link, *Papers of Woodrow Wilson*, Ishii Kikujiro to Robert Lansing, June 26, 1918, vol. 48, 449; Wilson to Robert Lansing, June 28, 1918, vol. 48, 457; Fowler, *British-American Relations*, 180–81.

29. Eugene P. Trani, "Woodrow Wilson and the Decision to Intervene in Russia: A Reconsideration," *Journal of Modern History* 48 (September 1976): 452.

30. Link, *Papers of Woodrow Wilson*, Sir William Wiseman to Sir Eric Drummond and Lord Arthur Balfour, February 4, 1918, vol. 46, 248; Memorandum by Sir William Wiseman, March 9, 1918, vol. 46, 591; Frederick Palmer, ed., *Bliss, Peacemaker: The Life and Letters of General Tasker Howard Bliss* (New York: Dodd, Mead, 1934), Bliss to Newton D. Baker, June 4, 1918, 295; Newton D. Baker to Bliss, July 8, 1918, 302.

31. Link, *Papers of Woodrow Wilson*, Colonel Edward House to Wilson, June 21, 1918, vol. 48, 390–91.

32. Fowler, *British-American Relations*, 167–68.

33. U.S. Department of State, *Foreign Relations, Russia, 1918*, Jean Jusserand to Robert Lansing, January 8, vol. 2, 20–21; March 12, vol. 2, 75–77; April 8, vol. 2, 109–12; April 21, vol. 2, 128–29; April 23, vol. 2, 132–33; Lord Reading to Robert Lansing, January 28, vol. 2, 35–36; April 25, vol. 2, 135–37; April 27, vol. 2, 140; May 1, vol. 2, 148–49; Arthur Hugh Frazier to Robert Lansing, July 2–3, vol. 2, 241–46; Link, *Papers of Woodrow Wilson*, Jean Jusserand to Robert Lansing, March 12, 1918, vol. 47, 21–23; Jean Jusserand to Wilson, June 25, vol. 48, 415. For the texts of the Supreme War Council's December 14, 1917, resolution and Balfour's June memorandum, see Lloyd George, *War Memoirs*, vol. 6, 161–62, 177–78. These represent but a small fraction of British and French attempts to pressure Wilson into Siberian intervention.

34. Link, *Papers of Woodrow Wilson*, Wilson to John S. Williams, February 6, 1918, vol. 46, 257.

35. Ibid., Colonel Edward House to Wilson, March 3, 1918, vol. 46, 518–19.

36. Ibid., Tasker H. Bliss to Newton D. Baker, June 8, 1918, vol. 48, 385; Colonel Edward House to Wilson, June 11, 1918, vol. 48, 283; Diary of Colonel Edward House, June 14, 1918, vol. 48, 317; U.S. Department of State, *Lansing Papers, 1914–1920*, Woodrow Wilson to Lansing, March 22, 1918, vol. 2, 357. Wilson's chief military advisers, Bliss and March, agreed with Wilson that intervention was militar-

ily impracticable. See Link, *Papers of Woodrow Wilson*, Tasker H. Bliss to Henry P. McCain, February 19, 1918, vol. 46, 391–92; Tasker H. Bliss to Newton D. Baker, May 26, 1918, vol. 48, 181; Peyton C. March to Tasker H. Bliss, May 28, 1918, vol. 48, 182; Peyton C. March to Newton D. Baker, June 24, 1918, vol. 48, 419–21.

37. William Appleman Williams, "The American Intervention in Russia, 1917–1920," *Studies on the Left* 3 (Fall 1963): 29–30, 35–36, 41–43, 47; 4 (Winter 1964): 40, 54–56. This article was published in two parts in back-to-back issues.

38. Ray Stannard Baker and William E. Dodd, eds., *The Public Papers of Woodrow Wilson* (New York: Harper, 1925–1927), Speech to the American Federation of Labor, November 27, 1917, vol. 5, 120; Fourteen Points Speech, January 1918, vol. 5, 155–62; Link, *Papers of Woodrow Wilson*, Chief Danger of Revolutions and Revolutionary Movements in Eastern Europe: Revolutionary Movements in Western Europe, February 9, 1918, vol. 46, 310–13; Wilson to Robert Lansing, February 13, 1918, vol. 46, 334; Robert Lansing to Wilson, February 15, 1918, vol. 46, 349–50; Robert K. Murray, *Red Scare: A Study of National Hysteria, 1919–1920* (New York: McGraw-Hill, 1955), 13, 22–32.

39. Link, *Papers of Woodrow Wilson*, Statement by Robert Lansing, December 4, 1917, vol. 45, 206; Robert Lansing to Woodrow Wilson, December 10, 1917, vol. 45, 264; David Lloyd George, *Memoirs of the Peace Conference* (Boston: Little, Brown, 1939), vol. 1, 213; vol. 6, 149.

40. Jane Degras, ed., *Soviet Documents on Foreign Policy, 1917–1945* (Oxford: Oxford University Press, 1951–1954), vol. 1, 43; Link, *Papers of Woodrow Wilson*, Wilson to Robert Lansing, January 20, 1918, vol. 46, 65; William G. McAdoo to Robert Lansing, January 17, 1918, vol. 46, 66; David S. Foglesong, *America's Secret War against Bolshevism: U.S. Intervention in the Russian Civil War, 1917–1920* (Chapel Hill: University of North Carolina Press, 1995), 55.

41. Degras, *Soviet Documents on Foreign Policy*, "To the Toiling, Oppressed, and Exhausted Peoples of Europe," vol. 1, 18–21; Link, *Papers of Woodrow Wilson*, Josephus Daniels's Diary, November 27, 1917, vol. 45, 147; December 21, 1917, vol. 45, 342.

42. Link, *Papers of Woodrow Wilson*, Wilson to Robert Lansing, January 20, 1918, vol. 46, 46n3; Wilson to Samuel Gompers, January 21, 1918, vol. 46, 53.

43. Degras, *Soviet Documents on Foreign Policy*, Trotsky's Speech at Brest-Litovsk, February 10, 1918, vol. 1, 43–45; Cumming and Pettit, eds., *Russian-American Relations*, 81–82, 104; Link, *Papers of Woodrow Wilson*, Lord Arthur Balfour to Lord Reading, April 19, 1918, vol. 47, 356; Sir William Wiseman to Eric Drummond, June 14, 1918, vol. 48, 315; John K. Caldwell to Robert Lansing, June 25, 1918, vol. 48, 429.

44. David W. McFadden, *Alternative Paths: Soviets and Americans, 1917–1920* (Oxford: Oxford University Press, 1993), 60; Richard K. Debo, *Revolution and Survival: The Foreign Policy of Soviet Russia, 1917–1918* (Toronto: University of Toronto Press, 1979), 59–60, 77, 125.

45. Degras, *Soviet Documents on Foreign Policy*, vol. 1, 34–39, 57–61, 78–79, 86; Link, *Papers of Woodrow Wilson*, Lord Reading to Wilson, February 27, 1918, vol.

46, 472n3; Lord Reading to Lord Arthur Balfour, April 25, 1918, vol. 47, 440; Debo, *Revolution and Survival*, 143, 173–74; Fowler, *British-American Relations*, 177; Lockhart, *British Agent*, 236, 243.

46. Link, *Papers of Woodrow Wilson*, Roger C. Tredwell to Robert Lansing, December 5, 1917, vol. 45, 216; Robert Lansing to Wilson, May 16, 1918, vol. 48, 38; Woodrow Wilson Papers, Manuscripts Division, Library of Congress, extract of Ariadna Tyrkova-Williams letter, April 26, 1918; Hornel to Wilson, June 11, 1918; Memo of Vance Thompson, June 12, 1918; David R. Francis to Wilson, June 22, 1918.

47. Link, *Papers of Woodrow Wilson*, Ferdinand Foch to Wilson, June 27, 1918, vol. 48, 445; March, *Nation at War*, 120; Edward M. Coffman, *The War to End All Wars: The American Military Experience in World War I* (Oxford: Oxford University Press, 1968), 179, 212.

48. Kennan, *Russia and the West under Lenin and Stalin*, 105; Robert J. Maddox, *The Unknown War with Russia: Wilson's Siberian Intervention* (San Rafael, Calif.: Presidio, 1977), 48–50.

49. Kennan, *Russia and the West under Lenin and Stalin*, 97.

50. Eduard Beneš, *My War Memoirs*, trans. Paul Selver (Boston: Houghton-Mifflin, 1928), 353; James Bunyan, ed., *Intervention, Civil War, and Communism in Russia, April–December 1918, Documents and Materials* (Baltimore: Johns Hopkins University Press, 1936), 81, 85, 88; Link, *Papers of Woodrow Wilson*, Tasker H. Bliss to Robert Lansing, May 3, 1918, vol. 47, 514.

51. John Bradley, *Allied Intervention in Russia* (New York: Basic Books, 1968), 83, 86–89.

52. Richard Goldhurst, *The Midnight War: The American Intervention in Russia 1918–1920* (New York: McGraw-Hill, 1978), 31–32; Richard Luckett, *The White Generals: An Account of the White Movement and the Russian Civil War* (New York: Viking, 1971), 163–64; Unterberger, *The United States, Revolutionary Russia, and the Rise of Czechoslovakia*, 173–74; Beneš, *War Memoirs*, 367.

53. Ackerman, *Trailing the Bolsheviki*, 129; Peter Fleming, *The Fate of Admiral Kolchak* (London: Rupert Hart-Davis, 1963), 18–23; Bunyan, *Intervention, Civil War, and Communism in Russia*, 86–88, 91.

54. Thomas G. Masaryk, *The Making of a State: Memories and Observations, 1914–1918*, trans. and introduced by Henry Wickham Steed (New York: Frederick A. Stokes, 1927), 276.

55. Jefferson Caffery Papers, University of Louisiana at Lafayette, May 20, 1918, *Times of London* clipping; Ray Stannard Baker, ed., *Woodrow Wilson: Life and Letters* (New York: Doubleday, 1939), vol. 8, 187–88, 191, 193.

56. Coffman, *War to End All Wars*, 158, 213.

57. Ibid., 10, 49, 171; B. H. Liddell Hart, *The War in Outline, 1914–1918* (New York: Random House, 1936), 245–49.

58. Baker, *Woodrow Wilson*, John J. Pershing to Newton D. Baker, June 17, 1918, vol. 8, 217; Coffman, *War to End All Wars*, 177, 180, 182; John Ellis, *Eye-Deep in Hell: Trench Warfare in World War I* (New York: Pantheon, 1976), 178.

59. Baker, *Woodrow Wilson*, Tasker H. Bliss to Newton D. Baker, June 1, 1918, vol. 8, 182; Georges Clemenceau, David Lloyd George, and Vittorio Orlando to Wilson, June 2, 1918, vol. 8, 185–86; Wilson Papers, Newton D. Baker to Wilson, June 21, 1918; Jefferson Caffery Papers, Jefferson Caffery to family, July 6, 1918; Coffman, *War to End All Wars*, 213.

60. Link, *Papers of Woodrow Wilson*, Lord Arthur Balfour to Lord Reading, April 15, 1918, vol. 47, 355; Sir William Wiseman to Colonel Edward House, May 1, 1918, vol. 47, 503–4.

61. U.S. Department of State, *Foreign Relations, Russia, 1918*, Paul S. Reinsch to Robert Lansing, June 13, vol. 2, 206–7; U.S. Department of State, *Lansing Papers, 1914–1920*, Woodrow Wilson to Lansing, June 17, 1918, vol. 2, 363.

62. Seymour, *Intimate Papers of Colonel House*, vol. 3, 407; U.S. Department of State, *Lansing Papers, 1914–1920*, Woodrow Wilson to Lansing, June 19, 1918, vol. 2, 364.

63. U.S. Department of State, *Foreign Relations, Russia, 1918*, John K. Caldwell to Robert Lansing, June 25, vol. 2, 227; Alexander Konovalov to Robert Lansing, June 25, vol. 2, 228–29.

64. Baker, *Woodrow Wilson*, Wilson to Thomas Dixon, June 26, 1918, vol. 8, 233; Ferdinand Foch to Wilson, June 27, 1918, vol. 8, 235.

65. Link, *Papers of Woodrow Wilson*, Supreme War Council memo, July 2, 1918, vol. 48, 496–97; U.S. Department of State, *Foreign Relations, Russia, 1918*, Austin M. Knight to Josephus Daniels, June 26, vol. 2, 231; Robert Lansing to Roland S. Morris, July 6, vol. 2, 263–64.

66. U.S. Department of State, *Foreign Relations, Russia, 1918*, John K. Caldwell to Robert Lansing, July 8, vol. 2, 267; Robert Lansing memo, July 8, vol. 2, 267–68; Robert Lansing to Thomas B. Hohler, August 21, vol. 2, 352; Fowler, *British-American Relations*, 190; Bunyan, *Intervention, Civil War, and Communism in Russia*, 109–11; Link, *Papers of Woodrow Wilson*, Paul J. Mantoux's notes of a meeting of the Council of Four, June 26, 1919, vol. 61, 206.

67. Bradley, *Allied Intervention in Russia*, 47; Debo, *Revolution and Survival*, 273; Melton, *Between War and Peace*, 62.

68. U.S. Department of State, *Foreign Relations, Russia, 1918*, Robert Lansing Memo, July 6, vol. 2, 262.

69. Ibid., July 17 *aide memoire*, vol. 2, 288.

CHAPTER THREE

~

Walking on Eggs
Loaded with Dynamite

VI. The evacuation of all Russian territory and such a settlement of all questions affecting Russia as will secure the best and freest cooperation of the other nations of the world in obtaining for her an unhampered and unembarrassed opportunity for the independent determination of her own political development and national policy. . . . The treatment accorded Russia by her sister nations in the months to come will be the acid test of their good will, of their comprehension of her needs as distinguished from their own interests, and of their intelligent and unselfish sympathy.

—President Woodrow Wilson, Fourteen Points Speech, January 1918.[1]

On the evening of August 4, 1918, Major General William S. Graves, a tall, fifty-three-year-old Texan, stepped off a train in Kansas City. He was immediately led to a railroad station, where he was greeted by Secretary of War Newton D. Baker. Graves held his breath. The War Department had wired him in the afternoon, instructing him to leave his Eighth Infantry Division at Camp Fremont in Palo Alto, California, and to proceed immediately to Kansas City to meet Baker.

Graves feared that Baker would tell him that he could not lead his division into battle in France as scheduled. Graves's fear proved well founded. Baker told Graves that he and his soldiers were going to Siberia, then handed him a sealed envelope containing Wilson's *aide memoire*, saying, "This contains the policy of the United States in Russia which you are to follow. Watch your

*Major General William S. Graves. Robert L. Eichelberger Papers,
David M. Rubenstein Rare Book & Manuscript Library, courtesy of
Duke University, Durham, North Carolina.*

*General Graves and his staff. Robert L. Eichelberger Papers, David M. Rubenstein Rare
Book & Manuscript Library, courtesy of Duke University, Durham, North Carolina.*

step; you will be walking on eggs loaded with dynamite." With that, Baker was gone. Having no other knowledge of the situation in Siberia, Graves decided that he must honor the *aide memoire*'s injunction against intervention in Russian internal affairs. Graves's strict interpretation of the *aide memoire* would earn him the intense hatred of anti-Bolsheviks of all nationalities, Russian, British, French, and American alike.[2]

Chaos

On September 2, General Graves arrived in Vladivostok, a city with a prewar population of 100,000 now swelled far beyond that number, with the first contingent of approximately 5,000 men, including support personnel, selected from his Eighth Division.

Graves found chaos when he stepped down from the transport. The Czechs had overthrown the Bolshevik government at Vladivostok but had not replaced it with any organized administration. The only government that existed consisted of a few troublesome czarist officials whom the Allied contingents had placed in power. Thus, Graves noted that he was met neither by customs inspectors nor by quarantine officials. Furthermore, Allied supplies, including bales of cotton, piles of rubber badly needed on the Western Front, and more than 1,000 automobiles lay unused and unguarded throughout the

Vladivostok. Robert L. Eichelberger Papers, David M. Rubenstein Rare Book & Manuscript Library, courtesy of Duke University, Durham, North Carolina.

area. The latter had not even been removed from their crates. The Wilson Administration had declared the rescue of these forlorn artifacts to be one of the primary goals of intervention, yet these relics of civilization, quaintly out of place in Siberia, would remain largely unutilized and unappreciated.[3]

Colonel Henry D. Styer had arrived from the Philippines over two weeks earlier with approximately 3,500 soldiers from the Twenty-Seventh and Thirty-First Infantry Regiments. Styer immediately informed Graves that the Twenty-Seventh Infantry was participating in a joint action with the Japanese against a group of Bolsheviks and German prisoners to the north at Khabarovsk. The Japanese alleged that the Germans had organized 15,000 men in an effort to seize the stores at Vladivostok. Another 50,000 Bolsheviks and Germans were allegedly blocking the Czechs west of Irkutsk.[4]

The Japanese commander, General Otani Kikuzo, also told Graves that he must place his force under Otani's command because all of the Allied governments had agreed that the Japanese commander would be the Supreme Allied Commander in Siberia. This news astounded Graves since he had received no order to recognize the Japanese commander as his superior, though President Wilson had indeed privately "agreed to let the Japanese have the supreme command when they landed at Vladivostok," nor had Graves expected to find any Allied forces besides the Japanese in Siberia. He

Twenty-Seventh Infantry on Parade in Vladivostok. Robert L. Eichelberger Papers, David M. Rubenstein Rare Book & Manuscript Library, courtesy of Duke University, Durham, North Carolina.

Japanese Infantry on Parade in Vladivostok. Robert L. Eichelberger Papers, David M. Rubenstein Rare Book & Manuscript Library, courtesy of Duke University, Durham, North Carolina.

knew that Wilson's intervention plan involved only American and Japanese troops, yet he saw over 2,000 British, French, Italian, and Chinese soldiers milling about Vladivostok. In addition, although Graves knew that Wilson's plan called for a Japanese force of 7,000, and the Japanese had subsequently promised to send only 12,000, it was quite obvious that the Japanese had sent many more men to Siberia than even the latter figure.[5]

If all of this was not confusing enough to Graves, he soon found that the Japanese were not telling the truth about the Ussuri River campaign around Khabarovsk. Only a small Bolshevik force opposed them there, and this force was quickly routed, ending all Bolshevik resistance east of Lake Baikal. The Japanese were attempting to destroy all opposition to them, Bolshevik and non-Bolshevik, and to justify the large numbers of troops they had dispatched to Siberia by exaggerating the strength of their opponents. They kept the Twenty-Seventh Infantry away from the front so that its officers could neither identify the enemy nor estimate its strength. Even so, an American intelligence officer finally concluded that Japanese and other Allied reports on the strength of the enemy were "greatly exaggerated." Graves's own inspection tour of the region in October produced the same result. The Twenty-Seventh Infantry was returned to Vladivostok and, thereafter, Graves viewed the Japanese with great suspicion.[6]

Guarding the Suchan Coal Mines

Although Graves was unwilling to engage in a war against the Bolsheviks, he was willing to help guard the Suchan coal mines. Located seventy-five miles west of Vladivostok, the Suchan mines supplied fuel for the eastern portion of the Trans-Siberian Railway. Early in September 1918 Allied commanders in Vladivostok agreed that the mines would be placed under American control. Graves ordered a company of Americans to join a company of Japanese troops and another of Chinese soldiers in guarding the mines.[7]

American commanders found themselves plagued by disputes between the mines' old managerial elite and its workers. The Allied commanders insisted that the mines' former manager, who had been removed from his position by the Bolsheviks, be restored to his former rank. Graves later wrote, "The manager said he was an engineer and politics never entered into his calculations, but we found he changed considerably after he got his old job back, and he soon became an ardent advocate of the old czarist methods in dealing with the miners." The manager's predilection for such methods was obviously heightened by his desire for revenge against those workers who had been instrumental in his dismissal.[8]

In fact, Graves had trouble restraining his own men from arresting Bolsheviks. Apparently, some American soldiers believed that they were in Siberia to fight bolshevism. It was understandable that they should think so since by guarding the Suchan mines, they were allowing supplies to reach anti-Bolshevik armies via the Trans-Siberian Railway. However, though Graves understood that guarding the mines was not a neutral act, he insisted that his instructions bound him to act in as impartial a manner as possible. Thus, he ordered his men at the Suchan mines to stop arresting Bolsheviks: "Troops must take no part in arresting people because of their political affiliations; they have no authority to arrest and confine a Russian citizen because he has taken part in some meeting." *New York Times* reporter Carl Ackerman witnessed Graves rebuking an officer for arresting a man because he claimed to be a Bolshevik. Graves declared, "The United States is not at war with the Bolsheviki or any other faction of Russia. . . . You are to arrest only those who attack you."[9]

The Peak and Decline of the Czechs

The *aide memoire* instructed Graves that the primary goal of intervention was to aid the Czechs. But the Czechs did not seem to require much aid. In fact, by the late summer of 1918, the Czechs controlled the Trans-Siberian

Railway from the Volga River to Vladivostok and were carrying on offensive operations as much as 200 miles from the railway.[10]

Indeed, it was the Czechs' approach to Ekaterinburg that caused the Bolsheviks to execute Czar Nicholas II, his wife, their five children, and four attendants, all of whom were being held in the former house of a military engineer. Lenin personally approved the executions because he feared that if the Czechs freed the czar and his family, they would become a powerful rallying point for anti-Bolsheviks. Whether because of the firing squad's poor marksmanship caused by drunkenness or because the daughters were wearing jewel-incrusted corsets, the executioners had to dispatch the writhing bodies of the latter with bayonets and pistols. The corpses were then left in an abandoned mine. Recent forensic evidence suggests that the remains were then removed, burned, and buried in a nearby forest. The Bolsheviks lied to the Russian public, claiming that only the czar had been executed, and not his family, which included a ten-year-old invalid son, and that the rest of the family was "sent to a safe place." (On the same night the czarina's sister, her husband, and other members of the imperial family were also hurled alive down a mine shaft at Alapaevsk.) When the Czechs arrived at the house in Ekaterinburg in whose cellar the czar was executed, they allegedly found one of his dogs still whimpering for him.[11]

But though the Czechs were the dominant force in Siberia, their forces were dispersed too widely. They did not consolidate their forces because the Allies instructed them not to. On June 18, 1918, the U.S. Consul at Omsk received this message from the new U.S. Consul-General in Moscow, DeWitt C. Poole: "You may inform the Czecho-Slovak leaders, confidentially, that pending further notice the Allies will be glad, from a political point of view, to have them hold their present position." This message, authorized after the fact by U.S. Ambassador to Russia David R. Francis, was naturally construed by the Czechs to mean that an Allied force of sufficient size was coming to reinforce them, especially since a French liaison officer, Major Alphonse Guinet, was continually assuring them of such aid. Guinet boasted to the Czechs, "Now you will witness how we will with body and soul support the liberation movement of the Czecho-Slovak army. Thanks to you a new Russian front is established." Unfortunately, however much soul Guinet's government was prepared to offer the Czechs, it could offer only a few bodies. Yet French Prime Minister Georges Clemenceau tipped the scales by sending instructions for the Czechs to seize the Trans-Siberian Railway in preparation for Allied intervention, instructions that must have increased the Czech perception that a sizable Allied force would be coming to reinforce them. Based on these assurances, on July 7 a representative of the Czech Executive

Committee traveling with the corps ordered the westernmost units to "stand fast and act as the advance guard of the Allies with a view to forming a new Eastern Front against the Germans."[12]

As a result, the Czechs were confused and demoralized when no Allied reinforcements arrived. They suffered a string of defeats at the hands of the Bolsheviks in September and October 1918, causing some units to refuse to fight. Despite these defeats and mutinies, and despite numerous pleas from the Czechs, the British, and the French, both the Japanese and the Americans refused to send reinforcements to aid them. Following President Wilson's instructions, Secretary of State Lansing informed the Czechs that no reinforcements would proceed to Omsk to aid them and advised them to fall back east of the Ural Mountains. The Czechs naturally felt betrayed by the Allies, representatives of whom had instructed them to hold their positions. Wilson's decision not to send reinforcements to aid the Czechs will be discussed in the next chapter.[13]

The Armistice

Two events in November ended any possibility of the Czechs operating effectively in Siberia. First, on November 11, an armistice was signed between the representatives of the Allies and those of the Central Powers, ending World War I. The Czechs had been fighting to re-create an Eastern Front against the Central Powers, and now such a front was no longer necessary. The Czech independence for which they had fought so well was now becoming a reality. They felt certain that it was time to go home.[14]

The Kolchak Coup

Yet the Czechs might have been persuaded to continue fighting the Bolsheviks had it not been for the second event of November 1918, the overthrow of the All-Russian Provisional Government. In April 1918 the Siberian government, dominated by members of the Socialist Revolutionary Party, merged with the Ufa Government, another fairly liberal government, and others to form the All-Russian Provisional Government. The All-Russian Provisional Government, led by a directorate of five members, pledged to surrender power to a constituent assembly once it was organized. On the evening of November 17, a group of Cossacks, led by Captain Ivan Krasilnikov, arrested the Directorate's two socialist members. Several ministers in the government and one of the remaining members of the Directorate then urged Admiral Alexander V. Kolchak, the government's war minister and the former commander of Russia's Black Sea fleet, to assume supreme power.

Kolchak accepted the offer, proclaiming himself "The Supreme Ruler of All the Russias." Kolchak's officials then promoted Krasilnikov two ranks to colonel, abolished the Constituent Assembly being organized in Ekaterin-burg, arrested several members for their alleged opposition to the regime, and executed some of them the following month.[15]

The British seemed pleased by the coup. Perhaps it was a mere coincidence that the Twenty-Fifth Middlesex Battalion arrived in Omsk a few days before Kolchak seized power, but General Graves later wrote, "There can be no question that the British troops were marching around the streets of Omsk the night of the coup and this had the effect of giving aid to the Russians engineering the change. There can also be no doubt that [British] General [Alfred] Knox had much influence with Admiral Kolchak, and he seemed to want everyone to know of this influence." (It was, after all, to the British that Kolchak had offered his military services in order to continue fighting the Central Powers after the Bolshevik Revolution.) This was the same Knox who was suspected of having worked to overthrow the Kerensky government in order to replace it with a stronger one. It was also the same Knox who, according to Graves, once complained bitterly that Graves "was getting the reputation of being a friend of the poor and didn't I know they were only swine." (Graves disagreed, calling the Siberian peasants "generous, kindly, and very hospitable.") It was the same Knox who, on October 25, had "threatened to gather a gang and overthrow" the All-Russian Provisional Government. It was the same Knox who had been attempting to maneuver reactionaries into key ministries within the government. (Not that Knox liked all of Kolchak's underlings. When Knox asked Kolchak why he kept his chief of staff, a young colonel that even Kolchak acknowledged to be inefficient and sadistic, Kolchak replied, "I am sure he will not stab me in the back," prompting Knox to note dryly, "Kolchak forgets the post requires more positive qualities.") Finally, it was the same Knox who, on October 27, had urged that the Directorate be reduced to a single member. Indeed, while serving as Britain's secretary of war the following year, Winston Churchill referred to the policy of continuing aid for the Kolchak regime as "an honourable obligation, seeing that the British Government had called it into being when necessity demanded it," thereby essentially acknowledging Knox's role in the coup that brought Kolchak into power.[16]

The coup distressed the Czechs, who had been friends of the Socialist Revolutionaries, the majority faction in Siberia. If the Czechs had continued to fight in Siberia following the armistice with the Central Powers, it would have been largely out of loyalty to their Socialist Revolutionary allies. The soldiers of the Czech Corps did not need to hear that the Czech National Council had denounced Kolchak's regime as government without the consent of the governed on November 22 to reach the same conclusion. They had seen Kolchak's reactionary clique firsthand. By his own account, the hot-tempered Kolchak made matters worse by speaking harshly to Czech leaders; when they asked why they were not consulted about the coup in advance, Kolchak retorted, "We are neither interested in nor obliged to consider your opinion." These were strong words considering that the Czechs remained the only effective force fighting the Bolsheviks at the time. Thus, when one of the Czech generals ordered the Fifth Regiment to the front for an attack on Perm a few days after the Kolchak coup, the soldiers refused. Henceforth, the Czechs would not fight the Bolsheviks. By January 20, 1919, all Czech troops on the front had been replaced by Russians. By June 16, Colonel John F. Stevens, head of America's Russian Railway Service Corps, was writing about the Czechs: "They are thoroughly dissatisfied, want to go home and Commanding General [Jan Syrový] tells me they cannot be held under discipline longer than three months. Four regiments have already refused duty, in other words will fight Bolsheviki no longer. There is very grave danger that they will defy their officers and by arrangements with Bolshevik[s] try to go home through Russia. This would mean war with Siberian army and defeat of latter and overthrow of government and consequent anarchy under Bolshevik[s]."[17]

On June 23, Czech leader Eduard Beneš wrote to the French Government, "Our soldiers in Siberia have already suffered so intensely that their desire is to return home as soon as possible." He later concluded regarding the deterioration of Czech morale: "They were disappointed because no help had arrived from the Japanese or the rest of the Allies, and they saw that the anti-Bolshevik Russians were incapable of rallying any firm resistance which might lead to a restoration of the Russian State authority. . . . Kolchak's coup on November 18, 1918, removed our troops from military cooperation with the Russians."[18]

General Graves agreed. He wrote:

> The Czechs in Siberia were naturally liberally minded men. They had had enough of autocracy and were willing to fight bolshevism because they visualized it as being an agent of Germany and Austria, and because it seemed to stand between them and their aspiration to establish a republican Czecho-Slovakia. As soon as they realized that fighting bolshevism meant not only combating all forms of liberalism, but it meant the placing of what governmental power was left into the hands of people who had held office during the Romanoff dynasty

and who probably had the Czarist ideas as to Government, then the Czechs could no longer march in step with England, France, and Japan.[19]

Secretary of War Baker concurred with Graves's assessment of Czech sentiment. On February 11, 1919, he wrote to the State Department concerning the Czechs:

> Many are not in sympathy with the kind of government they believe Kolchak is trying to establish in Siberia and a feeling has developed in the ranks that by fighting against the Bolsheviks they are helping to maintain a government with ideas directly opposed to the Czechs' idea of a democratic form of government. . . . There is also a belief among the Czech soldiers that it is not just to keep them on the fighting line where they continually suffer losses unless other allies send their troops to fight the Bolsheviks with them. I consider the morale bad and the Czechs do not constitute a dependable force for use against the Bolsheviks.

The U.S. Consul-General at Irkutsk, Ernest L. Harris, although an ardent supporter of Kolchak, agreed that the Czechs despised him as a reactionary.[20]

The Czechs were not the only ones who disapproved of the Kolchak coup. Many Whites, the name commonly used to refer to anti-Bolshevik Russians, were shocked and dismayed by it. To cite one indication of Siberian sentiment, approximately 55 percent of eastern Siberians and 80 percent of western Siberians had voted for the Socialist Revolutionaries and another 10 percent of Siberians for the Bolsheviks in the Russian elections for the Constituent Assembly in 1917; these Russians were hardly pleased by the advent of a reactionary regime and its arrest and execution of members of the Siberian Constituent Assembly of 1918. From the standpoint of the ordinary White soldier, the new regiments Kolchak now organized were chiefly distinguishable by the haughtiness of their officers, who wore ostentatious epaulets, which most Russians considered aristocratic emblems of czarist days and, thus, symbolic of the desire to restore the hated monarchy.[21]

Anton Ovchinnikov, a White soldier who had fought enthusiastically alongside the Czechs against the Bolsheviks but who was demoralized by the Kolchak coup, later recalled, "Our military spirit was broken." After one of Kolchak's new regiments consisting of arrogant officers and demoralized peasants fled the battlefield ignominiously, Ovchinnikov's unit composed a song that included the lyrics:

Here's your Kolchak army!
Here's your new Russian regiment!

> As they deserted at Belebei,
> So they will do again.

The members of Ovchinnikov's unit begged the Czechs to be allowed to accompany them eastward away from the front, but the Czechs were unable to grant such a request to Russian soldiers. Ovchinnikov ultimately deserted Kolchak's army, found peasants willing to give him clothes and a clergyman willing to write a fraudulent birth certificate for him, and fled to Sakhalin, the farthest east he could go and still remain in Russian territory. Like many Siberians, he ultimately became a partisan against the Kolchak regime. Although appalled by the partisans' own atrocities at Nikolaevsk, he felt he had little choice but to remain with them, given his complete opposition to the restoration of a monarchy. (His story ended more happily than most, though, because he managed to escape Soviet rule by hitching a ride to Shanghai on a steamer at the beginning of 1921, later immigrating to the United States.) Ovchinnikov's story illustrates the impossible position of decent Russians, forced to choose between equally barbaric Whites and Reds.[22]

The Canadian contingent of the British army in Siberia was also distressed by the Kolchak coup. A Canadian soldier later remembered: "However much one may deprecate the Bolshevik methods, we Canadians in Siberia could neither see nor hear anything which inspired in us any confidence in the Kolchak Government. . . . There came to our ears stories of the workings of that government which savoured more of Caesar Borgia than of 20th-century democracy." Partly as a result of these reports and partly because its officials doubted the legality of stationing in Siberia soldiers that had been conscripted under a law that restricted their use to "defense of the realm," the Canadian government withdrew its contingent after only a few months. Though the government allowed any soldier who wished to serve under the British or the Whites to remain in Siberia, only a few Canadians volunteered.[23]

Most American soldiers were equally unhappy with the Kolchak coup. Only four days after the coup Graves wrote to the War Department:

> The opinion just now is that this crowd could not remain in power 24 hours in eastern Siberia after allied troops are removed. . . . I think some blood will be shed when troops move out but the longer we stay the greater will be the bloodshed when allied troops do go, as in effect each day we remain here, now that war with Germany is over, we are by our mere presence helping establish a form of autocratic government which the people of Siberia will not stand for and our stay is creating some feeling against the allied governments because of the effect it has. The classes seem to be growing wider apart and the feeling between them more bitter daily.[24]

The War in Washington

Meanwhile, just as the arrival of cold weather brought a virtual end to hostilities in Siberia, it witnessed the beginning of a war in Washington. Bolstered by Republican gains in the congressional elections of November 1918 and by the signing of an armistice with the Central Powers the same month, Republican senators Hiram Johnson of California, William E. Borah of Idaho, and Robert M. La Follette of Wisconsin began attacking Wilson's Russia policy. On December 12, 1918, in a speech introducing his resolution demanding information from the war and state departments, Johnson read from Wilson's own *aide memoire* and then asserted that it provided no answer as to why American soldiers remained in Russia following the armistice. Johnson asked, "What is the policy of our nation toward Russia? I do not know our policy, and I know no other man who knows our policy. . . . I warn you of the policy, which God forbid this nation ever should enter upon, of endeavoring to impose by military force upon the various peoples of the earth the kind of government we desire for them and that they do not desire for themselves." Johnson's speech attracted so many congratulatory letters from across the country that he was compelled to draft a form letter in response to them. Though Johnson's resolution was bottled in the Senate Committee on Foreign Relations, the issue did not die. By February 14, 1919, the opponents of intervention had won so much bipartisan support that Johnson's resolution calling for the withdrawal of American troops from Russia lost by only one vote, that of Vice President Thomas Marshall. Had the Congress known about Wilson's secret funding of the Whites, which will be discussed in the next chapter, Johnson's resolution might have passed. Johnson was also insinuating during this time that the Wilson administration was using the fraudulent Sisson Documents to justify a course in Russia that was at variance with its announced policy. It was a shrewd guess.[25]

Each of the senators was asking the same question: if the object of intervention had been to aid the Czechs in fighting the Central Powers, why were American troops still present in Siberia months after the armistice? Why, indeed.

Notes

1. Arthur S. Link, ed., *The Papers of Woodrow Wilson* (Princeton, N.J.: Princeton University Press, 1966–1994), An Address to a Joint Session of Congress, January 8, 1918, vol. 45, 537.

2. William S. Graves, *America's Siberian Adventure, 1918–1920* (New York: Cape and Smith, 1931), 2–4.

3. Ibid., 55–57, 80; Robert L. Willett, *Russian Sideshow: America's Undeclared War, 1918–1920* (Washington, D.C.: Brassey's, 2003), 191; Robert J. Maddox, *The Unknown War with Russia: Wilson's Siberian Intervention* (San Rafael, Calif.: Presidio, 1977), 61–62.

4. Graves, *America's Siberian Adventure*, 57, 60–61; Maddox, *Unknown War with Russia*, 62. According to Secretary of State Lansing, the United States dispatched 7,398 soldiers and approximately 1,400 auxiliary personnel to Siberia. See U.S. Department of State, *Papers Relating to the Foreign Relations of the United States, Russia, 1918* (Washington, D.C.: Government Printing Office, 1931–1932; reprint, New York: Kraus, 1969), Robert Lansing to Ishii Kikujiro, August 15, 1918, vol. 2, 346.

5. Graves, *America's Siberian Adventure*, 57–59. For reference to Wilson's agreement to allow the Japanese the supreme command, see Link, *Papers of Woodrow Wilson*, Diary of Frank L. Polk, July 16, 1918, vol. 48, 639; Polk to Wilson, July 26, 1918, vol. 49, 108.

6. Graves, *America's Siberian Adventure*, 63–64; Maddox, *Unknown War with Russia*, 62–63; George F. Kennan, *Russia and the West under Lenin and Stalin* (Boston: Little, Brown, 1960), 109.

7. Graves, *America's Siberian Adventure*, 93–94; Maddox, *Unknown War with Russia*, 63.

8. Graves, *America's Siberian Adventure*, 94–95; Maddox, *Unknown War with Russia*, 64.

9. Graves, *America's Siberian Adventure*, 95; Carl W. Ackerman, *Trailing the Bolsheviki: Twelve Thousand Miles with the Allies in Siberia* (New York: Charles Scribner's Sons, 1919), 188; Betty M. Unterberger, *America's Siberian Expedition, 1918–1920* (Durham, N.C.: Duke University Press, 1956; reprint, New York: Greenwood, 1969), 90.

10. Maddox, *Unknown War with Russia*, 65.

11. Richard Goldhurst, *The Midnight War: The American Intervention in Russia, 1918–1920* (New York: McGraw-Hill, 1978), 64; Richard Luckett, *The White Generals: An Account of the White Movement and the Russian Civil War* (New York: Viking, 1971), 165; Peter Fleming, *The Fate of Admiral Kolchak* (London: Rupert Hart-Davis, 1963), 87; Joshua Hammer, "Resurrecting the Czar," *Smithsonian*, November 2010, 38–48.

12. Graves, *America's Siberian Adventure*, 70; Fleming, *Fate of Admiral Kolchak*, 83; Ackerman, *Trailing the Bolsheviki*, 136; Betty M. Unterberger, *The United States, Revolutionary Russia, and the Rise of Czechoslovakia*, 2nd ed. (College Station: Texas A & M University Press, 2000), 211, 238; David W. McFadden, *Alternative Paths: Soviets and Americans, 1917–1920* (Oxford: Oxford University Press, 1993), 140; Willett, *Russian Sideshow*, 159.

13. Graves, *America's Siberian Adventure*, 72; U.S. Department of State, *Foreign Relations, Russia, 1918*, British Embassy to Robert Lansing, August 12, vol. 2, 341–

42; John K. Caldwell to Robert Lansing, August 15, vol. 2, 346–48; Ernest L. Harris to Robert Lansing, September 4, vol. 2, 365; September 10, vol. 2, 374; September 12, vol. 2, 377; September 13, vol. 2, 379; John K. Caldwell to Robert Lansing, September 12, vol. 2, 377; September 16, vol. 2, 383; Robert Lansing to Roland S. Morris, September 26, vol. 2, 393–94; U.S. Department of State, *Papers Relating to the Foreign Relations of the United States: The Lansing Papers, 1914–1920* (Washington, D.C.: Government Printing Office, 1939–1940), Jean Jusserand to Robert Lansing, August 17, 1918, vol. 2, 376–77.

14. Fleming, *Fate of Admiral Kolchak*, 103.

15. Graves, *America's Siberian Adventure*, 98–99; U.S. Department of State, *Foreign Relations, Russia, 1918*, John K. Caldwell to Robert Lansing, August 3, vol. 2, 363; Ernest L. Harris to Robert Lansing, November 18, vol. 2, 435; November 19, vol. 2, 435; Maddox, *Unknown War with Russia*, 67; Fleming, *Fate of Admiral Kolchak*, 109–11; H. H. Fisher and Elena Varneck, eds., *The Testimony of Kolchak and Other Siberian Materials*, trans. Elena Varneck (Stanford, Calif.: Stanford University Press, 1935), 192; Ackerman, *Trailing the Bolsheviki*, 147, 153; N. G. O. Pereira, *White Siberia: The Politics of Civil War* (Montreal: McGill-Queen's University Press, 1996), 106.

16. Graves, *America's Siberian Adventure*, 87, 99–100; Maddox, *Unknown War with Russia*, 67; James Bunyan, ed., *Intervention, Civil War, and Communism in Russia, April–December 1918, Documents and Materials* (Stanford, Calif.: Stanford University Press, 1936), 359; Link, *Papers of Woodrow Wilson*, William S. Graves to Adjutant General Peter Harris, June 21, 1919, vol. 62, 89; Goldhurst, *Midnight War*, 153; Fleming, *Fate of Admiral Kolchak*, 32.

17. Kennan, *Russia and the West under Lenin and Stalin*, 114; Graves, *America's Siberian Intervention*, 113–14; Fisher and Varneck, *Testimony of Kolchak*, 187; Link, *Papers of Woodrow Wilson*, John F. Stevens to William Phillips, June 16, 1919, vol. 60, 608; Woodrow Wilson to Carter Glass, September 25, 1919, vol. 63, 518n1; Newton D. Baker to Wilson, February 17, 1920, vol. 64, 436.

18. Link, *Papers of Woodrow Wilson*, Maurice Hankey's notes of a meeting of the Council of Four, June 26, 1919, vol. 61, 201; Eduard Beneš, *My War Memoirs*, trans. Paul Selver (Boston: Houghton-Mifflin, 1928), 371.

19. Graves, *America's Siberian Intervention*, 82.

20. U.S. Department of State, *Papers Relating to the Foreign Relations of the United States, Russia, 1919* (Washington, D.C.: Government Printing Office, 1937; reprint, New York: Kraus, 1969), Newton D. Baker to Frank L. Polk, February 11, 277–78; U.S. Department of State, *Foreign Relations, Russia, 1918*, Ernest L. Harris to Robert Lansing, November 22, vol. 2, 441.

21. David S. Foglesong, *America's Secret War against Bolshevism: U.S. Intervention in the Russian Civil War, 1917–1920* (Chapel Hill: University of North Carolina Press, 1995), 152; Bunyan, *Intervention, Civil War, and Communism in Russia*, 372.

22. Anton Ovchinnikov, "Memoirs of the Red Partisan Movement in the Russian Far East, 1918–1920," in *Testimony of Kolchak*, ed. Fisher and Varneck, 271–74, 278, 283–84, 306–9, 324.

23. Roy MacLaren, *Canadians in Russia, 1918–1919* (Toronto: Macmillan of Canada, 1976), 148, 183–84, 189, 206, 213; Graves, *America's Siberian Adventure*, 83.

24. Link, *Papers of Woodrow Wilson*, William S. Graves to Newton D. Baker, November 21, 1918, vol. 53, 168–69.

25. Maddox, *Unknown War with Russia*, 85; McFadden, *Alternative Paths*, 172–74, 181; Foglesong, *America's Secret War against Bolshevism*, 71; William Appleman Williams, *American-Russian Relations, 1781–1947* (New York: Rinehart, 1952), 153; Leonid I. Strakhovsky, *American Opinion about Russia, 1917–1920* (Toronto: University of Toronto Press, 1961), 94–95; Link, *Papers of Woodrow Wilson*, Newton D. Baker to Wilson, January 1, 1919, vol. 53, 583n6; Colonel Edward House to Wilson, February 17, 1919, vol. 55, 204n1.

CHAPTER FOUR

~

To Make the
World Safe for Democracy

Mankind must make up its mind either for Wilson or for Lenin.

—Swiss essayist and playwright Hermann Kesser, October 27, 1918[1]

Thomas Woodrow Wilson. Adoc-photos/Art Resource, NY.

Vladimir Ilyitch Oulianov, called Lenin. Adoc-photos/Art Resource, NY.

There were three reasons that American forces remained in Siberia after the armistice between the Allies and the Central Powers in November 1918. First, Wilson wanted the soldiers to aid the anti-Bolsheviks in overthrowing the Soviet government. Second, he wanted them to prevent the Japanese from achieving complete control over eastern Siberia and northern Manchuria. Third, he was disinclined to alter his Russian policy until he had conferred with Allied leaders at the Paris Peace Conference.

The Defeat of the Central Powers

By the autumn of 1918 the Germans, who had threatened to seize Paris only a few months earlier, were at their last gasp. The same German army that had advanced twenty miles along a fifty-mile front toward the French capital in the spring of 1918 bogged down amid the obstacles presented by old battlefields—a wilderness of abandoned trenches, shattered roads and railroads, and massive shell craters—its starving soldiers more interested in raiding pantries and wine cellars than in advancing. The arrival of the Spanish influenza among soldiers already weakened by a poor diet made matters worse. The Allies wisely dug new trench lines, forcing the Germans into costly attacks. On the evening of July 18–19, the Germans fell back across the Marne, which they had crossed only three days earlier, thus ending the Second Battle of the Marne and all hope of a German victory in the war. By August, the presence of 1.3 million inexperienced but enthusiastic American doughboys, who were continuing to arrive at the rate of 250,000 to 300,000 per month, had revived British and French morale and seriously undermined that of the Germans. As General Paul von Hindenburg later recalled, "Unlike the enemy, we had no fresh reserves to throw in. Instead of inexhaustible Americans, we had only weary allies who were themselves on the point of collapse."

In the late summer and early fall the Americans assumed the brunt of the fighting from their exhausted allies; one million Americans fought in the bloody Meuse-Argonne campaign. The Allies' virtual monopoly on tanks, the quality of which steadily improved throughout the war, proved decisive as well. The Allies achieved breakthroughs on August 8 and September 28 that removed the Germans from French and Belgian territory they had occupied since the beginning of the war. When Germany's Austrian and Turkish allies were forced to sue for peace due to similar disasters on the Italian and Middle Eastern fronts, and German suffering from the severe famine caused by the Allied blockade reached epic proportions, there was a revolution that ended the kaiser's reign and ushered in the Weimar Republic, the first democracy in German history. Only two days later, on November 11, representatives of the republic signed an armistice with the Allies.[2]

The Bolshevik Menace

Yet President Wilson could not relax. The more he thought about the European situation, the more uneasy he became. Wilson had initially considered the Bolsheviks a temporary phenomenon, a misguided group of radicals who would not last as rulers. Now he realized that the Soviet government had consolidated its power and was far stronger than it had been the previous year. Looking across the Atlantic at Europe, he saw a collection of nations torn by four years of the bloodiest war in history and on the verge of economic collapse. This was a ripe field for bolshevism, if there ever was one, Wilson thought. Indeed, communist revolutions would occur briefly in Hungary and Bavaria in 1919. Now that the German government was suing for peace, the Soviet government was clearly the principal threat to the democratic postwar world Wilson was determined to forge.[3]

The Red Terror that began in September 1918 increased Wilson's opposition to the Bolsheviks. The Terror began as a Bolshevik response to the events of August 30. On that day the head of the Petrograd branch of the Cheka, the Bolshevik secret police, was assassinated. On the same evening in Moscow, after concluding a speech at the Mikhelson Armaments Factory with the shout, "There is only one issue, victory or death!" Vladimir Lenin was shot in the left shoulder and the left side of the neck. Soviet authorities blamed the Left Socialist Revolutionaries for both attacks. The evidence is unclear; while the party's central committee disclaimed any responsibility for the assaults on Bolshevik leaders, party members had certainly been enraged by a recent Bolshevik crackdown on the party and arrest of its leaders. The following day a Bolshevik mob who believed that British agents were behind the assassination attempt on Lenin attacked the British embassy building in Petrograd, killing a naval attaché. The Soviet government then arrested and executed thousands of Russians, evicted many wealthy and middle-class people from their homes, and detained numerous British and French diplomatic and consular officials and civilians on the charge of counterrevolutionary activity. One of these diplomats was R. H. Bruce Lockhart, the unofficial British envoy to the Bolsheviks.[4]

Although Lenin, who was in critical condition for a while, may not have been responsible for the actions taken against Western diplomats, whom he was still trying to woo, he had certainly justified the use of terror against anti-Bolsheviks in a well-publicized address to American workers only eleven days before the shooting. In that letter Lenin declared: "No revolution can be successful unless the resistance of the exploiters is crushed. When we, the workers and toiling peasants, captured state power, it became our duty to crush the resistance of the exploiters. We are proud that we have been doing this. We regret that we are not doing it with sufficient firmness and determination. . . . Only traitors or idiots can demand formal equality of rights for the bourgeoisie." Privately, Lenin was even more immoderate, raging against affluent farmers, known as kulaks, whom he called "spiders," "leeches," and "vampires," and calling for their complete destruction. He demanded "Ruthless war on the kulaks! Death to them! Hatred and contempt for the parties which defend them!" In another letter to both American and European workers a few months later, he added: "Every state, including the most democratic republic, is nothing but a machine for the suppression of one class by another. The proletarian state is a machine for the suppression of the bourgeoisie by the proletariat." This cynical view of government horrified Wilson, who had spent decades, both as a political science professor and as a government official, touting American-style democracy.[5]

After meeting with Wilson on September 14, Sir William Wiseman wrote that the president had "lost faith . . . in the Bolsheviks and is, I think, much more inclined to fall in with our programme than he was a few months ago." The program to which Wiseman referred was a Siberian intervention that was actively rather than just incidentally anti-Bolshevik.[6]

On September 20, based on information received from the U.S. Consul-General in Moscow, DeWitt C. Poole, Wilson approved the transmission of a telegram to all American diplomatic stations and its release to the press. The telegram asserted:

> This Government is in receipt of information from reliable sources revealing that the peaceable Russian citizens of Moscow, Petrograd, and other cities are suffering from an openly avowed campaign of mass terrorism and are subject to wholesale executions. Thousands of persons have been shot and without even a form of trial; ill administered prisons are filled beyond capacity and every night scores of Russian citizens are recklessly put to death; and irresponsible bands are venting their brutal passions in the daily massacre of untold innocents.
>
> In view of the earnest desire of the people of the United States to befriend the Russian people and lend them all possible assistance in their struggle to reconstruct their nation upon principles of democracy and self-government and acting therefore solely in the interest of the Russian people themselves, the Government feels that it cannot be silent or refrain from expressing its horror at this existing state of terrorism. Furthermore, it believes that in order successfully to check the further increase of the indiscriminate slaughter of Russian citizens all the civilized nations should register their abhorrence of such barbarism.

You will inquire, therefore, whether the Government to which you are accredited will be disposed to take some immediate action, which is entirely divorced from the atmosphere of belligerency and the conduct of war, to impress upon the perpetrators of these crimes the aversion with which civilization regards their present wanton acts.

The same month Eugene Debs, the leader of the Socialist Party in the United States, was sentenced to ten years for violating the Espionage Act by giving a speech that criticized World War I in the Bolshevik fashion, as a war generated by a few capitalists in pursuit of their own interests at the expense of millions of workers, and in which he declared, "Our hearts . . . are with the Bolsheviki of Russia."[7]

On October 16, after Wiseman met with Wilson again, he wrote, "The Bolsheviki, he agreed, were impossible. He had watched with disgust their treatment of Lockhart, who had tried to help them." (Although Lockhart was innocent of some of the crimes with which the Soviet government charged him, namely plotting to kill both Lenin and Trotsky and to destroy all of the railway bridges leading into Moscow and Petrograd, he was not as innocent as Wilson imagined. His own papers and letters reveal that, though having supported closer relations with the Bolsheviks, he had also funneled one and a half million rubles to White organizations dedicated to overthrowing the Soviet government, in essence playing both sides of the fence.) Wilson also told Wiseman, "If we humiliate the German people and drive them too far, we shall destroy all form of government there and Bolshevism will take its place." At a cabinet meeting on November 5, Wilson "spoke at length" about the threat of bolshevism to Europe due to the influence of economic hardship and Bolshevik propaganda. Wilson even asked Secretary of State Robert Lansing if he could get neutral European countries, such as Switzerland, to seize Bolshevik funds and expel Bolshevik agitators. In fact, two days later, Wilson told his chief adviser, Colonel House, that the reason he desired to hold the peace conference at Versailles, rather than in Switzerland, was that the latter nation was "saturated with every poisonous element and open to every hostile influence in Europe." Wilson was referring to Bolshevik propagandists. By early 1919 Allied pressure had resulted in the expulsion of Soviet representatives from Switzerland, the Netherlands, Spain, Sweden, Norway, and Denmark.[8]

The telegram dispatched to American diplomatic stations was largely written by Secretary of State Lansing. On September 24, he denounced the Bolsheviks in a letter to the president, claiming that they had "committed such monstrous crimes within the past six weeks in Moscow and other cities" as could scarcely be believed. His sentences were filled with such phrases as "in view of the recent examples of the blood-thirsty character of the Bolsheviks" and "the extreme terrorism which has recently been resorted to by the Bolsheviks." On October 26, he wrote in his diary that bolshevism was "the most hideous and monstrous thing that the human mind has ever conceived." On November 21, he recommended to the president that the U.S. government issue an official statement on the Russian situation that included these remarks:

> In all parts of Russia where the people desire to safeguard the principles of democratic freedom won by their Revolution, the United States purposes to assist by all the means in its power. Exceptional conditions, however, exist in that part of Russia which is dominated by the regime established at Moscow and Petrograd. To judge from the words of its own leaders and from the known practice of its adherents, this regime is as much opposed to democracy as was the autocratic militarism of Germany. Under its control a class war of extermination has been encouraged. . . . The United States cannot take part in measures which would tend to prolong the control of such a regime. It cannot, therefore, undertake to render assistance in this part of Russia until the authorities at Moscow and Petrograd definitely abandon government by mass terror and murder and at the same time obligate themselves, openly and in a manner which will leave no opportunity for evasion, to restore order and the due process of law and set up a government based on the freely expressed will of the whole people.

Thus, the memorandum of W. C. Huntington, commercial attaché to the American Embassy in Russia, received a favorable hearing the following day. The memo stated, "Humanitarianism and economic interests are both potent reasons for aiding Russia, but a still graver reason is to 'make the world safe for democracy,'" thereby repeating the war goal made famous by the president himself. Huntington explained regarding democracy, "It will not be safe as long as Russia goes on like a volcano, occasionally throwing hot lava on everything round about." Therefore, the first goal of American aid to Russia should be "to stamp out Bolshevism and its attendant tyranny and cruelty."[9]

But just as Wilson and Lansing were beginning to consider the Bolsheviks the chief threat to their postwar plans, the great difficulties involved in overthrowing the Soviet government became apparent to them. The Czechs and Allies began to call for large-scale American intervention on the Volga front to save the overextended Czechs from destruction. On September 23, 1918,

U.S. Ambassador to Japan Roland S. Morris joined the chorus. However, un-like the Czechs and other Allies, Morris realized the impossibility of sending a large force to Russia, so he suggested only that General Graves's small force proceed to Omsk in order to aid the Czechs. On the following day Lansing wrote to the president that, based on the reports of the Czech Corps, Czech leader Thomas Masaryk did not believe that Wilson's original intervention plan of having the Czechs provide a focal point for the re-creation of the Eastern Front by Russian forces would succeed, because "he did not believe we could count upon the Russians reorganizing as a military force." In short, Russians were not behaving as the Allies had envisioned; they were not ral-lying in large numbers with the purpose of restoring the Eastern Front against the Central Powers. That this development surprised the Allies demonstrates how little they understood the war weariness of nearly all Russians.[10]

Lansing was confused. On September 24, he wrote to Wilson:

> I do not see how, with the small force which we have in Siberia, we can do more than hasten arms and ammunition to them [the Czechs] and refrain from urging them to withdraw at the present time. But, even with sufficient muni-tions and supplies, I doubt if so small a body of troops can avoid final annihila-tion unless a considerable force is sent to cooperate with them in repelling the Bolsheviks. Where is such a large force to come from? . . .
>
> The more I consider the matter the more perplexing and distressing it be-comes. We cannot abandon the Czecho-Slovaks on the ground that they will not abandon their Russian friends. Of course that would never do. And yet, what is the alternative, or is there any?

On September 26, Lansing replied to Morris in words taken almost verbatim from the president, "Strongly as our sympathies constrain us to make every possible sacrifice to keep the country on the Volga front out of the hands of the merciless Red Guards, it is the unqualified judgment of our military authorities that to attempt military activities west of the Urals is to attempt the impossible." Lansing suggested that the Czechs be advised to withdraw east of the Urals, and to consolidate themselves into a defensive position. The next day General Graves was informed that American forces would not go west of Lake Baikal.[11]

Even if Wilson had been able to spare a large number of troops for the Volga front, and even if he had believed that Congress would have ap-proved large-scale intervention in Russia, it is unlikely that he would have dispatched a large army there. From the beginning, Wilson had believed that intervention should involve as few soldiers as possible so as to be as unobtrusive as possible. These troops should merely guard the Trans-Siberian

Railway so that supplies could reach the Czechs and White Russians, forces he considered more acceptable to the Russian people. Wilson greatly disapproved of the presence of the British and French at Omsk, where their visibility vastly exceeded their effectiveness in support of the Czechs and Whites fighting at the front. On August 23, Wilson wrote to Lansing, "The other governments are going much further and much faster—are, indeed, acting upon a plan which is altogether foreign from ours and inconsistent with it."[12]

By late September 1918 both Wilson and Lansing had come to question both the necessity and the practicality of re-creating the Eastern Front. Two developments caused this dramatic change in thought. First, the situation on the Western Front changed completely. In early July it had seemed as though the French might be doomed, but by late September it was clear that it was the Central Powers that were doomed. Second, the Czechs' situation changed completely. In early July they had held all 5,000 miles of the Trans-Siberian Railway from the Volga River to Vladivostok, but by late September it was obvious that they were overextended and, thus, that a new Eastern Front could not be created in time to be a factor in the war. Thus, Lansing wrote to Morris on September 26 concerning Allied plans to push for a re-creation of the Eastern Front, "We do not believe them to be practical or based upon sound reason or good military judgment." For these reasons Lansing had told Sir William Wiseman five days earlier that "the policy of the U.S. Government is perfectly clear. . . . [It is] to rescue the Czechs and not to assist them in recreating an Eastern Front." This statement flatly contradicted those made by Lansing in July 1918, but by late September, the situation had changed completely. Nevertheless, Lansing's statement was not even a completely accurate statement of American policy at that time, either: the U.S. government did not want to "rescue" the Czechs but to have them maintain their position east of the Urals until such time as they could support an offensive against the Bolsheviks led by anti-Bolshevik Russians. For this reason the U.S. government still made no arrangements to transport either the Czechs or its own soldiers out of Siberia.[13]

Aid to the Czechs and Whites

In the meantime Wilson was content to send whatever aid he could to both the Czechs and the Whites. On the very day that Wilson decided to intervene in Siberia, July 6, 1918, he forwarded $7 million in credits to the Czech Corps. On July 15, Assistant Secretary of State Frank L. Polk informed U.S. Ambassador to France William G. Sharp regarding the request for aid from Whites in Paris, "The President has asked the Department to be kind enough to request you to say to the gentlemen who sent him this interesting and impressive message that he has received it and that they may rest assured that the United States is diligently endeavoring to find a way in which to give wise assistance to the Russian people." On November 5, Lansing assured Sharp that U.S. consuls in Russia were keeping in close touch with "the leaders of all movements having for their purpose the restoration of orderly government in Russia." He added, "As you are aware, this Government is determined to devise means to render economic assistance to the Russian people and has not modified its purpose to assist Russia." The "Russia" referred to in such dispatches was most certainly not Soviet Russia.[14]

The U.S. government gave various kinds of aid to the Czechs and Whites by various means. The American Red Cross, with the full support of the government, supplied the Czechs and Whites with clothing and medical services. Furthermore, the Russian embassy of the Provisional Government in Washington, which had never been disbanded, was used by the State Department to funnel supplies to the Whites. The Russian embassy was supposedly still in existence only to cancel contracts that the former government had made and to pay the Russian debt, and yet one significant contract with the Remington Rifle Company for 245,000 rifles was allowed to proceed, and the money in the embassy's account at the First National City Bank of New York was never used to pay the Russian debt. The State Department talked many creditors out of demanding payment from the embassy by offering to defer payments on loans that these individuals and companies had received from the U.S. government. Rather, the embassy's money was used to buy military supplies that the War Department had obligingly declared to be "surplus," making them available quickly and at a fraction of the usual cost. The embassy obtained additional funds by reselling some of the items contracted for by the Provisional Government for use against the Central Powers, such as barbed wire, that were no longer needed. Every payment made by the embassy required approval from the treasury and state departments. In total more than $50 million worth of rifles, machine guns, boots, and other equipment passed to White armies via the Russian embassy. By using both the Russian embassy and the $50 million War Fund that Congress had granted him in July 1918 Wilson was able to send hundreds of thousands of rifles and machine guns and other supplies to the Czechs and Whites without the consent of Congress. This American aid supplemented the almost one hundred million pounds worth of aid the British gave the Whites in 1918–1919, including one million hand grenades, 600,000 rifles, 6,800 machine guns, 192 field guns, 300,000 artillery shells, and 200,000 uniforms dispatched to Kolchak's forces. For a while in 1919, the French added another eighteen million francs per month in aid to the Kolchak government, in addition to its continual support of the Czechs. Allied aid to the Czechs and Whites was especially crucial since they occupied areas that lacked major munitions factories. Allied supplies reached these groups via the Chinese Eastern and Trans-Siberian Railways, which American soldiers were helping to guard by February 1919.[15]

As is often the case with massive aid programs, this program was characterized not only by waste but by sheer absurdity as well. General Graves complained, "A great number of automobiles and trucks are being sent over, which it is absolutely impossible, with the railroad as it is, to get out to the Czech troops. This is true with a great deal of other property being sent here. I am convinced that the Czechs are satisfied that they are not going to use it and these expensive Cadillac cars will remain on the dock in all kinds of weather for a long time unless the Russians take the property and use it for purposes for which it was not sent to Vladivostok. I do not know under what conditions or supervision this property was purchased in the United States."[16]

Nothing better epitomized the sea change in the Allied perspective on the relative dangers posed by the Germans and the Bolsheviks than the armistice agreement between the Allies and Germany. Despite Wilson's insistence in the Fourteen Points Speech ten months earlier that any armistice provide for the immediate and complete evacuation of German troops from Russian territory, the armistice signed on November 11 allowed German forces to remain in the Baltic territories until directed to withdraw by the Allies. Even the final Treaty of Versailles the following year did not mandate German withdrawal from the Baltic region because Wilson, Lansing, and the Allies were all worried about the potential spread of bolshevism to this region after a German withdrawal.[17]

The Japanese Menace

The second reason that American troops remained in eastern Siberia after the armistice with the Central Powers was to prevent Japan from achieving complete control of the Chinese Eastern and Trans-Siberian Railways, the lifelines of northern Manchuria and Siberia. Such a policy became necessary when, in the late summer and autumn of 1918, Japanese actions destroyed the relatively high degree of trust that had existed between the United States and Japan during the previous year.

On July 23, 1918, U.S. Ambassador to Japan Morris informed Secretary of State Lansing that the Japanese were sending their Eighth Division to

Harbin in northern Manchuria to protect a section of the Chinese Eastern Railway. The Japanese were alleging that this action was taken out of military necessity. The region had to be protected from Bolsheviks and German war prisoners, they claimed. On the next day Lansing told Wilson that Japanese Ambassador Ishii Kikujiro had informed him that Japan could not accept Wilson's 7,000-man limit for its Siberian intervention force, since the Japanese public would consider the limit an indication of American distrust in Japanese motives. Nevertheless, Ishii assured Lansing that the Japanese intervention force would not exceed 12,000 troops—though he added ominously that Japan reserved the right to dispatch more soldiers later if it became necessary. Also, on July 24, a U.S. chargé d'affaires in China requested information from the State Department concerning Japanese statements to the effect that they alone would be protecting the entire Chinese Eastern Railway. The Chinese foreign minister had "professed his surprise" that such a task would not be entrusted to Chinese troops.[18]

In August the Japanese intention to exert sole control over northern Manchuria and eastern Siberia became manifest. On August 3, Wilson learned that Ishii was still saying that he was fairly certain that Japanese intervention would be limited to 12,000 troops and assuring the State Department that the Japanese had no plans to send troops anywhere but Siberia (not to northern Manchuria, for instance). On August 5, Lansing learned that Japanese Foreign Minister Motono Ichiro was saying this also, but adding that 12,000 soldiers might be insufficient "to meet the increasingly serious conditions developing in northern Manchuria and eastern Siberia." On August 13, Lansing learned that the Japanese had sent a brigade consisting of 1,700 men to Manchouli, a town in northern Manchuria near Chita, the location of the crucial junction between the Chinese Eastern and Trans-Siberian Railways. The Japanese claimed that the invasion of China by a force of Bolsheviks and German prisoners had necessitated this action. On August 15, Lansing learned that the Japanese were sending 5,000 more soldiers to Manchouli. A chargé d'affaires in China wrote to him, "The Chinese absolutely deny that Maximalist [Bolshevik] or enemy forces have bombarded Manchouli or otherwise made military encroachment on Chinese territory."[19]

By August 21, the State Department estimated that 12,000 Japanese troops were situated along the Chinese Eastern Railway, including 6,000 at Harbin and 3,000 at Manchouli. The Chinese government had not been consulted on this matter, as they should have been under the terms of the military agreement they had contracted with the Japanese in May 1918. On August 26, Lansing learned that Japan's Twelfth Division, consisting of 10,000 men, was being dispatched from Japan to Vladivostok, and that its Third Division, consisting of 20,000 soldiers, was being sent to northern Manchuria from Japanese-controlled southern Manchuria. The Japanese foreign minister explained that the ultimate destination of both divisions was the area around Khabarovsk, where the Japanese were allegedly encountering heavy Bolshevik and German resistance.[20]

As we have seen, General Graves had serious doubts about the veracity of Japanese claims concerning the Ussuri campaign around Khabarovsk. Graves later wrote, "At the time General Otani [the Japanese commander] asked for heavy reinforcements, he ordered an offensive which must be construed as indicating that he had confidence that the troops at his disposal could defeat the enemy long before the requested reinforcements could arrive in Siberia, and, as a matter of fact, the actual military movements ordered by General Otani proved to be little more than skirmishes." Worse, Graves was concerned that Japanese brutality in Siberia would reflect badly on American forces. On October 1, Graves wrote to his superiors in Washington, "It is very likely, and I believe such will be the case, that the actions of the Japanese troops [in the Ussuri campaign] with whom we are so closely associated will soon be considered by the Russian people as the actions of the Allied troops and it will not be long before no distinction will be made, whether such actions are committed by Japanese or American troops."[21]

Japanese justifications for their actions were dubious at best. Ambassador Ishii attempted to justify the large Japanese presence in northern Manchuria and eastern Siberia by explaining that it was vital to relieve the Czechs before winter, and that an enemy force of "not less than 30,000" was opposing the Czechs. Not only was this estimate of enemy strength unsupported by the reports of American officials in Russia, but months after September 5, when Ambassador Morris declared the railways cleared of enemy forces, the Japanese had not withdrawn any soldiers, prompting the president to write, "In such circumstances I can see no necessity for a large Japanese force in Siberia." On October 18, General Graves reported, "Returned Wednesday from inspection of troops to the north. Found all towns and villages occupied by what appeared to be ten times as many Japanese troops as are necessary. . . . I feel sure that there are fully sixty thousand of these troops in all. . . . I can see no reason for such a number of troops in this country." A week later he added regarding the Japanese, "It is evidently their desire to keep American troops from being stationed alone at any station in Siberia, and they have already accomplished their desire by occupying all of the places." Graves estimated that there were 40,000 Japanese troops in Siberia and another 20,000 in northern Manchuria. On October 27, Ambassador Morris reported that the Japanese had refused a British request that they send troops to support the

Czechs in the Volga region, thus making it clear that, in dispatching much larger numbers of troops than the intervention agreement with the United States mandated, Japan was pursuing its own interests in the East rather than implementing the Anglo-French plan to have Allied forces re-create the Eastern Front. By November 6, Japanese soldiers occupied "every possible entrance into Siberia and Manchuria." By November 20, the Japanese foreign minister himself placed the number of Japanese troops in northern Manchuria and eastern Siberia at 72,000.[22]

The Japanese controlled these areas economically as well as militarily. On September 9, U.S. Consul in Vladivostok John K. Caldwell complained that the Japanese were using their own currency in the Vladivostok area and that this was resented by the Russians "as indicating more than temporary occupation and as tending to further depreciate [the] ruble." By December 16, the State Department had received reports to the effect that the Japanese were using their control of the Chinese Eastern Railway to prevent all but Japanese goods from reaching Chinese markets. Not only were those reports accurate, but Japanese goods were also being exempted from import duties, and Japanese merchants were receiving every conceivable advantage in northern Manchuria.[23]

Lansing had foreseen some of these developments as early as August 18. On that day, after learning that the Japanese were sending troops to Manchouli under false pretenses, he wrote to Wilson regarding the reports he had received:

> A careful consideration of the facts as disclosed by these communications convinces me that the situation is developing in a way which differs considerably from the plan originally determined upon and compels a consideration of the policy which should be adopted in reference to the new conditions presented. . . . I believe that the evidence points to an intention on the part of the Japanese to send a larger number of troops to Vladivostok than the 13,500 already sent. . . . I do feel that we must assume that Japan, with the pressure of the present situation together with the undoubted approval of the Allied Governments, will assert that military conditions require her to send a much larger force both to Vladivostok and to the western border of Manchuria.

As we have seen, Lansing's prediction proved correct. Two days later, after conversing with the president, Lansing wrote, "This Government is not in favor of proceeding west of Irkutsk in relieving the Czecho-Slovaks in western Siberia." Thus, Wilson and Lansing declined to send the American Expeditionary Force to Omsk not only because it was impractical and violated their conception of intervention but also because they feared leaving all of northern Manchuria and eastern Siberia to the Japanese. In view of Japanese actions in the late summer and autumn of 1918 the Bolsheviks were not the only threat to Wilson's vision of a new democratic order in the postwar world.[24]

But not everyone agreed that the small American force in Siberia had the power to obstruct Japanese schemes. On November 6, Secretary of War Newton Baker, after reading General Graves's reports concerning Japanese activity in Siberia, wrote to President Wilson, "I heartily wish it were possible for us to arrange affairs in such a way as to withdraw entirely from that expedition." Three weeks later he wrote to Wilson, declaring that the removal of American troops from Siberia was necessary because "the presence of our troops is being used by the Japanese as a cloak for their own presence and operations there." Furthermore, Baker added,

> The longer we stay, the more Japanese there are and the more difficult it will be to induce the Japanese to withdraw their forces if we set the example. . . . I am especially fearful that the Japanese intervention in Siberia is growing so rapidly and is so obviously beyond any interest Japan could have of a humanitarian or philanthropic character that the difficulty of securing Japanese withdrawal is growing every hour and I dread to think how we shall all feel if we are rudely awakened some day to a realization that Japan had gone in under our wing and so completely mastered the country that she cannot be either induced out or forced out by any action either of the Russians or of the Allies.[25]

The president and the State Department decided, however, that the presence of American troops in eastern Siberia was desirable. On November 16, flirting briefly with Baker's view, Lansing asked Ambassador Morris whether he deemed it advisable, in the event that the Japanese did not modify their policy in the Far East, that the United States withdraw its forces from Siberia in protest and declare to the world its reasons for doing so. On November 20, Morris, having met with Japanese Foreign Minister Goto Shinpei, advised against the action. Goto had been completely unmoved by the threat of the American withdrawal and proclamation. Morris wrote, "The withdrawal of our troops from Siberia . . . would, I fear, be welcomed by the Japanese military authorities and interpreted as an abandonment of our efforts to assist in the reconstruction of Siberia." Thereafter, there was little talk of withdrawal. In fact, after meeting with Wilson on December 30, British Prime Minister David Lloyd George reported, "He was not very much in favour of the Siberian expedition, though as regards that his principal anxiety was as to the conduct of the Japanese, who were apparently taking the whole of Eastern Siberia into their own hands, sending sealed wagons [with goods for sale] into the interior, and generally behaving as if they owned the country. His whole attitude, in fact, was strongly anti-Japanese." Indeed, on January 30, 1919, Wilson told one of his advisers that "he did not trust the Japanese; that he had trusted them before—in fact they had broken their agreement about Siberia. We had sent 7,000 troops to Siberia and they promised to send about the same number but had sent 70,000 and had occupied all the strategic points as far as Irkutsk, and that he would not trust them again."[26]

But aside from retaining the American Expeditionary Force in eastern Siberia, Wilson and Lansing were completely at a loss as to what action they could take against the Japanese. One of the feeble actions taken was that the War Department never instructed Graves, as the other Allies instructed their Siberian commanders, to treat the Japanese commander as the Supreme Commander of Allied Forces in Siberia. Thus, despite repeated Japanese requests, Graves never placed himself and his soldiers under Japanese command. Ignoring the president's earlier assurances to the Japanese, the State Department merely let the matter of a supreme command drop.[27]

It was not until November 16 that Lansing vigorously protested Japanese actions in the Far East as a violation of their agreements with the United States and China. Lansing tried to get the British and French to join the U.S. protest, but both refused, still hoping that the Japanese would send some of their troops to western Siberia to fight the Bolsheviks.[28]

The Inter-Allied Railway Agreement

Although the presence of a small number of American troops in eastern Siberia did not make Japanese generals quake with fear, it did, in combination with American diplomatic pressure and the influence of Japanese liberals, lead to the withdrawal of some Japanese troops and to an inter-allied railway agreement that was favorable to the United States. On December 29, Ambassador Morris reported that the Japanese had announced the withdrawal of 34,000 soldiers from northern Manchuria and eastern Siberia. While this still left approximately 38,000 Japanese troops there, Morris believed that the new Japanese premier had won a great "victory over the reactionary forces of the General Staff." A few days later the Japanese government declared that it would "reexamine the Siberian situation in light of changed circumstances."[29]

The result was the Inter-Allied Railway Agreement. The agreement called for the creation of the Inter-Allied Committee, which would be composed of one representative each from China, France, Great Britain, Italy,

Japan, Russia, and the United States. The Inter-Allied Committee would determine general policy for the maintenance of the Chinese Eastern and Trans-Siberian Railways. Each member of the committee would also choose one railway expert for membership on the Technical Board, which would manage the day-to-day operation of the railways. These men had their work cut out for them because the Trans-Siberian Railway possessed very light rails that were frequently crushed under the burden of heavy freight cars, its embankments and roadbeds were often inadequate, and heavy rains sometimes caused trains to derail—and that was before it was assaulted by partisans, who destroyed 826 bridges, twenty stations, and fourteen water supply depots during the civil war. As noted earlier, its chronic shortages of equipment and qualified personnel had helped doom the czarist and provisional governments. Britain, France, the United States, and Japan each agreed to contribute $5 million to the maintenance of the railways. The Allies agreed to appoint Colonel John F. Stevens, head of America's Russian Railway Service Corps, a unit of approximately 300 experienced American railway men that had originally been established to aid the Provisional Government, president of the Technical Board. Most important, Japan agreed to surrender its monopoly of the railways. Thereafter, American soldiers would not only continue to guard the Suchan coal mines but would also protect the Trans-Siberian Railway from Vladivostok to Nikolsk (144 miles), from Spaskoe to Ussuri (70 miles), and from Verkhne-Udinsk to Baikal City (also known as Mysovaya; 316 miles). The Japanese would also relinquish to the Czechs the railway west of Baikal City and to the Chinese most of the Chinese Eastern Railway, though the agreement still left the Japanese with control over approximately 2,300 miles of track.[30]

Unfortunately, this agreement, which American officials had worked so hard to negotiate, was soon endangered by financial problems. On January 24, 1919, Acting Secretary of State Frank L. Polk informed Lansing and Wilson, then in Paris for the peace conference, that Congress was extremely critical of Wilson's Russian policy and that there was little prospect of receiving funds from it for the maintenance of the Trans-Siberian and Chinese Eastern Railways. On January 31, after close consultation with the president, Lansing instructed Polk:

> You are requested to ask for a second [secret] hearing before such committee or committees in Congress as you think best. At this hearing you will state that it is the President's wish that the Siberian situation and the activities of the administration thereto be made known fully and frankly, though in strict confidence, to the members of these committees. You will then develop the strate-

gic importance both from the point of view of Russia and of the United States of the Trans-Siberian Railway as being a principal means of access to and from the Russian people and as affording an opportunity for economic aid to Siberia where the people are relatively friendly and resistant to Bolshevik influence. . . . You may then narrate in considerable detail the difficulties which we have had with Japan with reference to this railway and in particular the action of Japan in practically seizing the Chinese Eastern Railway, thereby in effect controlling all intercourse to and from Russia via the Pacific. You might mention the number of troops sent by Japan for the purpose and point out that such number was far in excess of that contemplated by the arrangement under which troops of the Associated Governments were landed in Siberia. The nature of the activities of Japan including disposition of their troops and Japanese commercial activities should then be referred to [followed by] a statement of the efforts of the Government of the United States to restore the railroad to a condition where it would not be exclusively dominated by any one power.

Lansing added that American efforts to obtain both a new railway agreement and the withdrawal of a substantial number of Japanese troops had been successful and that these efforts should be "followed through, thereby giving practical effect to the principle of the open door." Lansing concluded: "The consequence of failure to support Stevens . . . should be developed and the responsibility of Congress made clear. . . . It is desired that you treat the matter with the utmost frankness, giving all information at your disposal under, of course, a pledge of confidence. . . . We feel that it may be a wise practice to take Congress more into confidence on such matters and we at least desire to make the experiment in this case." Note that this dispatch indicates both reasons for the maintenance of troops in Siberia, the Bolshevik and Japanese threats to the postwar order Wilson envisioned.[31]

On February 4, Polk replied that Congress, having just agreed to appropriate $100 million for the feeding of Europe, was not in a giving mood. In addition, Senator Hiram Johnson was raging against Wilson's Russia policy. It was the unanimous opinion of the cabinet, with whom Polk had met, that to discuss the Russian situation with Congress in any form would be to jeopardize all appropriations bills. The cabinet advised that the president accept the Inter-Allied Railway Agreement, putting off the question of funding until later. Five days later Lansing responded, writing that the president would follow the cabinet's recommendation but hoped that Polk would keep alert for the first available opportunity to secure the support of the appropriate congressional committees. Lansing reminded Polk, "It is felt that this matter can be treated entirely apart from the general Russian problem, as irrespective of what our policy may be toward Russia, and irrespective of further Russian developments, it is essential that we maintain the policy of the open door with reference to the Siberian and particularly the Chinese Eastern Railway." In the meantime, the Russian Bureau, a subsidiary of the War Trade Board established in October 1918 and charged with providing economic assistance to, and encouraging and regulating American trade with, the non-Bolshevik areas of Russia, should advance such funds as it could spare for the support of the Russian Railway Service Corps, a transfer of funds later approved by Congress. On the next day the United States formally accepted the Inter-Allied Railway Agreement.[32]

In March 1919, Wilson decided to fund the maintenance of the railways through his War Fund, though he knew that he could do so only until June, when the fund would expire. In June the president issued an executive order that declared that the money obtained from the recent liquidation of the Russian Bureau would be used by the secretary of state for the "maintenance or improvement" of the Trans-Siberian and Chinese Eastern Railways.[33]

Semenov and Kalmikov

Although U.S. officials succeeded in securing both an end to the Japanese monopoly of the Far Eastern railways and the withdrawal of 34,000 Japanese troops from Manchuria and Siberia, they underestimated the ingenuity of the Japanese military. The Japanese generals soon settled on a plan to drive American forces out of Siberia. They would use two erratic, reactionary Cossacks, Gregori Semenov and Ivan Kalmikov, to harass the Americans into leaving, all the while pleading innocence to any complicity in their acts.

Leader of a motley army consisting of approximately 2,000 Trans-Baikal Cossacks and other groups, the half-Mongolian Semenov fancied himself another Napoleon. He always carried Bonaparte's *Maxims* in his pocket, though it is uncertain that he ever read the book, and was constantly thrusting his hand into his coat. Whenever Japanese funds proved insufficient to sustain his lavish lifestyle, he robbed banks and Chinese merchants. His wife, who lived in Nagasaki, deposited some of his loot in Japanese banks. The British subsidized him for a while in early 1918 but dropped him as a client after he refused to allow them to organize and train his men. At any rate, the chaos he created in eastern Siberia suited the Japanese, whose intention was to prevent Russia from uniting under any government that might restore its place as a rival to Japan in the Far East, far better than it did the British, whose goal was to unite Siberia under a government powerful enough to resist the Germans and overthrow the Bolsheviks. The Semenov-Japanese partnership, so well suited to the nefarious goals of each partner, was a marriage

Gregori Semenov. Courtesy of The Czech Legion Project, www.czechlegion.com.

made in hell. The same was true for Kalmikov, who had become the leader of the Ussuri Cossacks by murdering the rightful heir to that position and then bribing the Cossacks with money derived from the sale of a boxcar of sugar, a rare commodity in Siberia, provided by the Japanese.[34]

General Graves despised both men. In his memoirs he called Semenov a "murderer, robber, and a most dissolute scoundrel" and wrote that if he "had committed, in the United States, one one-hundredth of the offenses that he committed in Siberia, he would have been legally or illegally killed, for such a character could not exist in this country." Graves was even harsher in his estimate of Kalmikov: "He was the worst scoundrel I ever saw or heard of and I seriously doubt, if one should go through the entire Standard Dictionary, looking for words descriptive of crime, if a crime could be found that Kalmikoff had not committed. . . . Kalmikoff murdered with his own hands, where Semenoff ordered others to kill, and therein lies the difference between Kalmikoff and Semenoff."[35]

Many of Graves's soldiers shared his assessment. Corporal Leslie H. Head, stationed at Khabarovsk, recalled:

From the very beginning the American troops and the Cossacks disagreed and each heartily detested the other. We regarded them as a bunch of

Ivan Kalmikov (center). Robert L. Eichelberger Papers, David M. Rubenstein Rare Book & Manuscript Library, courtesy of Duke University, Durham, North Carolina.

Semenov's soldiers. Courtesy of The Czech Legion Project, www.czechlegion.com.

swashbuckling bandits and they termed us foreign interlopers and even accused us of being sympathetic with the Bolsheviki, simply because we didn't go
around dealing blows to the general public and paid for what we got instead of
requisitioning it and handing out worthless promissory notes as they did. . . . I
recall seeing Kalmykoff's armored train on numerous occasions and our trigger
fingers often itched as we saw the obscene gestures to us and heard their epi-
thets as their frowsy and lousy but heavily armed train guards contemptuously
looked us over while their armored trains passed our lonely posts. I think it a
credit to our discipline and common sense that we didn't "let them have it."[36]

In the beginning Kalmikov was the more hesitant of the two Cossacks
to inflame the Americans. For a long time his chief offense was to throw
dead horses from his trains as he passed American encampments, apparently
hoping to expel the Americans by mere force of stench. As we shall see, his
offenses later became more serious.[37]

Acting more like Jesse James than his revered Napoleon, Semenov
preferred robbing American trains that traveled through Chita. When
Semenov's troops stole a railway car that was being used by the Russian
Railway Service Corps as an office, the Japanese promised to help retrieve it,
one Japanese general saying that he was certain that its seizure was a mere
misunderstanding since Semenov was an honorable man. Months went by,
and more protests were registered, but the car was never returned.[38]

When the theft of a railway car proved insufficient to drive the Americans out of Siberia or place his name in the annals of history beside that of
Napoleon, Semenov decided to adopt a policy of direct confrontation with
American forces. In initiating this policy Semenov was setting himself on
a collision course with fiery Lieutenant Colonel Charles H. Morrow, affec-
tionately known to his troops as the "Bull of the Woods." Colonel Morrow
commanded the two battalions of the Twenty-Seventh Infantry that had
been sent, in accord with the Inter-Allied Railway Agreement, to guard the
Verkhne-Udinsk to Baikal City sector of the Trans-Siberian Railway.[39]

One day in early June 1919 Semenov entered Colonel Morrow's sector
and attempted to arrest several Russian railway employees he termed Bolsheviks. Colonel Morrow refused to allow the railway employees to be arrested
and told Semenov never to attempt to arrest people in his sector again. According to General Graves, "Semenoff claimed to be horrified at the thought
that any foreigner could tell him what he could or could not do in Russia,
and he notified Morrow that he was going to repeat his former act." Colonel
Morrow replied that if Semenov entered his sector with his armored train
again, "he would blow him to perdition or some similar place." Semenov

possessed a fleet of nine armored trains, including the *Merciless*, the *Terrible*, and the *Horrible*. The most formidable of these trains, called the *Destroyer*, was shielded by steel plate and eighteen inches of reinforced concrete, and was equipped with four mounted cannons and numerous machine guns.[40]

On June 9, Semenov approached Colonel Morrow's sector. Colonel Morrow arranged his thirty-seven-millimeter cannons on each side of the railroad track, though he was uncertain whether their shells could pierce the *Destroyer*. A Japanese force five times the size of Colonel Morrow's appeared on the scene; its commander told Colonel Morrow that he would support Se-menov if Morrow launched any attack on his armored train when it entered the sector. Colonel Morrow refused to back down, preparing his cannons to fire on Semenov. The *Destroyer* lumbered down the tracks. When the Japa-nese saw that Colonel Morrow was serious, they rode out to stop Semenov's train before it reached the sector, ordering him to turn back. He did so. War with the Cossacks and the Japanese had been narrowly avoided. It was now apparent that if the Japanese could order Semenov about in this fashion, they could certainly have retrieved one stolen railway car if they had desired.[41]

The incident produced various reactions. The Japanese now acted with greater caution in their dealings with Colonel Morrow. As one of his fellow officers later wrote, "The Japanese regarded Colonel Morrow as a sort of bomb with the fuse already lighted." For their part, the Czechs were now so convinced that Colonel Morrow would have to fight both the Cossacks and the Japanese that they formed a plan to send him 10,000 troops in two days should the need arise. As for Semenov, he reacted with his usual petulance, claiming that it had all been a misunderstanding purposely fostered by the interpreters employed by Colonel Morrow and that it would not happen again.[42]

Indeed, it did not happen again, both because Semenov and the Japanese now regarded Colonel Morrow as a hothead and because they determined on a new plan to have Semenov harass American railway workers in Japanese-controlled areas. On July 27, 1919, Ambassador Morris complained to the State Department about "the refusal of the Japanese military authorities to protect, when called upon to do so, the representatives of the Technical Board from interference in the performance of their duties and the enforce-ment of their orders." On August 15, Stevens reported, "Semenoff's hostile acts against our inspectors [are] worse than ever. Japan [is] giving me ab-solutely no protection; [they are] apparently in sympathy with Semenoff. I have ordered [the] removal of inspectors as perhaps even their lives may be in danger." On the same day Morris reported:

The Japanese Government now for the first time definitely refuses to protect the representatives of the Inter-Allied Technical Committee in the performance of their duties; Semenoff, emboldened by the passive attitude of Japan, is apparently defying the authority of the Inter-Allied representatives, terrorizing the railway employees and controlling the operation of the railway to suit his own purposes. The Department will appreciate the fact that the engineers are alone at widely separated stations surrounded by hostile Cossacks and unable to rely on the protection of the Japanese soldiers. Under these circumstances Stevens and Emerson [another leader of the Russian Railway Service Corps] feel that they are not justified in risking the lives of the engineers and are preparing to withdraw them from the Semenoff section.[43]

As a result of these dispatches, on August 30, Secretary of State Lansing formally protested Japan's unwillingness to protect American railway workers, and threatened to withdraw U.S. forces from Siberia, "to be followed, if need be, by a public statement of the reasons for such an action, since it might be misunderstood if no explanation [is] made." This was, of course, precisely what the Japanese military desired.[44]

In fact, it was quite obvious to everyone that although Semenov and Kalmikov were officially the subordinates of Kolchak, it was the Japanese who pulled their strings. Neither Cossack ever stirred far from his Japanese umbilical cord because both were so detested by the Siberian people, whom they terrorized, that to do so would have placed their lives in jeopardy. As early as December 16, 1918, the State Department had protested the Japanese backing of the two generals. Both then and later, the Japanese retorted that all Russian armies were independent, so that to threaten the use of force against them would be to interfere in Russian internal affairs, something Japan would never dream of doing.[45]

Leave It to the Conference

A third reason that President Wilson maintained troops in Siberia after the armistice with the Central Powers was that he realized that for any Russian policy to be effective, it would have to be agreed upon by all of the Allies. Thus, Wilson was not inclined to alter his Russian policy until he had conferred with Allied leaders at the Paris Peace Conference. After meeting with Wilson on October 16, 1918, Sir William Wiseman wrote, "The question of Russia, he thought, should also be left to the Peace Conference." For the same reason, Wilson declined to issue the official statement on the Russian situation that Lansing had prepared on November 24. Assistant Secretary of

State Polk repeated the same reason for inaction in a dispatch transmitted on December 4. That was the day the president and the secretary of state set sail for France.[46]

Notes

1. Arno J. Mayer, *Political Origins of the New Diplomacy, 1917–1918* (New Haven, Conn.: Yale University Press, 1959), 393.

2. John Keegan, *The First World War* (New York: Alfred A. Knopf, 1999), 372, 374, 404, 408–19; Edward M. Coffman, *The War to End All Wars: The American Military Experience in World War I* (Oxford: Oxford University Press, 1968), 214, 237, 247, 298–300; John Ellis, *Eye-Deep in Hell: Trench Warfare in World War I* (New York: Pantheon, 1976), 128–29, 136, 181. For the armistice terms, see Arthur S. Link, ed., *The Papers of Woodrow Wilson* (Princeton, N.J.: Princeton University Press, 1966–1994), An Address to a Joint Session of Congress, November 11, 1918, vol. 53, 36–41.

3. For reference to the alarm caused by the brief communist revolutions in Hungary and Bavaria, see Link, *Papers of Woodrow Wilson*, Robert Lansing to Wilson, March 24, 1919, vol. 56, 239–41; Diary of Ray Stannard Baker, April 19, 1919, vol. 58, 509.

4. Ibid., Robert Lansing to Wilson, September 14, 1918, vol. 51, 5n2; Semion Lyandres, "The 1918 Attempt on the Life of Lenin: A New Look at the Evidence," *Slavic Review* 48 (Fall 1989): 432–48; David W. McFadden, *Alternative Paths: Soviets and Americans, 1917–1920* (Oxford: Oxford University Press, 1993), 155, 157; R. H. Bruce Lockhart, *British Agent* (New York: G. P. Putnam's Sons, 1933), 314–22.

5. C. Leiteizen, ed., *Lenin on the United States: Selected Writings by V. I. Lenin* (New York: International Publishers, 1970), "Letter to American Workers," August 20, 1918, 344, 347; "Letter to the Workers of Europe and America," January 21, 1919, 376–377; Richard K. Debo, *Revolution and Survival: The Foreign Policy of Soviet Russia, 1917–1918* (Toronto: University of Toronto Press, 1979), 357.

6. Link, *Papers of Woodrow Wilson*, Sir William Wiseman to Arthur C. Murray, September 14, 1918, vol. 51, 8.

7. Ibid., Wilson to Robert Lansing, September 20, vol. 51, 78n2; David S. Foglesong, *America's Secret War against Bolshevism, U.S. Intervention in the Russian Civil War, 1917–1920* (Chapel Hill: University of North Carolina Press, 1995), 38.

8. W. B. Fowler, *British-American Relations, 1917–1918: The Role of Sir William Wiseman* (Princeton, N.J.: Princeton University Press, 1969), 288; McFadden, *Alternative Paths*, 156, 176; Robert J. Maddox, *The Unknown War with Russia: Wilson's Siberian Intervention* (San Rafael, Calif.: Presidio, 1977), 80; Ray Stannard Baker, ed., *Woodrow Wilson: Life and Letters* (New York: Doubleday, 1927–1939), vol. 8, 553, 560.

9. U.S. Department of State, *Papers Relating to the Foreign Relations of the United States: The Lansing Papers, 1914–1920* (Washington, D.C.: Government Printing

Office, 1939–1940), Lansing to Woodrow Wilson, September 24, 1918, vol. 2, 387; Linda Killen, *The Russian Bureau: A Case Study in Wilsonian Diplomacy* (Lexington: University Press of Kentucky, 1983), 79; Link, *Papers of Woodrow Wilson*, Memorandum of William C. Huntington, November 22, 1918, vol. 53, 178.

10. U.S. Department of State, *Papers Relating to the Foreign Relations of the United States: Russia, 1918* (Washington, D.C.: Government Printing Office, 1931–1932; reprint, New York: Kraus, 1969), Roland S. Morris to Robert Lansing, September 23, vol. 2, 389–90; Link, *Papers of Woodrow Wilson*, Robert Lansing to Wilson, September 24, 1918, vol. 51, 95.

11. U.S. Department of State, *Lansing Papers, 1914–1920*, Lansing to Woodrow Wilson, September 24, 1918, vol. 2, 387; U.S. Department of State, *Foreign Relations, Russia, 1918*, Robert Lansing to Roland S. Morris, September 26, vol. 2, 393; William S. Graves, *America's Siberian Adventure, 1918–1920* (New York: Cape and Smith, 1931), 67.

12. U.S. Department of State, *Lansing Papers, 1914–1920*, Woodrow Wilson to Lansing, August 23, 1918, vol. 2, 378.

13. U.S. Department of State, *Foreign Relations, Russia, 1918*, Robert Lansing to Roland S. Morris, September 26, vol. 2, 393; Fowler, *British-American Relations*, 194.

14. U.S. Department of State, *Foreign Relations, Russia, 1918*, Frank L. Polk to William G. Sharp, July 15, vol. 2, 282; Robert Lansing to William G. Sharp, November 5, vol. 2, 425; Richard Goldhurst, *The Midnight War: The American Intervention in Russia, 1918–1920* (New York: McGraw-Hill, 1978), 21–22.

15. U.S. Department of State, *Foreign Relations, Russia, 1918*, Robert Lansing to Woodrow Wilson, August 29, vol. 2, 379; September 9, vol. 2, 382; U.S. Department of State, *Papers Relating to the Foreign Relations of the United States: Russia, 1919* (Washington, D.C.: Government Printing Office, 1937; reprint, New York: Kraus, 1969), Executive Order 3094-A, June 5, 265; Link, *Papers of Woodrow Wilson*, Wilson to Bernard Baruch, September 17, 1918, vol. 51, 26; Robert Lansing and Vance C. McCormick to Frank L. Polk, April 16, 1919, vol. 57, 420–22; Maddox, *Unknown War with Russia*, 81–84; Foglesong, *America's Secret War against Bolshevism*, 61, 70; Ilya Somin, *Stillborn Crusade: The Tragic Failure of Western Intervention in the Russian Civil War, 1918–1920* (New Brunswick, N.J.: Transaction, 1996), 9, 57; N. G. O. Pereira, *White Siberia: The Politics of Civil War* (Montreal: McGill-Queen's University Press, 1996), 105, 122.

16. Link, *Papers of Woodrow Wilson*, William S. Graves to Adjutant General Peter Harris, December 29, 1918, vol. 55, 402.

17. Foglesong, *America's Secret War against Bolshevism*, 254.

18. U.S. Department of State, *Foreign Relations, Russia, 1918*, Roland S. Morris to Robert Lansing, July 23, vol. 2, 300; Robert Lansing to Woodrow Wilson, July 24, vol. 2, 301; J. V. A. MacMurray to Robert Lansing, July 24, vol. 2, 303.

19. Ibid., Frank L. Polk to Woodrow Wilson, August 3, vol. 2, 325–26; Roland S. Morris to Robert Lansing, August 5, vol. 2, 330; August 13, vol. 2, 344; J. V. A. MacMurray to Robert Lansing, August 15, vol. 2, 349.

20. Ibid., Breckinridge Long Memo, August 21, vol. 2, 353; Roland S. Morris to Robert Lansing, August 26, vol. 2, 355–57.

21. Graves, *America's Siberian Adventure*, 62; Link, *Papers of Woodrow Wilson*, William S. Graves to Adjutant General Peter Harris, October 1, 1918, vol. 51, 609.

22. U.S. Department of State, *Foreign Relations, Russia, 1918*, Ishii Kikujiro to Robert Lansing, August 27, vol. 2, 357–58; Roland S. Morris to Robert Lansing, September 5, vol. 2, 368; November 6, vol. 2, 427; November 20, vol. 2, 436; Link, *Papers of Woodrow Wilson*, Wilson to Robert Lansing, September 17, 1918, vol. 51, 25; William S. Graves to Peter Harris, October 18, 1918, vol. 51, 384; October 25, vol. 51, 449; Roland S. Morris to Robert Lansing, October 27, vol. 51, 481.

23. U.S. Department of State, *Foreign Relations, Russia, 1918*, John K. Caldwell to Robert Lansing, September 9, vol. 2, 372; Frank L. Polk to Roland S. Morris, December 16, vol. 2, 462; Betty M. Unterberger, *America's Siberian Expedition, 1918–1920* (Durham, N.C.: Duke University Press, 1956; reprint, New York: Greenwood, 1969), 103–4.

24. U.S. Department of State, *Lansing Papers, 1914–1920*, Lansing to Woodrow Wilson, August 18, 1918, vol. 2, 374–75; U.S. Department of State, *Foreign Relations, Russia, 1918*, Robert Lansing Memo, August 20, vol. 2, 351.

25. Link, *Papers of Woodrow Wilson*, Newton D. Baker to Wilson, November 6, 1918, vol. 51, 608; November 27, 1918, vol. 53, 227–28.

26. U.S. Department of State, *Foreign Relations, Russia, 1918*, Robert Lansing to Roland S. Morris, November 16, vol. 2, 435; Roland S. Morris to Robert Lansing, November 20, vol. 2, 436–37; Link, *Papers of Woodrow Wilson*, Memorandum of David Lloyd George, December 30, 1918, vol. 53, 560; Diary of David H. Miller, January 30, 1919, vol. 54, 379.

27. Graves, *America's Siberian Adventure*, 57–59; U.S. Department of State, *Lansing Papers, 1914–1920*, Colville Barclay to Lansing, August 16, 1918, vol. 2, 373.

28. U.S. Department of State, *Foreign Relations, Russia, 1918*, Robert Lansing to Walter Hines Page, November 16, vol. 2, 433; Robert Lansing to Roland S. Morris, November 16, vol. 2, 434; William G. Sharp to Robert Lansing, November 22, vol. 2, 440; Irwin B. Laughlin to Robert Lansing, December 9, vol. 2, 477.

29. U.S. Department of State, *Foreign Relations, Russia, 1918*, Roland S. Morris to Robert Lansing, December 29, vol. 2, 465–66; Unterberger, *America's Siberian Expedition*, 106.

30. U.S. Department of State, *Foreign Relations, Russia, 1919*, Roland S. Morris to Frank L. Polk, January 9, 236; Ishii Kikujiro to Frank L. Polk, January 15, 239; Katsuji Debuchi to Breckinridge Long, January 18, 242–43; Charles H. Smith to Frank L. Polk, April 22, 555; Robert L. Willett, *Russian Sideshow: America's Undeclared War, 1918–1920* (Washington, D.C.: Brassey's, 2003), 206–7; Killen, *Russian Bureau*, 61–62, 117, 189.

31. U.S. Department of State, *Foreign Relations, Russia, 1919*, Frank L. Polk to Commission to Negotiate Peace, January 24, 245; Commission to Negotiate Peace to Frank L. Polk, January 31, 246–48.

32. Ibid., Frank L. Polk to Commission to Negotiate Peace, February 4, 248–49; Commission to Negotiate Peace to Frank L. Polk, February 9, 251; Frank L. Polk to Ishii Kikujiro, February 10, 251–52; Killen, *Russian Bureau*, 42, 50, 117–19.

33. U.S. Department of State, *Foreign Relations, Russia, 1919*, Woodrow Wilson to Frank L. Polk, March 3, 262; Executive Order No. 3094-A, June 5, 265–66.

34. Unterberger, *America's Siberian Expedition*, 119; Carol Willcox Melton, *Between War and Peace: Woodrow Wilson and the American Expeditionary Force in Siberia, 1918–1921* (Macon, Ga.: Mercer University Press, 2001), 57–58.

35. Graves, *America's Siberian Adventure*, 86, 90–91, 314.

36. R. Ernest Dupuy, *Perish by the Sword: The Czechoslovakian Anabasis and Our Supporting Campaigns in North Russia and Siberia, 1918–1920* (Harrisburg, Pa.: Military Service Publishing, 1939), 235–36.

37. Maddox, *Unknown War with Russia*, 71.

38. U.S. Department of State, *Foreign Relations, Russia, 1919*, Paul S. Reinsch to Frank L. Polk, May 31, 505; Roland S. Morris to Robert Lansing, July 17, 566–67.

39. Graves, *America's Siberian Adventure*, 183; Dupuy, *Perish by the Sword*, 232.

40. Graves, *America's Siberian Adventure*, 183–84; Maddox, *Unknown War with Russia*, 71–72; Dupuy, *Perish by the Sword*, 257.

41. Graves, *America's Siberian Adventure*, 184, 206; Maddox, *Unknown War with Russia*, 72.

42. Maddox, *Unknown War with Russia*, 73; U.S. Department of State, *Foreign Relations, Russia, 1919*, Paul S. Reinsch to Frank L. Polk, June 14, 507.

43. U.S. Department of State, *Foreign Relations, Russia, 1919*, Roland S. Morris to Robert Lansing, July 27, 567; August 15, 571; John F. Stevens to Robert Lansing, August 15, 570.

44. Ibid., Robert Lansing to American Embassy in Tokyo, August 30, 576–77.

45. For early dispatches noting Japanese control of Semenov and Kalmikov, see U.S. Department of State, *Foreign Relations, Russia, 1918*, Ernest L. Harris to Robert Lansing, October 31, vol. 2, 419–20; December 9, vol. 2, 456; Roland S. Morris to Robert Lansing, November 7, vol. 2, 428; Charles Moser to Robert Lansing, November 27, vol. 2, 448; Alfred Thomson to Robert Lansing, December 6, vol. 2, 454; December 9, vol. 2, 458; December 13, vol. 2, 462; Sergei Ughet to Frank L. Polk, December 14, vol. 2, 461; Frank L. Polk to Roland S. Morris, December 16, vol. 2, 462.

46. Ibid., Frank L. Polk to DeWitt C. Poole, December 4, vol. 2, 457; Fowler, *British-American Relations*, 288. For reference to Wilson's reason for deciding against the issuance of Lansing's statement, see Link, *Papers of Woodrow Wilson*, Frank L. Polk to Robert Lansing, January 6, 1919, vol. 53, 627.

CHAPTER FIVE

~

In Search of a Russian Policy

[Russia] was the Banquo's ghost sitting at every Council Table.

—Herbert Hoover, regarding the Paris Peace Conference.[1]

In the first half of 1919 the Allies made five attempts to formulate a common policy for Russia at the Paris Peace Conference. All of these attempts failed.

The Prinkipo Proposal

The first attempt was the Prinkipo proposal. In early December 1918 an inter-Allied conference, lacking only American participation, was held in London. At this conference the subject of the representation of Russia at the Paris Peace Conference (see photo p. 101) was discussed. French Prime Minister Georges Clemenceau vehemently opposed any Russian participation in the conference. The secretary recorded, "He would resist with great energy any representation of Russia, which had betrayed the Allied cause during the war. The peace which was yet to be settled did not concern her." British Prime Minister Lloyd George strongly disagreed:

It must be recognized that, great as had been the suffering of the other Allies, Russia had probably lost more lives than any. Their troops had fought without arms or munitions; they had been outrageously betrayed by their Government, and it was little to be wondered at if, in their bitterness, the Russian people had rebelled against the Alliance. He doubted whether any other country would have borne as much as Russia and remained in the war so long. . . . It was not possible to say that the Tartars, the Finns, the Letts, should come to the Peace Conference and not the Bolsheviks, who stood for two-thirds of the whole population. The Bolsheviks, whatever might be thought of them, appeared to have a hold over the majority of the population. This was a fact, a sinister one no doubt, but facts could not be neglected because they were unpalatable. He reminded the meeting that 120 years ago similar feelings had been experienced, and similar views expressed, in that very room, with Mr. [William] Pitt, whose portrait was hanging on the wall, in the Chair, in regard to the French revolutionaries, and the dissidents in Vendee, and in the south of France. He therefore strongly deprecated the adoption of any fixed attitude towards Central Russia.

A further reason which weighed with him was the danger that the military intervention would only strengthen the very force which we set out to destroy. It was impossible to ignore the parallel of the French Revolution. There, too, had been horrors as bad as, or worse than, those of the Bolsheviks, perpetrated by a small faction, who had secured the control of the French. There, too, we were invited to help. Toulon and La Vendee corresponded to Riga and the Ukraine. But the very fact that we intervened enabled Danton to rally French patriotism and make the terror a military instrument. When the Revolution was followed by a military dictatorship we were worse off. France became organized as a great military machine imbued with a passionate hatred against us.

Were we prepared to face a revolutionary war against a population of over 100,000,000, associating ourselves in this intervention with allies like the Japanese, against whom feeling in Russia was so passionately strong? He knew of no authority on the strength of which we could be justified in hypothecating our resources and our manhood in the belief that the Russians would regard us as deliverers. For Russia to emancipate herself would be a redemption, but the attempt to emancipate her by foreign armies might prove a disaster to Europe as well as to Russia. The one sure method of establishing the power of the Bolsheviks would be to create more Bolsheviks. The best thing was to let Bolshevism fail of itself, as it might and probably would if it did not represent Russian sentiment.[2]

But Clemenceau's disgust with the Bolsheviks made any sort of neutrality in the Russian Civil War unthinkable to him. Instead, he began to promote the *cordon sanitaire* strategy. This strategy involved crushing the Soviet government economically, by establishing a ring of hostile states around Soviet Russia. Clemenceau called the circle of nations the cordon sanitaire because he compared bolshevism to a disease, the sufferers of which must be quarantined. As Clemenceau explained to his foreign minister, Pichon, on December 13, 1918, "The inter-allied plan of action is not of an offensive character,

The Big Four at Versailles(left to right); David Lloyd George, Vittorio Orlando, Georges Clemenceau, and Woodrow Wilson during peace conference. Gianni Dagli Orti/The Art Archive at Art Resource, NY.

but it simply interdicts to the Bolsheviks access to the Ukraine regions, the Caucasus, and Western Siberia, which are economically necessary to them for their endurance, and where the elements of Russian order are being orga-nized." Thus, Clemenceau was unmoved by an official statement from Soviet envoy Maxim Litvinov that offered peace to the Allies on December 24.[3]

By contrast, seizing the opportunity offered by Litvinov's statement, Lloyd George ordered notes transmitted to each Allied government, on January 3, 1919, proposing that every organized group in Russia be invited to send representatives to Paris for the peace conference. Two days later, Pichon re-plied, in the strongest possible language, that the French government would negotiate with anyone *but* the Bolsheviks. The foreign minister proposed the cordon sanitaire strategy instead, making it quite clear that the French government could not tolerate the presence of Bolsheviks in Paris and that if Lloyd George insisted upon inviting them, there might be wholesale resigna-tions within the French foreign ministry.[4]

On January 12, Lloyd George again pressed his views, this time at the peace conference. All of the Big Four, Wilson, Lloyd George, Clemenceau, and Orlando, were now present. As Lloyd George spoke, the secretary recorded:

> The peasants accepted Bolshevism for the same reason as the peasants had accepted it in the French Revolution, namely, that it gave them land. . . . We had formally recognized the Czar's Government, although at the time we knew it to be absolutely rotten. Our reason had been that it was the *de facto* Government . . . but we refused to recognize the Bolshevists. To say that we ourselves should pick the representatives of a great people was contrary to every principle for which we had fought. It was possible that the Bolshevists did not represent Russia. But certainly [prominent anti-Bolshevik] Prince [Georgi] Lvoff did not. . . . The British Government made exactly the same mistake when they said the émigrés represented France. This led them into a war which lasted about twenty-five years. The Russian peasants probably felt towards Trotsky much as the French peasants did towards Robespierre.

Unimpressed with Lloyd George's arguments, the French claimed that the Soviet government would fall if the Allies did not increase its prestige by negotiating with it. Wilson was silent.[5]

On January 16, at another meeting of the Big Four, Lloyd George outlined what he considered the three Russian policies available to the Allies. The first was a full-scale invasion of Russia, an option at which Lloyd George scoffed:

> The Germans, at the time when they needed every available man to reinforce their attack on the Western Front, had been forced to keep about a million men to garrison a few provinces of Russia which were a mere fringe of the whole country; and, moreover, at that moment Bolshevism was weak and disorganized. Now, it was strong and had a formidable army. Was anyone of the Western Allies prepared to send a million men into Russia? He doubted whether a thousand would be willing to go. All reports tended to show that the Allied troops in Siberia and in Northern Russia were most unwilling to continue the campaign and determined to return to their homes. . . .
>
> [Anton] Denikin was said to have recognized Kolchak, but he was quite unable to get into touch with him, as an immense Bolshevik area intervened between them. Kolchak, moreover, appeared to pursue the revival of the old regime in Russia. . . . This would not help to create a new world.

The second policy that could be adopted, Lloyd George said, was the cordon sanitaire strategy. But, he argued: "Our blockade of Russia would lead to the killing, not of the ruffians enlisted by the Bolsheviks, but the ordinary population, with whom we wish to be friends. This was a policy which, if only on the grounds of humanity, we could not support."

The third alternative, which Lloyd George considered the most sensible one, was to invite representatives from all of the Russian governments to come to Paris to negotiate:

> We could not leave Paris at the conclusion of the Peace Conference congratulating ourselves on having made a better world if at that moment half of Europe and half of Russia were in flames. It had been alleged that if Bolshevik emissaries came to France and England they would proselytise the French and British peoples. It was possible that Bolshevism might gain ground in these countries, but it would not be as a consequence of the visit of a few Russian emissaries. He himself had no fears on this score. Moreover, conditions could be imposed on the delegates, and if they failed to observe them they could be sent back to Russia. With this threat over them it was most likely that they would avoid giving offense as they would be anxious to explain their case.

Finally breaking his silence, Wilson declared that he agreed entirely with Lloyd George. The secretary recorded:

> There was certainly a latent force behind Bolshevism which attracted as much sympathy as its more brutal aspects caused general disgust. There was throughout the world a feeling of revolt against the large vested interests which influenced the world both in the economic and in the political sphere. The way to cure this domination was, in his opinion, constant discussion and a slow process of reform; but the world at large had grown impatient of delay. . . . We should be fighting against the current of the times if we tried to prevent Russia from finding her own path in freedom. Part of the strength of the Bolshevik leaders was doubtless the threat of foreign intervention. With the help of this threat they gathered the people round them. The reports of the American representatives in Russia were to this effect. He thought, therefore, that the British proposal contained the only suggestion that led anywhere. If the Bolsheviks refrained from invading Lithuania, Poland, Finland, & co., he thought we should be well advised to allow as many groups as desired to do so to send representatives to Paris. We should then try to reconcile them, both mutually and with the rest of the world.

This is one of many instances in which Wilson spoke sensibly about Russia, in stark contrast to his often foolish actions. It is not that Wilson was insincere in his pronouncements, only that his fear of bolshevism constantly overrode his good judgment.[6]

In any case, the proponents of the British proposal to invite the representatives of the various Russian governments to Paris received a boost on January 18, when William H. Buckler filed his report. Buckler, a special assistant to the American Embassy in London, had traveled to Stockholm to speak with Litvinov, with the express permission of Wilson. Having met with Litvinov from January 14 to 16, Buckler now cabled:

> The Soviet Government is prepared to compromise on all points, including the Russian foreign debt, protection to existing foreign enterprises and the granting of new concessions in Russia. . . . The conciliatory attitude of the Soviet Government is unquestionable. . . .
>
> Litvinov and his associates fully realize that for a long time Russia will need expert assistance and advice, especially in technical and financial matters and that she cannot get on without foreign machinery and manufactured imports. If peace were made, Russian Bolshevist propaganda in foreign countries would cease at once. The war declared on Russia by the Allies called forth that revolutionary propaganda as a measure of retaliation just as it has produced violence and terror in other [sectors of Russia]. These [activities] will all cease as soon as the war stops. . . . Russians realize that in certain western countries conditions are not favorable for a revolution of the Russian type.

Buckler claimed that the Bolsheviks were willing to offer amnesty for Whites and the cessation of combat with the Finns, Poles, and Ukrainians. The Bolsheviks would even support Wilson's pet project, the League of Nations, provided it "could prevent war without encouraging reaction." After adding that extremists in Soviet Russia were opposed to these concessions, Buckler concluded regarding Allied intervention in Russia, "The continuance of such intervention plays into the hands of these extremists whereas a policy of agreement with the Soviet Government will counteract their influence, will strengthen the moderates, and by reviving trade and industry will procure prosperity, the best of all antidotes to Bolshevism."[7]

On January 21, President Wilson read Buckler's report at another meeting of the Big Four, who discussed it the same afternoon. Out of deference to Clemenceau's feelings, Wilson then amended Lloyd George's original proposal, saying that the "various organized groups in Russia should be asked to send representatives, not to Paris, but to some other place." Lloyd George responded that one advantage of Wilson's proposal was that the site of the meeting could be chosen in such a way that the Bolsheviks would not have to pass through any other country, thus alleviating the fears of many governments. Wilson added, rather curiously, that he wanted the representatives of the various Russian governments "all in one room." Whether Wilson was willing to risk his own life by sitting between them in this room is unclear.

At this point Italian Foreign Minister Baron Sidney Sonnino cried that the Bolsheviks were enemies of the Allies and did not deserve to be heard. Only the various anti-Bolshevik groups should be invited. The secretary recorded: "Mr. Lloyd George expressed the view that the acceptance of M. Sonnino's proposal would amount to their hearing a string of people, all of whom held the same opinion, and all of whom would strike the same note. But they would not hear the people who at the present moment were actually controlling European Russia." When Lloyd George finished, Wilson made an interesting series of statements:

> As M. Sonnino had implied, they were all repelled by Bolshevism, and for that reason they had placed armed men in opposition to them. . . . The Allies were making it possible for the Bolsheviks to argue that Imperialistic and Capitalistic Governments were endeavoring to exploit the country and to give the land back to the landlords, and so bring about a reaction. If it could be shown that this was not true and that the Allies were prepared to deal with the rulers of Russia, much of the moral force of this argument would disappear. The allegation that the Allies were against the people and wanted to control their affairs provided the argument which enabled them to raise armies. If, on the other hand, the Allies could swallow their pride and the natural repulsion which they felt for the Bolsheviks, and see the representatives of all organized groups in one place, he thought it would bring about a marked reaction against Bolshevism.

While some allowance must be made for Wilson's desire to placate the ardently anti-Bolshevik Italians and French at this meeting, it is nevertheless striking that Wilson here portrays the proposed conference solely as a means of discrediting the Soviet government. There is no suggestion that the Allies should engage in serious negotiations with the Bolsheviks, should the conference fail to "bring about a marked reaction against Bolshevism."

Clemenceau now took the floor. He argued once again that bolshevism was spreading throughout Europe and that something must be done to stop it. He said that he did not trust Litvinov, who was laying a trap for the Allies, but he would support Wilson's proposal in the interest of unity. Sonnino agreed completely with Clemenceau on each of these points. British Foreign Secretary Arthur Balfour suggested only that abstention from hostilities be made a condition for representation in the proposed conference. Everyone agreed to this stipulation, and it was decided that Wilson should draft a proclamation inviting all organized parties in Russia to attend a meeting "at some selected place" to discuss "the means of restoring order and peace in Russia."[8]

Finding the "selected place" that would admit the Bolsheviks proved difficult. As Lloyd George later recalled, "No country could be found willing to receive their envoys. It was as if I had proposed that we should invite a delegation of lepers from the stricken isle of Molokai." But, working through the evening, Lloyd George and Wilson found a place. On January 22, Wilson read the text of his proclamation to the rest of the Big Four. Each organized group in Russia that agreed to cease military activity for the duration of the conference would be invited to send up to three representatives to Prinkipo Island, in the sea of Marmara near the Turkish Straits. The Prinkipo conference would begin on February 15, 1919. The Allies would furnish transportation to the island if necessary. The Big Four approved Wilson's proclamation, which was transmitted from a powerful wireless transmitter atop the Eiffel Tower so that the Allies would not have to issue a direct invitation to Soviet leaders.[9]

Secretary of State Robert Lansing then moved swiftly to ensure that the Prinkipo proposal was not misunderstood. On January 27, Lansing informed Assistant Secretary of State Frank L. Polk that any fears of the Allies negotiating seriously with the Bolsheviks could be laid to rest. After noting that Allied leaders had concluded that they were incapable of mustering a large army to defeat the Bolsheviks, Lansing explained:

> In these circumstances the best and humane thing to do seemed to be to make an appeal of some sort to the warring elements to cease violence while the Peace Conference is in session. . . . It very probably will not accomplish anything but we could not do less than make an attempt to stay the slaughter and horror which the Russians are enduring. The only alternative since force was out of the question was to remain silent and let things take their course. That would have satisfied no one. . . .
>
> You can use the [this] information discreetly where you think it would do good and correct [a] wrong impression.[10]

Nevertheless, misunderstandings were inevitable. On February 4, DeWitt C. Poole, now chargé d'affaires at Archangel, tendered his resignation in protest against the Prinkipo proposal, arguing that the Bolsheviks were completely immoral and that the Allies should not give them any respectability by listening to them. But on February 10, Lansing informed the State Department that he had written Poole to assure him that "it is not the intention of the American Government in agreeing to this meeting to barter in matters of principle with the Bolshevik Government. The purpose of the meeting is rather that of investigation." In view of this new information and Lansing's request that he remain at his post, Poole withdrew his resignation.[11]

Meanwhile, on the very day that Poole tendered his resignation, the Soviet government agreed to send representatives to the Prinkipo conference.

In fact, Soviet Commissar for Foreign Affairs Georgi V. Chicherin reiterated the Soviet government's position, previously conveyed through Litvinov, that it was now willing to discuss the payment of Russian debts through raw materials if necessary. Furthermore, the Soviet government was willing to grant concessions to the "nationals of the Entente Powers" and did not even exclude the cession of territory to the Allies. The Allies could then maintain troops on this territory if they desired. The Soviet government also agreed to cease the dissemination of revolutionary propaganda in Allied nations. Chicherin concluded by pointing to the recent military victories of the Bolsheviks and to their rapprochement with the Socialist Revolutionaries and the Mensheviks, two sizable rival factions, as signs of their growing strength.[12]

The reaction of the White governments to the Prinkipo proposal was very different. It must first be noted that the governments of Archangel and Southern Russia, dominated by czarist generals Nicholas N. Yudenich and Anton Denikin respectively, had recognized Alexander Kolchak as their leader. On February 12, the "unified governments of Siberia, Archangel, and Southern Russia" announced that "under no circumstances whatever would there be any question of an exchange of ideas on this matter with the participation of the Bolshevists, in whom the conscience of the Russian people sees only traitors." The announcement added, "They have fomented anarchy and trodden underfoot the democratic principles which guide civilized states, and they maintain themselves in power only by terrorism." This last statement was hypocritical, coming from committed czarists whose leader had himself overthrown a democratic government in Siberia and who engaged in terrorism of his own.[13]

Although Wilson soon discovered that it was the French who had undermined the Prinkipo proposal by urging the White governments to refuse to attend, he did not protest their interference, nor did he make even the mildest attempt to pressure Kolchak into sending representatives to the Prinkipo conference, though a considerable portion of Kolchak's weapons and supplies came from the United States. The State Department did urge the Kolchak government on February 15, the scheduled date for the opening of the conference, to send representatives to Prinkipo Island, but added that the invitation to the Bolsheviks "did not imply any willingness to barter principles with the Bolsheviks, but has for its sole purpose investigation and obtaining complete information." With such an assurance, there was no reason for the Whites to have sent representatives to Prinkipo Island. Indeed, even after Kolchak thumbed his nose at Wilson's proposal, American aid to him continued unabated. Wilson merely expressed disappointment at a press conference that "the Allies' invitation to Prinkipo Island had attracted the factions least desirable, to the exclusion of those who might restore order." In case the journalists failed to deduce the identity of those "factions least desirable," Wilson added that "he regarded the Soviet reply to the Allies as rather insulting because their intimation of a willingness to make good the Russian debt apparently revealed the Bolshevik desire to . . . buy recognition." Wilson had gone from complaining about the Bolshevik repudiation of the Russian debt to grousing about their expression of a willingness to pay it. Two weeks later he explained his visceral reaction to the Bolshevik offer in a speech to the Democratic National Committee, declaring that the Bolsheviks "are the most consummate sneaks in the world; I suppose, because they know they have no high motives themselves, they do not believe that anybody else has." The moralistic Wilson interpreted their offer as an attempt to buy him and, thus, as an insult to his character. Yet there is no record to suggest that the sensitive president felt insulted two months earlier when the Kolchak government promised to pay Russian debt as part of its own campaign to obtain Allied recognition.[14]

The Churchill Initiative

The second attempt made at the Paris Peace Conference to formulate an Allied policy for Russia may be called the Churchill initiative. According to Lloyd George, British War Minister Winston Churchill was "the most formidable and irrepressible protagonist of an anti-Bolshevik war." Lloyd George recalled, "He was horrified, as we all were, at the savage murder of the Czar, the Czarina, and their helpless children. His ducal blood revolted against the wholesale elimination of Grand Dukes in Russia." Although, as prime minister of Britain during World War II, Churchill would later form an alliance of convenience with the Soviet Union to stop Adolf Hitler, and then become a prominent spokesman for the containment of communism after the war, his earliest proposal for dealing with the Soviet regime was a massive invasion. In a December 31, 1918, meeting Churchill contended that each of the Allies should contribute troops to the formation of a large force that would crush the Soviet government and establish national elections in Russia. Churchill then played a role in helping the French sabotage the Prinkipo proposal by encouraging the Whites to resist it.[15]

Churchill found support for his proposal of a massive invasion of Soviet Russia in General Ferdinand Foch, Supreme Allied Commander in the recent war, who had a similar plan. Foch proposed enlisting troops from the peoples who lay on the fringes of Russia, such as the Poles, Finns, and nationals of the Baltic states, all of whom he claimed greatly feared the Bolsheviks, in an attack on Soviet Russia. Of course, Foch proposed that these troops be led by Allied officers—no doubt because they had proved their tactical genius on the Western Front. According to Wilson's chief adviser Colonel Edward House, Foch would even "go so far as to accept German cooperation" in overthrowing the Bolsheviks "after the signing of the preliminary treaty of peace," an idea made more palatable by the fact that the kaiser's regime had been replaced by a democratic government. Foch also proposed repatriating the 1.2 million Russian prisoners of war in Germany to Denikin's territory. Foch oddly assumed that Russian soldiers who had surrendered to the Germans would wish to fight for the Whites rather than make trouble for them, forgetting that one of the principal causes of the Bolshevik Revolution was large-scale desertion and mutiny by common soldiers, many of whom had then joined the revolutionaries.[16]

Churchill seized the opportunity presented by the absence of Lloyd George and the impending departure of Wilson to introduce his plan at a meeting of the Supreme War Council in the early evening of February 14. Churchill began by stating that a new Russian policy was necessary in view of the failure of the Prinkipo proposal. President Wilson replied that there were only two facts of which he was certain:

> The first was that the troops of the Allied and Associated Powers were doing no sort of good in Russia. . . . His conclusion, therefore, was that the Allied and Associated Powers ought to withdraw their troops from all parts of Russian territory. . . . The second related to Prinkipo. . . . As far as he was concerned, he would be quite content that informal American representatives should meet representatives of the Bolsheviks. . . . What we were seeking was not rapprochement with the Bolsheviks, but clear information. The reports received from various official and unofficial sources were so conflicting that it was impossible to form a coherent picture of the state of the country.

Churchill responded that, although there was some logic to the argument that the Allies should withdraw from Russia, such a withdrawal would lead only to "an interminable vista of violence and misery." Wilson retorted that existing Allied forces could do nothing and that no more troops could be sent. Churchill replied that volunteers and material aid could be sent to help the White forces. Wilson answered that an insufficient number of volunteers could be found and that any aid sent would probably be used by reactionaries. One is again struck by the contrast between the good sense of Wilson's statements and the foolishness of his actions. Churchill responded by asking if Wilson's last statement meant that he thought that no further aid should be sent to the White forces. The secretary recorded: "President Wilson said that he hesitated to express any definite opinion on this question. He had explained to the Council how he would act if alone. He would, however, cast in his lot with the rest."[17]

The following day, with Wilson on a ship bound for the United States and Lloyd George still absent from Paris, Churchill proposed, at a meeting of the Council of Four governments, that a telegram be sent to the Bolsheviks demanding that they cease all military operations and asserting that if they failed to do so, they would be considered ineligible for the Prinkipo conference. This proposed telegram was rather illogical since the original announcement of the conference already stipulated the cessation of hostilities as a requirement for attending and since the conference could not be held anyway, owing to the refusal of the White governments to send representatives, a refusal he himself had secretly encouraged. In response to this proposal Clemenceau again urged the adoption of his cordon sanitaire strategy. Colonel House, who was present in place of President Wilson, said that he thought "the question to be decided was how to finesse the situation against the Bolsheviks." Balfour agreed: "Mr. Balfour thought it was necessary to take steps to put the Bolsheviks in the wrong, not only before public opinion, but before those who held the view that Bolshevism was democracy gone astray with large elements of good in it. Personally, he thought Bolshevism was the worst form of class tyranny. . . . He thought, therefore, some sort of message should be sent to the Bolsheviks, which would compel them either to cease hostilities or to refuse negotiations." But Clemenceau argued that the Prinkipo proposal had been such an embarrassing failure for the Allies that they should never again communicate with the Soviet government. No decision was reached concerning Churchill's proposed telegram.[18]

Churchill was not finished yet. On February 17, he submitted a resolution to the Supreme War Council directing its military representatives to examine the possibility of landing a large Allied force in Russia to aid the Whites. This resolution was opposed by American representatives to the council. In a compromise resolution the council finally decided that its military representatives should discuss the matter secretly and then inform their respective governments. Churchill had introduced the resolution under the delusion that Wilson, having said that he would "cast in his lot with the rest," would agree to large-scale intervention if the Allies favored it. On February 19, Wilson, having received the news of Churchill's action while aboard the USS *George Washington*, cabled Paris: "Am greatly surprised by Churchill's Russian suggestion. . . . What I said at the hurried meeting Friday afternoon was meant only to convey the idea that I would not take any hasty action myself. . . . It would be fatal to be led further into the Russian chaos." Wilson was particularly distressed at this time because during the voyage home a fellow passenger, former U.S. Ambassador to Russia David R. Francis, was badgering him with his own plan for large-scale intervention, a plan based on the extreme improbability of attracting 100,000 volunteers. (Francis actually stated that he expected 200,000, but 100,000 should be sufficient.) Perhaps this is why Wilson cabled House in Paris only four days after his previous message to emphasize his opposition to large-scale intervention and his irritation with Churchill: "Hope you will be very plain and decided to the effect that we are not at war with Russia and will in no circumstances that we can now foresee take part in military operations there against the Russians. I do not at all understand why Churchill was allowed to come to Paris on such an errand after what Lloyd George had said with regard to the British sending troops to Russia."[19]

Lloyd George was equally upset with Churchill. He wrote to him: "I beg you not to commit this country to what would be a purely mad enterprise out of hatred of Bolshevik principles. . . . [Chancellor of the Exchequer Austen] Chamberlain tells me we can hardly make both ends meet on a peace basis even at the present crushing rate of taxation and if we are committed to a war against a continent like Russia it is the direct road to bankruptcy and Bolshevism in these islands." On this point Balfour was in complete agreement.[20]

It was obvious that without the support of either Wilson or Lloyd George, Churchill's plan could not be adopted. On February 23, Lansing wrote, "Churchill's project is dead and there is little danger that it will be revived again by the Conference." Indeed, by June, the plan's prospects were so dim that an increasingly desperate Churchill was trying to sell another improbable scheme for overthrowing the Soviet government: that the Allies should compel half of the Czech Corps to help Kolchak overthrow that government by repatriating them to Czechoslovakia via Archangel, a route that would require these soldiers, who were badly demoralized even by Churchill's own account, to fight their way through most of Soviet Russia.[21]

Like this latter proposal, Churchill's original plan was impractical from the start. Great Britain, France, and Italy were too exhausted and economically insolvent from a devastating world war to support a large-scale invasion of Russia. The American Congress and public, already bristling at the massive cost of the war and of postwar foreign aid, would never have favored it; indeed, it was difficult enough for Wilson to find the funds to maintain a few thousand troops in Russia in the face of passionate opposition. The Japanese understood the huge logistical problems involved in transporting and supplying a massive army thousands of miles westward via the rickety

Trans-Siberian Railway and were much more interested in exploiting eastern Siberia than in helping to establish a strong, unified Russia; therefore, they made it abundantly and repeatedly clear that they had no intention of sending forces into western Siberia, much less beyond the Urals. Furthermore, Churchill's grandiose talk of a massive army of Allied volunteers was sheer fantasy, as was General Foch's alternate plan to use Poles, Finns, and Baltic nationalists to overthrow the Soviet government. While these peoples were quite willing to fight the Bolsheviks to achieve the widest possible borders for their new nations, formed in the wake of the Russian and German collapses, they had little interest in fighting a protracted war deep inside Russia for ideological purposes, especially since the White Russian governments refused to recognize their independence while the Bolsheviks did so readily. In July 1919 elections in Finland brought to power a center-left coalition that was opposed to intervention in the Russian Civil War. Likewise, the Poles were content with the advantageous peace they eventually signed with the Bolsheviks (though they briefly tussled with the Soviets over parts of the Ukraine in 1920), and the Baltic peoples reached similar agreements.[22]

The Bullitt Mission

The third attempt made at the Paris Peace Conference to formulate an Allied policy for Russia was the Bullitt mission. Journalist Lincoln Steffens had recommended to Colonel House that informal American representatives be selected to meet with the Bolsheviks. Colonel House submitted this proposal to President Wilson. Wilson chose William C. Bullitt, an attaché of the American Commission to Negotiate Peace, to head the secret mission. Not only were the British consulted, but Lloyd George's secretary gave Bullitt a list of conditions on which the Allies might withdraw from Russia. The two principal conditions were the cessation of hostilities and amnesty for the Whites. The French were not informed of the Bullitt mission since it was feared that they might attempt to sabotage it as they had the Prinkipo conference.[23]

Bullitt, accompanied by Steffens, arrived in Moscow in early March 1919. Bullitt issued three preliminary reports throughout March, as well as an extensive final report on March 25. Let us examine Bullitt's final report in detail.[24]

The Food Situation

Due to the effective blockade of Soviet Russia produced by the Allied control of the ports of Murmansk, Archangel, and Vladivostok, by the continuing Allied blockade of the Baltic Sea (begun as an anti-German war measure but continued against Soviet Russia even after Germany signed the Treaty of Versailles), and by Allied backing of anti-Bolshevik troops in the food-producing regions of southern Russia and Siberia, Moscow and Petrograd were now facing starvation. The mortality rate was particularly high among newborns, whose mothers could not suckle them, among the new mothers themselves, and among the aged. The Allied backing of the Whites had not only severed European Russia from much of its usual food supply in the Ukraine and Siberia but was also forcing the Soviet government to allocate many of its best minds and much of its rail capacity to defense rather than to food distribution. Bullitt wrote:

> Everyone is hungry in Moscow and Petrograd, including the People's Commissaries [Commissars]. The daily ration of Lenin and the other Commissaries is the same as that of a soldier in the army or of a workman at hard labor. In the hotel which is reserved for Government officials the menu is the following: Breakfast: a quarter to a half pound of black bread, which must last all day, and tea without sugar. Dinner: a good soup, a small piece of fish, for which occasionally a diminutive piece of meat is substituted, a vegetable, either a potato or a bit of cabbage, more tea without sugar. Supper: what remains of the morning ration of bread and more tea without sugar. . . . Whenever the Government is able to get its hands on such "luxuries" [as sugar, butter, or chicken] it turns them over to the schools where an attempt is made to give every child a good dinner every day. . . .
>
> The food control works well so that there is no abundance alongside of famine. Powerful and weak alike endure about the same degree of starvation.

In fact, Bullitt alleged, the Soviet government was paying industrial managers and technical experts as much as $45,000 per year, while Lenin himself received only $1,500 per year. Bullitt wrote, "This very anomalous situation arises from the principle that any believing Communist must adhere to the scale of wages established by the Government, but if the Government considers it necessary to have the assistance of any anti-Communist, it is permitted to pay him as much as he demands."

The Medical Situation
Due to the Allied blockade, medicines could not be imported into Soviet Russia. Thus, the people there were facing terrible typhoid and smallpox epidemics.

The Red Terror
According to Bullitt, the Red Terror was finished. While it lasted, about 5,000 people had been executed in all of Soviet Russia. Bullitt claimed:

"These figures agree with those which were brought back from Russia by Major [Allen] Wardwell [head of the American Red Cross Commission in Russia, May–October 1918] and inasmuch as I have checked them with Soviet and neutral sources, I believe them to be approximately correct. It is worthy to note in this connection that in the White Terror in Southern Finland alone, according to official figures, General [Carl] Mannerheim executed without trial 12,000 working men and women."

The Theater
The Soviet government was funding Russian theater. The program was being funded by "the Department of Education which prefers classics and sees to it that working men and women and children are given an opportunity to attend the performances and that they are instructed beforehand in the significance and beauties of the productions."

Morals
Rumors concerning Soviet debaucheries, rampant in the West, were false. Lenin, Chicherin, and Litvinov had practically fallen on the floor with merriment when Bullitt informed them of the Western rumor that Soviet women had been "nationalized."

Education
Education was thriving in Soviet Russia, according to Bullitt. Bullitt wrote, "Not only have all the Russian classics been reprinted in editions of three and five million copies and sold at a low price to the people, but thousands of new schools for men, women, and children have been opened in all parts of Russia." Films, lectures, and art galleries were being organized for the working classes. Children who were "defective and over-nervous" were being taught to compose music, paint, sculpt, and write poetry in accord with the Soviet belief that a fine line divided "defective" qualities from those of genius. In short, "the Soviet Government seems to have done more for the education of the Russian people in a year and a half than Czardom did in fifty years."

Morale
Morale was surprisingly high in Soviet Russia, Bullitt claimed. He wrote:

> Perhaps the most striking fact in Russia today is the general support which is given the Government by the people in spite of their starvation. Indeed, the people lay the blame for their distresses wholly on the blockade and on the Governments which maintain it. The Soviet form of government seems

to have become to the Russian people the symbol of their revolution. Unquestionably it is a form of Government which lends itself to gross abuse and tyranny but it meets the demand of the moment in Russia and it has acquired so great a hold on the imagination of the common people that the women are ready to starve and the young men to die for it.

Opposition Leaders

According to Bullitt, N. V. Volsky and Julius Martov, the leaders of the Right Socialist Revolutionaries and the Mensheviks respectively, were being allowed free speech but were not inclined to criticize the Soviet government as long as Allied troops remained on Russian soil in support of czarists. Volsky said:

> Intervention of any kind will prolong the regime of the Bolsheviki by compelling us, like all honorable Russians, to drop opposition and rally around the Soviet Government in defense of the revolution. . . .
>
> If by any chance Kolchak and Denikin were to win, they would have to kill in tens of thousands where the Bolsheviks have had to kill in hundreds and the result would be the complete ruin and collapse of Russia into anarchy. Has not the Ukraine been enough to teach the Allies that occupation by non-Bolshevist troops merely turns into Bolsheviki those who of the population who were not Bolsheviki! It is clear that the Bolsheviki are really fighting against bourgeois dictatorship. We are, therefore, prepared to help them in every possible way.

Martov agreed, saying:

> The Mensheviki are against every form of intervention, direct or indirect, because by providing the incentive to militarization it is bound to emphasize the least desirable qualities of the revolution. Further, the needs of the army overwhelm all efforts at meeting the needs of social and economic reconstruction. Agreement with the Soviet Government would lessen the tension of defense and would unmuzzle the opposition, who while the Soviet Government is attacked are prepared to help in its defense, while reserving until peace their efforts to alter the Bolshevik regime.
>
> The forces that would support intervention must be dominated by those of extreme reaction because all but the revolutionaries are prepared temporarily to sink their differences with the Bolsheviki in order to defend the revolution as a whole.

Other opposition groups included the Left Socialist Revolutionaries and the anarchists, both of whom went so far as to call Lenin and Chicherin "the

paid bourgeois gendarmes of the Entente" because the Bolsheviks were paying bourgeois experts large sums to hold high offices and were attempting
to obtain peace with the Allies. These groups called for the slaughter of the
bourgeoisie.

The Red Army

The Red Army contained approximately one million soldiers, nearly all between the ages of seventeen and twenty-seven. Bourgeois officers from the
old Russian Army were occupying important posts in the Red Army, though
closely watched by Bolshevik supervisors. Morale was high: "Discipline has
been restored and on the whole the spirit of the army appears to be very
high, particularly since its recent successes. The soldiers no longer have the
beaten-dog look which distinguished them under the Czar but carry themselves like freemen and curiously like Americans. They are popular with the
people." The Red Army possessed adequate equipment, except that it lacked
heavy artillery, airplanes, and gas shells.

Vladimir Lenin

Lenin's influence and prestige were extraordinarily high. Bullitt wrote:

> The hold which Lenin has gained on the imagination of the Russian people
> makes his position almost that of a dictator. There is already a Lenin legend.
> He is regarded as almost a prophet. His picture, usually accompanied by that
> of Karl Marx, hangs everywhere. In Russia, one never hears Lenin and Trotsky
> spoken of in the same breath as is usual in the Western world. Lenin is re-
> garded as in a class by himself. Trotsky is but one of the lower order of mortals.
>
> When I called on Lenin at the Kremlin I had to wait a few minutes until a
> delegation of peasants left his room. They had heard in their village that Com-
> rade Lenin was hungry. And they had come hundreds of miles carrying 800
> poods of bread as the gift of the village to Lenin. Just before them was another
> delegation of peasants to whom the report had come that Comrade Lenin was
> working in an unheated room. They came bearing a stove and enough firewood
> to heat it for three months. Lenin is the only leader who receives such gifts.
> And he turns them into the common fund.

Concessions

The Soviet government was willing to grant important concessions to the
Allies. Bullitt wrote:

> The Soviet Government recognizes very clearly the undesirability of granting
> concessions to foreigners and is ready to do so only because of necessity. The

members of the Government realize that the lifting of the blockade will be illusory unless the Soviet Government is able to establish credits in foreign countries, particularly the United States and England, so that goods may be bought in those countries. . . . Russia must, therefore, obtain credit at any price. The members of the Soviet Government realize fully that as a preliminary step to the obtaining of credit the payment of foreign debts must be resumed, and, therefore, are ready to pay such debts. But even though these debts are paid the members of the Soviet Government believe that they will not be able to borrow money in foreign countries on any mere promise to pay. They believe, therefore, that they will have to grant concessions in Russia to foreigners in order to obtain immediate credit. They desire to avoid this expedient if in any way it shall be possible, but if absolutely necessary they are ready to adopt it in order to begin the restoration of the normal life of the country.[25]

The credulous tone of some parts of Bullitt's report eerily resembles the glowing accounts penned by Westerners who visited the regimes of Mussolini, Hitler, and Stalin in the 1930s and were shown only what the dictators wished them to see. His assertion that the Red Terror was finished was sheer nonsense. Furthermore, he placed the responsibility for the famine entirely on the Allied blockade, unwilling to attribute it even partly to Bolshevik practices, such as strict price controls on food and efforts to collectivize farming, both of which greatly undermined agricultural production. His literal fellow traveler, Steffens, was even worse, originating the famous howler, "I have seen the future and it works!"[26]

Nevertheless, Bullitt's report did corroborate an important finding of Buckler. The discovery was that, like most extremists who achieve sudden power, the Bolsheviks had learned that they would have to make some compromises with their ideology in order to survive. Just as Lenin had been prepared to make humiliating concessions to the Germans in the Treaty of Brest-Litovsk in order to secure peace with them, he was now willing to make concessions to the Allies to make peace with them, since he believed that the very survival of the Soviet regime depended on a breathing spell from war. Since the Allies never accepted the Soviet offer, one can only speculate whether these concessions would have proved to be fleeting measures undertaken by fundamentally unchanging but opportunistic ideologues or would have fostered a pragmatic turn of mind among Soviet leaders, with long-term consequences.

After Bullitt filed this extensive report, he journeyed to Paris to meet with Allied officials. He received a warm reception from Colonel House, who wrote in his diary, "Bullitt got back tonight from Russia. His story is interesting and at last I can see a way out of that vexatious problem, that is, if we can get action by the Prime Ministers and the President." The next day House spoke to Italian Prime Minister Vittorio Orlando on behalf of negotiating a treaty with the Bolshevik regime as the *de facto* government of Russia. Orlando allegedly agreed to the proposal.[27]

But Bullitt found Lloyd George positively frantic regarding the anti-Bolshevik mania then sweeping Great Britain. When Bullitt implored Lloyd George to use his influence to bring some sanity to Allied policy towards Russia, Lloyd George, waiving a copy of the *Daily Mail*, cried, "As long as the British press is doing this kind of thing, how can you expect me to be sensible about Russia!?" He added that he doubted Bullitt's account of conditions in Soviet Russia would be believed in Britain and spoke of sending a prominent member of Britain's Conservative Party to Soviet Russia to corroborate Bullitt's findings. Lloyd George never carried out this plan.[28]

In fact, on April 16, under pressure from the Conservative Party, Lloyd George implied that the Bullitt mission was entirely Wilson's affair. After declaring to the House of Commons that the Soviet government had been guilty of heinous crimes and, therefore, could not be recognized, Lloyd George added, "It is not for me to judge the value of this [Bullitt's] communication, but if the President of the United States had attached any value to it he would have brought it before the conference, and he certainly did not."[29]

Everywhere Lloyd George turned he seemed to encounter panic regarding the Bolshevik menace. He later recalled an appearance by Joseph Noulens, the former French ambassador to Russia, at a meeting of the Big Four at the peace conference. According to Lloyd George's account, Noulens stated, "with histrionic emphasis," that he had seen on triumphal arches built to commemorate the anniversary of the Bolshevik Revolution the inscription, "He who does not work, neither shall he eat." Lloyd George wrote, "This Pauline dictum [2 Thessalonians 3:10] he evidently thought to be one of those nefarious doctrines propounded by Lenin, and designed to undermine the very foundations of respectable society."[30]

Lloyd George had other reasons besides conservative opposition for denying his association with the Bullitt mission. First, he did not wish to be accused of going behind the backs of the French, as he and Wilson had certainly done. More important, any attempt to negotiate with the Soviet government required Wilson's support, and Wilson was disinclined to grant such support.

Indeed, Bullitt found it impossible to speak with the president. Wilson developed a headache and could not meet with him. William Appleman Williams has written sarcastically, "Together with his 'cold' that prevented the conference with William Boyce Thomson [another advocate of negotiating with the Bolsheviks] in January 1918, Wilson's apparent susceptibility to everyday ailments would seem to have played a vital role in American relations with Russia." But medical historian Edwin Weinstein has contended that Wilson did indeed suffer from a severe cold accompanied by a high fever that may have caused heart and brain damage. Indeed, Wilson suffered a nervous and physical collapse several days later, on April 3. But whether Wilson had a headache on the particular day Bullitt wished to see him is largely irrelevant. The important fact is that Wilson never evinced the slightest desire to negotiate seriously with the Soviet government, either before or after the Bullitt mission. Similarly, while there is some controversy as to whether Wilson ever read the full version of Bullitt's report, which was never found among his papers, his papers do include a somewhat briefer version of the report and a resultant memorandum from the Russian Section of the American Commissioners to Negotiate Peace (of which Bullitt was a member) recommending that the Allies negotiate peace with the Soviet government, a memorandum about which Wilson even commented favorably on April 1. The bottom line is that Wilson certainly knew the gist of Bullitt's findings, at the very least, but made a conscious decision not to implement his recommendation. It did not help Bullitt's case with the president that a subcommittee of the Senate Judiciary Committee, under the leadership of Lee S. Overman, had just concluded a series of hearings in which a long list of anti-Bolsheviks, including Ambassador Francis, told hair-raising tales of the Red Terror.[31]

Bullitt resigned from the peace commission on May 17, not only over Wilson's Russian policy but also over the president's sanctioning of the mistreatment of Germany in the Treaty of Versailles, in contradiction to his famous advocacy of "a peace without victory" in January 1917. Bullitt reproached the president for having "so little faith in the millions of men, like myself, in every nation who had faith in you." At a final staff dinner at which the table was decorated with red roses and yellow jonquils, Bullitt tossed the roses to the nine staffers who had resigned with him, the yellow flowers to those who had, in his opinion, been too cowardly to do so. Bullitt told a journalist that he planned to lie in the sand on the Riviera and "watch the world go to hell." Soon after, he was telling his story to a senate committee led by Republicans anxious to discredit the president. Colonel House confided to his diary regarding Bullitt's testimony, "Candor compels me to record that in my opinion Bullitt told the truth." But Wilson never forgave Bullitt for what he regarded as rank disloyalty. In 1933, when the United States became the last major power to recognize the Soviet government, Franklin Roosevelt appointed Bullitt the nation's first ambassador to the Soviet Union.[32]

It has been suggested that Wilson did not wish to negotiate with the Bolsheviks because he faced the same obstacle of a virulently anti-Bolshevik press that plagued Lloyd George in Britain. Certainly, much of the American press seethed with anti-Bolshevism. Most American newspapers had opposed the Prinkipo proposal. The *New York Globe* had written that "those who sup with the devil need a long spoon," and the *Boston Transcript* added, "We are not in a situation where we need to parley with murderers and robbers." When the *New York Tribune* heard rumors that the Big Four were considering recognizing the Soviet government, it called this news "incredible" and "grossly insulting," the *Washington Post* adding that the American people would never stand for it: "They are at war with Bolshevism and will not compromise with the enemy for any reason whatever." As the historian Leonid I. Strakhovsky has written: "This fear of Bolshevik infiltration led to a new wave of anti-Bolshevik feeling. Newspaper editors felt perfectly justified in expressing this feeling when referring to the Bolsheviks as 'assassins and madmen' or 'human scum'; or as perpetrators of 'an atrocious campaign that shamed even the Germans and made the tyranny of Ivan the Terrible seem benevolent'; or as crime-mad leaders 'for whom the noose yearned'; or as 'beasts, drunk from their saturnalia of crime in Russia' and 'intent upon the destruction of civilization.' Indeed, the Huns of 1917 and 1918 had become benefactors to humanity in comparison with such monsters as these."[33]

It has also been suggested that Wilson did not wish to negotiate with the Bolsheviks because Kolchak's military position began to improve in the early spring of 1919. This is what Bullitt himself believed, citing the claim made by all of the leading Paris newspapers that Kolchak would be in Moscow within two weeks. Indeed, Kolchak's army captured Ufa on March 13. On March 29 Wilson received a cable from the State Department transmitting a message from U.S. Consul-General at Irkutsk Ernest L. Harris. Reporting from Omsk, Harris wrote, "At present I view things brighter than ever before. The railway of future [is about] to be taken over by the Allies. The campaign of the Siberian army against the Bolsheviks is progressing favorably. Kolchak government is stronger than ever before and growing in power. . . . Kolchak today does not ask for foreign soldiers to assist him in fighting Bolsheviks. He can do that himself and is doing it successfully. . . . Russia is now in a fair way to master Bolshevism with her own resources." As we shall see, this was sheer fantasy.[34]

But while the rabid anti-Bolshevism of the American press and Kolchak's spring successes were important, there is no evidence that Wilson had ever given any serious thought to negotiating seriously with the Bolsheviks. After hearing conflicting reports, Wilson had sent William H. Buckler to meet Litvinov in Stockholm. Buckler had declared that the Bolsheviks were sincere and rational. Wilson had still been uncertain so he had proposed that the representatives of the various Russian governments meet at Prinkipo Island. The Bolsheviks had accepted the invitation, while the Whites, egged on by the French, had refused to even consider the possibility of speaking to the Bolsheviks. Once again seeking information, Wilson had sent William C. Bullitt to Moscow. Bullitt echoed Butler's contention that the Bolsheviks were sincere and rational. Wilson ignored Bullitt's findings.

What are we to infer from this series of events? That President Wilson ignored the various reports because he thought the sources unreliable, though he himself had selected the sources? That he was insincere in his desire to seek information and simply decided to waste Buckler's and Bullitt's time? Certainly not. Wilson was struggling with his own fears, sincerely attempting to formulate a sensible Allied policy for Russia. In the end, he failed in this struggle. The tragedy was not only his but Russia's and the world's.

The Hoover-Nansen Initiative

The fourth attempt made at the Paris Peace Conference to formulate an Allied policy for Russia may be called the Hoover-Nansen initiative. By March 1919 the Big Four were becoming aware of the dreadful effects of the blockade they had imposed on Soviet Russia. The State Department cabled Paris on March 11 to report that the situation there was desperate. The number of deaths in the previous month alone was 113,000. Petrograd was being depopulated. It was alleged that horses and dogs were being eaten, and it was even rumored that cannibalism was being practiced. Assistant Secretary of State Frank L. Polk wrote, "Department is impressed with the question of how long the Allied Governments can properly delay some organized attempt to remedy conditions of distress such as those described in this report." By the end of the month the situation had worsened. A reliable source in Soviet Russia claimed that 100,000 people there were seriously ill and that only a small number of these could be received in hospitals. Another 100,000 were also ill but could move about. Only the children were well fed, though infants were among the principal casualties due to a lack of milk. Furthermore, Soviet Russia also suffered from epidemics of typhus and smallpox. Cholera and the bubonic plague were expected later in the spring.[35]

It soon became obvious to Allied leaders that they could not ignore the catastrophic state of Soviet Russia without losing a major battle in the propaganda war against the Bolsheviks. Their dilemma was that they did not want to appear heartless, yet they could not bring themselves to lift the blockade of Soviet Russia lest such an action strengthen the Soviet government. At this point a solution to this problem came from Herbert Hoover, the future president of the United States, then serving as director general of relief for the Supreme Economic Council. Hoover had become famous for his sterling performance as head of the Commission for Relief in Belgium. On March 28, 1919, he wrote to President Wilson, "As a result of Bolshevik economic conceptions, the people are dying of hunger and disease at the rate of some hundreds of thousands monthly in a country that formerly supplied food to a large part of the world." Note that Hoover assigned none of the blame for the starvation of Soviet Russia to the Allied blockade. In any case, Hoover proposed the establishment of a "second Belgian Relief Commission for Russia," which would be headed by some well-known humanitarian from one of the northern neutral countries. The Allies would fund this commission's relief work, but only if the Bolsheviks agreed to cease military action "across certain defined borders and cease their subsidizing of disturbances abroad." The Bolsheviks would also be required to agree to the fair distribution of the aid.[36]

Hoover declared that the primary advantage of his proposal was that, by working through a neutral relief commission, the Allies would not have to legitimate the Soviet government by dealing with any of its leaders. He wrote, "We cannot even remotely recognize this murderous tyranny without stimulating actionist radicalism in every country in Europe and without transgressing on every National ideal of our own."[37]

But there was another advantage to Hoover's proposal that was equally important and clear, though unstated. Hoover's condition that the Bolsheviks must cease all military operations before they could receive Allied aid put the Allies in a no-lose situation. If the Bolsheviks accepted this proposal, their government would be destroyed by White armies that would certainly not cease their own military operations. If, as was more likely, the Bolsheviks declined the Allied aid offer, it could be proclaimed that the Bolsheviks were so cruel that they declined a purely humanitarian offer from a neutral relief commission to feed their starving populace.

Wilson understood the significance of Hoover's proposal instantly and supported it. He hoped that the Bolsheviks would accept such an offer since, if the White armies did not destroy the Soviet government, he was certain that the food would. He was convinced that bolshevism thrived only where empty stomachs could be found. If the Russian peasants were well fed, they would be less inclined to follow the Bolsheviks. Thus, Wilson had written to Lansing on January 10, "The real thing with which to stop Bolshevism is food." Note, however, that such a belief was inconsistent with the policy of the Allied blockade, a blockade that Wilson supported or at least did nothing to hinder. Wilson did not seem to recognize the glaring inconsistency.[38]

Hoover was also well aware of the power of food. He would soon be the guiding force behind the economic blockade of Hungary that would destroy Béla Kun's Marxist government. Now he yearned for the destruction of the Soviet government. Not only did his conservatism incline him in this direction, but he was especially upset with the Bolsheviks for nationalizing Ural mining properties in which he held a large interest. Having expelled Hoover's American employees and having replaced, brutalized, and even killed some of his Russian experts, the Bolsheviks had then broken the furnaces and were unable to read the blueprints left behind that would have instructed them on how to do the repair work, so that thousands of Russians were thrown out of work. In fact, by 1919 Hoover's mining firm, which had grossed six million rubles in 1916, was actively aiding Kolchak in Siberia. Hoover's hatred of the Bolsheviks was so fierce that twice Colonel House and President Wilson had to prevent him from releasing to the press characterizations of his initiative that were laden with invective against the Bolsheviks, before they finally accepted a third version that was sufficiently moderate.[39]

But though he was supportive of Hoover's proposal, Wilson was occupied with German affairs, so he turned the project over to Colonel House shortly before his collapse on April 3, which kept him in bed for several days. It was also on April 3 that, as if by some miracle, well-known Scandinavian humanitarian Dr. Fridtjof Nansen wrote to Wilson with a proposal uncannily similar to Hoover's. In fact, Nansen even used phrases similar to Hoover's. For instance, Nansen, like Hoover, stressed the words "neutral" and "purely humanitarian" to describe his proposed commission. Also like Hoover, Nansen emphasized the fact that if the Allied aid was provided through such a commission, it would not involve any sort of recognition of the Soviet government.[40]

It is no coincidence that a well-known Scandinavian humanitarian who fit Hoover's description proposed the same relief plan that Hoover had suggested only a few days earlier and used almost precisely the same words to do so. In fact, Hoover had not only persuaded Nansen to sign the letter but had even drafted it himself. Yet there was one subtle but significant difference between the so-called Hoover and Nansen proposals. Hoover alluded vaguely to the necessity of guarantees by the Bolsheviks that Allied aid would be distributed fairly. By contrast, the Nansen proposal, though also written by Hoover, stated specifically that the "justice of distribution" should be guaranteed by the "neutral" commission.[41]

The Big Four preferred the Nansen proposal, as demonstrated by their reply on April 17. Considering the fact that the Allied blockade was one of the major causes of the famine in Soviet Russia, their opening statement was appallingly hypocritical: "It is shocking to humanity that millions of men, women, and children lack the food and necessities which make life endurable. The Governments and peoples whom we represent would be glad to cooperate without thought of political, military, or financial advantage." The Big Four then announced that they had accepted the substance of Nansen's proposal.

They altered the proposal in such ways, however, that no government could have accepted it. First, the Big Four announced that local governments in Soviet Russia should determine the distribution of the aid in consultation with the relief commission. This amendment to Nansen's proposal was an attempt to undermine the authority of the Soviet government by making the local governments dependent on the Allies.

Second, the Big Four stated that another requirement for Allied aid was that the Bolsheviks not only cease hostilities with the Whites, but also order "a complete suspension of the transfer of troops and military material of all sorts to and within Russian territory." Such a concession, absent a similar concession from the Whites that the proposal did not include, would have been suicidal.

A third new stipulation made by the Big Four, less objectionable to the Soviet government but nonetheless problematic for it, was that the Bolsheviks should pay for all of the "aid." The Hoover and Nansen proposals had only mentioned in passing that the Bolsheviks might be able to pay for some of it. Thus, what the Big Four's final proposal amounted to was not really aid but an agreement to temporarily lift the Allied blockade of Soviet Russia at a military and political cost that the Soviet government could not pay. This was the proposal made to the Bolsheviks in early May 1919.[42]

It is no surprise that the Bolsheviks rejected this "purely humanitarian" offer. As George F. Kennan has written: "What were the Soviet leaders to make of such a communication? A resignation of their powers over food distribution, over the transportation system, and over local government, coupled with the continued presence of foreign troops in Russia, would plainly spell the end of their regime." Also, by May, the Bolsheviks had taken the offensive militarily and were in a much better position than they had been in March or April. As Lloyd George had asked, as early as January, when Clemenceau had made a proposal similar to Hoover's and Nansen's, why should the Bolsheviks accept such conditions in exchange for food when they would soon be in the grain-rich Ukraine, anyway?[43]

Thus, on May 14, the Big Four learned that Soviet Commissar for Foreign Affairs Georgi Chicherin had denounced the Hoover-Nansen proposal as a fraud. Nevertheless, Chicherin offered to negotiate with the Allies whenever they had a serious proposal. Based on this statement, which held out a ray of hope, Nansen asked Hoover whether he ought to meet with Bolshevik representatives in Stockholm. Hoover, in Paris at the time, responded quickly, "Please inform Nansen that until [the] whole matter has been given further consideration by the Governments here, we consider it extremely inadvisable to arrange any meeting with Bolshevik representatives." That summer Hoover dispatched food supplies from the American Relief Administration, which he now headed, to various eastern Baltic ports, but only in support of anti-Bolshevik forces there and in anticipation of their capture of Petrograd, an event that never occurred. Ironically, Hoover did finally get to lead a successful effort to alleviate famine in Soviet Russia—in 1921, under a Republican administration, following the termination of the Allied blockade and the Bolshevik victory in the Russian Civil War.[44]

The Kolchak Proposal

The final attempt made at the Paris Peace Conference to formulate an Allied policy for Russia was the proposal to recognize and further assist the Kolchak government. A few days before the Big Four learned that the Bolsheviks had rejected the Hoover-Nansen proposal, President Wilson decided to send U.S. Ambassador to Japan Roland Morris, a former Princeton student of Wilson whom Wilson trusted deeply, to Siberia, an order he relayed to the State Department on May 14. On the following day, the State Department wired Morris, instructing him to proceed to Omsk, where he would confer with the leading ministers of the Kolchak government. The object of Morris's mission would be

> [t]o obtain from that Government, official definite assurances as to the objects that they have in view with regard to the future Governmental regime in Russia, and the methods by which they mean to set a new regime up, asking particular assurances with regard to the reform in land tenure, and the extension and security of the suffrage, and the choice and projected action of a constituent assembly, and also learn as definitely as possible the influences Kolchak is under. The President states his object is to satisfy himself as to whether the Kolchak Government deserves the recognition, or at least the countenance, if not the support, of our Government.

Two days later, the State Department cabled again to add that the president was particularly interested "as to the kind of men and influences surrounding

Kolchak and . . . [whether] Kolchak is strong enough to control them in the right direction." At the same time the State Department was sending these instructions to Morris, it was also helping the Russian Embassy to secure another 150,000 rifles for Kolchak. Apparently, department officials, having already made up their minds, felt that there was little point in waiting for Morris's report.[45]

Delayed by pressing matters in Japan, Morris did not begin his journey until July. In fact, as late as June 30, the president was adding another important instruction to Morris's list: "I am also desirous that Ambassador Morris should so utilize his visit to Omsk to impress upon the Japanese Government our great interest in the Siberian situation and our intention to adopt a definite policy which will include the 'open door' to Russia free from Japanese domination."[46]

Meanwhile, as Morris was preparing to depart for Omsk, the Allied leaders remained active in their war against the Bolsheviks. On May 26, 1919, the Council of Four sent a message to Kolchak regarding the Allied goal of "peace and self-government" for Russia that referred to their own nations in the third person: "They are convinced by their experiences of the last twelve months that it is not possible to attain these ends by dealing with the Soviet Government of Moscow. They are therefore disposed to assist the Government of Admiral Kolchak and his Associates with munitions, supplies, and food, to establish themselves as the government of all of Russia, provided that they receive from them definite guarantees that their policy has the same objects in view as that of the Allied and Associated Powers." The "definite guarantees" that the Allies required from the Kolchak government were assurances that the government would summon a constituent assembly once White forces reached Moscow, allow elections for local government immediately, disavow any intention to restore a czarist regime, recognize the independence of Finland and Poland, and agree to submit territorial disputes in the Baltic region, the Caucasus, and Rumania to settlement by the League of Nations. Finally, once a democratic government was established in Russia, the new government would have to join the League of Nations and pay Russia's national debts. Of course, Kolchak, in a response that was actually drafted by British and French representatives stationed at his headquarters who knew precisely what Wilson wanted to hear, readily agreed to these conditions since promises cost him nothing. As one of Kolchak's aides later recalled, "To get the support of the Allies—which was as necessary for the White government as air—required masquerading as a civil democratic regime." The only immediate requirement concerned local elections. Even so, the Kolchak government soon refused to allow the local elections it promised. Yet Allied aid continued unabated.[47]

The Allied leaders also made efforts to ensure that their blockade of Soviet Russia was both continued and tightened. On June 7, the Supreme Economic Council sent a note to the Council of Four expressing its concern over the legal basis for the blockade. The Allied governments' authority to enforce the blockade, the note stated, was based solely on war powers laws. When the Central Powers signed the Treaty of Versailles soon, these powers would lapse. To remedy this problem, the Supreme Economic Council recommended "that there should be an abstinence from any positive measures or public announcements indicating the resumption of trade." In other words, if the Allied governments did not declare the blockade laws void, Allied civilians and companies might consider them still intact. What these individuals and businesses did not know would not hurt them, or more to the point, would hurt the Soviet government.[48]

But the secretary of state, a man of unquestionable genius in the ancient executive art of bypassing legislatures, had a better idea. On August 2, Lansing wrote to the American Commission to Negotiate Peace from his desk in Washington, "In carrying out a general policy of non-intercourse with the Bolshevik territory this Government could deny clearance to all American vessels for the Baltic referred to, as well as passports to persons seeking to visit these regions, and the same action taken by other governments would accomplish the same purpose as a hostile blockade." A cry of gratitude went up from Allied officials yearning to breathe free from meddlesome legislators, who suffered from the annoying misconception that they had the right to a say in what occurred merely because they had been elected by the people. Thanks to Lansing's quick thinking, the Allied blockade had been saved.[49]

To ensure that the neutral governments agreed to follow Lansing's policy, a matter vital to the success of the blockade, Wilson ordered the State Department, also on August 2, to send each neutral government a strongly worded note. Wilson wrote that the notes should contain such statements as these:

> The avowed hostility of the Bolsheviks to all governments and the announced program of international revolution make them as great a menace to the national safety of neutral countries as to Allied countries. For any government to permit them to increase their power through commercial intercourse with its nationals would be to encourage a movement which is frankly directed against all governments and would certainly invite the condemnation of all peoples desirous of restoring peace and social order.

The President cannot believe that any government whose people might be in a position to carry on commerce with the Russian ports referred to would be so indifferent to the opinion of the civilized world as to permit supplies to be exported to those ports directly or indirectly.

On October 2, Clemenceau, in his capacity as president of the peace conference, was asked by the Council of Four to address similar notes to the neutral countries.[50]

The state of New York was determined to do its part in the war on bolshevism as well. On June 12, 1919, representatives of the New York State Legislative Committee to Investigate Bolshevism, accompanied by police, raided the offices of Ludwig Martens. Martens had been appointed Soviet representative to the United States on January 2, but had been ignored by the State Department, which continued to associate itself with the former Russian Embassy in Washington. The New York legislative committee seized all of Martens's records, and the New York attorney general interrogated him and his staff. Martens subsequently protested this action to the State Department, but his protests fell on deaf ears. Despite the absence of any evidence that Martens had dispensed any communist propaganda while in the United States—in fact, Martens had studiously avoided any involvement in American politics since his chief mission was to negotiate deals with American businesses—he was forced to leave the country in order to avoid deportation in December 1920.[51]

Meanwhile, Morris was making his way towards Omsk. On July 22, 1919, he issued his first report from the headquarters of the Kolchak government. It was not encouraging. Morris wrote: "I find the situation here extremely critical. Complete demoralization of Kolchak's Siberian Army." Morris claimed that the Czechs hated the Kolchak government and were determined not to spend another winter in Siberia. Who would guard the Trans-Siberian Railway west of Irkutsk when the Czechs left? Morris continued gravely:

I must report, however, that the Kolchak government has failed to command the confidence of anybody in Siberia except a small discredited group of reactionaries, Monarchists, and former military officials. It is the judgment of all with whom I have conferred—representative Czechs, British and French military officers, our own railway-service men, Allied Consuls, and even thoughtful and moderate Russians such as the Orthodox Bishop at Krasnoyarsk and Kolchak's appointed governor of the Province of Tomsk—that the withdrawal of the Czechs would be a signal for a formidable anti-Kolchak if not pro-Bolshevik uprising in every town on the railway from Irkutsk to Omsk.

Morris concluded by stating that there were five facts that had impressed him in his travels through the vast expanse of Siberia. First, the people greatly distrusted the Cossack generals who represented the Kolchak government in eastern Siberia. Second, Kolchak's officials had failed completely to note "the change in popular feeling" in Russia since the revolution. Morris wrote, "All careful observers of Russian affairs testify that there has been no improvement in the point of view, the conduct, or the methods of former officials, temporarily returned to power by the Kolchak Government." Third, Kolchak's officials had taken no constructive measures to meet Siberia's economic needs. On the contrary, Morris wrote, "I hear everywhere well-authenticated instances of speculation and corruption." Fourth, there was great "resentment, particularly among the peasants, against the system of conscription which has taken mere boys from the towns and villages, placed them under inefficient and criminal officers, and led them, untrained, un-equipped, and ill-fed, to mutilation and death at the front." Finally, the Kolchak government was engaging in the "suppression of all attempts at local self-government."[52]

What was Lansing's response to this disturbing report, which demonstrated that Kolchak could not be relied upon to keep his promises even for a couple of months? Three days after receiving Morris's report, Lansing wrote to Secretary of War Newton Baker, urging him to cooperate in the shipment of more supplies to Kolchak.[53]

Nevertheless, Lansing was sufficiently disturbed by Morris's report that he replied, on July 26, requesting that Morris investigate further regarding Kolchak's level of support in western Siberia. Lansing wrote: "The Department has had the opinion that Kolchak reverses were the result of overextension and that present weakness is due to Kolchak supporters having placed almost entire emphasis on military effort. It would seem that no Government in Russia can survive except by demonstrating its power to give better conditions of general welfare than the Bolsheviks are affording."[54]

On the next day Morris reported: "All over Siberia there is an orgy of arrest without charges; of execution without even the pretense of trial; and of confiscation without color of authority. Fear—panic fear—has seized everyone. Men suspect each other and live in constant terror that some spy or enemy will cry 'Bolshevik' and condemn them to instant death." Yet three days later Lansing sent Kolchak a message expressing pleasure at the leader's promises of reform.[55]

On July 31, Morris issued his third report. Morris reported that British General Alfred Knox and French General Maurice Janin, despite being staunch supporters of Kolchak, agreed that his general staff was so hopelessly inefficient and corrupt that no more Allied supplies should be sent unless the Allies also began supervising both the distribution of the aid and the organization of the army itself. Indeed, Kolchak's top-heavy command structure included more than 4,000 staff officers to oversee his relatively small force, compared to 1,000 in the entire German army during the recent war and forty-two in the million-man American army in France.[56]

In his fourth report, on August 4, Morris characterized Kolchak as weak and inexperienced and Kolchak's minister of finance as completely ignorant of financial matters. Morris continued:

> Of the military members and the officers of the General Staff, nothing favorable can be said. As a body they have shown themselves intolerant, reactionary, and corrupt. They have dominated the Government for the last six months. . . .
>
> The ministers, handicapped by inexperience and an astonishing ignorance of conditions and needs, seem quite incapable of conducting a government. . . . They have lost all touch, if they ever had any, with those groups in the population, the cooperatives, the Zemstvos, the existing party organizations, which know the conditions and might suggest practicable measures. The result has been inaction in every department, and this has offered to the military leaders the opportunity they have sought. On the ground that the only object of the Government was the destruction of Bolshevism by force, they have seized the power in every locality and have wielded it with a ruthlessness which has antagonized the populace and with a disregard of vital economic and financial problems which now endanger the success of the whole movement. . . . The result is now a total collapse—financial, economic, and sanitary. . . . To mistakes of military policy must be added an incredible amount of corruption among individual officials which Kolchak has not seriously attempted to correct or punish. . . .
>
> The Government has failed in administration; has failed in the organization of the army; has failed to retain the confidence of the moderate groups.

The only strengths that Morris could attribute to the Kolchak government were the personal honesty of Kolchak himself and the fact that every Russian moderate must choose between the Kolchak regime and the Soviet government. Morris did not explain why, in view of the conditions he had just described, and in view of the fact that Siberians had never experienced the brunt of the Red Terror as they now did the White, these moderates should choose Kolchak over the Bolsheviks.[57]

In his August 8 report Morris asked the important question, "Is the Kolchak Government, as it now exists, sufficiently strong to rescue Russia from the grip of Bolshevism?" His answer was clear:

I regret to report that in my opinion it is not. Only drastic changes in its personnel and methods would render it equal to such a task, no matter how much support the Allied governments might give it. . . . Neither Kolchak nor his civilian colleagues have been able to modify or control the forces of reaction and corruption which have surrounded them from the very beginning of the movement. I have discussed with Government officials who I believe are earnest and well-meaning men the feasibility of adopting certain immediate measures to win back popular support and confidence. These included some guarantees of personal security; an effort to at least punish military officials who are speculating in army supplies while the soldiers are without food, are commandeering railway cars and selling them at enormous prices; the creation of some provincial council of peasants and Zemstvo representatives with whom Kolchak could occasionally confer. But it is quite evident that they are powerless to even attempt such measures.

Morris had a second question: "Would it be possible with the assistance of the Allies to effect changes in personnel and methods?" Morris's second answer was a little more ambivalent than his first. He stated that "it would be a long and at times a most discouraging task," adding, "Should the [Kolchak] Government survive it can continue only provided that it receives immediate help from the Allies."[58]

Astonishingly, in spite of these bleak reports, Morris advocated recognition of the Kolchak government on August 11. He explained, "Without this recognition and the substantial assistance which it implies, the Kolchak Government, even though it should survive the present military crisis, could not in my judgment continue to function much longer." This statement, like Morris's previous ones, was hardly calculated to inspire confidence in the Kolchak government. But to Morris, as to Wilson and Lansing, the need to destroy the Soviet government overrode all other considerations. This fact is shown by Morris's August 16 report, in which he explained that the Kolchak government was the "only available agency through which we can give aid to Russia." Significantly, Morris added, referring to the Japanese occupation of eastern Siberia, that the "open door [was] now in imminent peril of being closed," oddly implying that giving more aid to Kolchak might somehow improve that situation as well, despite the fact that the Kolchak government's chief official representatives in eastern Siberia, Semenov and Kalmikov, were largely Japanese puppets.[59]

Morris estimated that $200 million more in credits would have to be granted to the Kolchak government so that it might buy necessary weapons and supplies. In order to ensure that these weapons and supplies reached Kolchak's armies via the railways, the number of Allied railway inspectors would have to be greatly increased, 40,000 additional troops would have to be sent to replace the Czechs guarding the western portion of the Trans-Siberian Railway, and $20 million would have to be spent on the operation and maintenance of the railway. Then, in order "to ensure an honest and efficient use of credits and distribution of supplies"—that is, in order to prevent the bandits on Kolchak's general staff from stealing everything—inspectors would have to be sent to oversee the distribution of all supplies.[60]

In view of Morris's sober assessment of the situation, Wilson would have been justified in reasoning that it would be more practical to recognize the dead czar as the true ruler of Russia and send him military aid. Instead, though obviously unable to make the Herculean efforts that Morris proclaimed indispensable, Wilson decided to spend millions of dollars more on a regime that had not the slightest chance of survival. When reading Morris's reports, one wonders why it did not occur to Wilson that a government so enormously difficult to save must be immensely unpopular and, thus, not worth saving.

At any rate, on August 12, Morris reported that the military situation was so bad for Kolchak that his advisers were urging him to abandon Omsk, and he was ordering all civil employees between the ages of eighteen and forty to the front for military service. Two days later Morris transmitted a secret resolution of the popularly elected zemstvo of the province of Irkutsk, which stated:

> As the measures taken by the Government at Omsk which have for their object the revival of government privileges existing under the old regime tend simply to further the economic deterioration and political ruin of the country, the people are loudly expressing their dissatisfaction, disappointment, and enmity towards stricter measures, such as the curtailment of the rights of local organs of administration, the systematic and organized fight with every form of social development, the suppression of all citizen rights, the employing of force in fighting the press and freedom of speech, the interference of military authorities with civilian life, [and] the self-assumed authority of many individual agents of government.

On August 18, Kolchak declared that he would not call any conference of zemstvos or other democratic groups until he had received definite assurances from the Allies as to future aid.[61]

On August 25, Lansing responded to Morris's recommendations. He declared that since the United States could not send any more troops to Siberia, it would not recognize the Kolchak government. Furthermore, Wilson was now sorely lacking in money for which he did not need congressional authorization. Nevertheless, Kolchak could be told that the United States government had secured him a $50 million loan from a consortium of American and British banks. Kolchak could also be told that another large shipment of rifles would be arriving in Siberia soon. This shipment will be the focus of further discussion in the next chapter. Finally, Kolchak could be told that this "meager" aid was not the result of "lack of appreciation of his own extraordinary efforts in overcoming great obstacles or of any change in our hope to assist Russia." Presumably, one of the "great obstacles" to which Lansing referred was the Siberian people's intense hatred of his government.[62]

On August 27, Morris replied, "Our inability to send any additional troops . . . renders the entire plan submitted in my August 11th impracticable." Thus, Morris's only advice now was to "await the outcome of the present crisis." The implication was that since the United States could not provide aid that was massive enough to save the Kolchak government from extinction, it should not waste any more money and materials on it. But the State Department not only proceeded with the $50 million loan and the shipment of rifles, but also dispatched more aid in September, when Kolchak's situation was even more hopeless. On September 19, Assistant Secretary of State William Phillips, noting that the British were supplying Denikin and the French were supplying both the Czechs and the anti-Bolsheviks in the countries bordering Russia, asked Wilson to authorize the Secretary of War to give the Kolchak forces clothing on a credit basis. Wilson agreed immediately.[63]

The Red Scare

Wilson was in Los Angeles when he replied to Phillips's request. On September 4, Wilson had begun a cross-country tour with the object of obtaining popular support for the Treaty of Versailles and the League of Nations. During this tour, Wilson used the Red Scare as a political tool, arguing that bolshevism was the inevitable product of the absence of a League of Nations. The result was that Wilson convinced many people of the terrible threat posed by bolshevism without convincing them of the need for the League of Nations. In fact, some historians believe that, by encouraging xenophobia, the Red Scare promoted the isolationist sentiment that destroyed any chance of American membership in the League of Nations.[64]

Although many American newspapers were virulently anti-Bolshevik from the outset of the Bolshevik Revolution—an attitude strengthened by Wilson's publication of the fraudulent Sisson Documents against the advice of the State Department in September 1918—the Red Scare did not begin in earnest until June 1919. On June 2, mysterious explosions in eight different cities at the same hour targeted public officials, judges, and businessmen, yet such was the amateurish nature of the bombers that they managed to kill only two people. One of the targeted officials was Attorney General Alexander Mitchell Palmer, who was retiring for the evening when a bomb exploded outside his home. The only person injured by the blast was the bomber himself, whose fragments were scattered about the neighborhood, one chunk landing across the street on the doorstep of Franklin D. Roosevelt, then assistant secretary of the navy, who called the police.[65]

The bomber, an Italian immigrant, was probably an anarchist since he appears to have left an anarchist pamphlet next door. Nevertheless, Palmer, who planned to run for president in 1920 at the end of Wilson's second and final term, hinted to the newspapers that the culprit had been a communist. No one claimed responsibility for this bomb or any of the others, but Congress, swayed by Palmer's dark hints and urgent requests, added a $500,000 supplement to the $1.5 million that had already been appropriated for the Justice Department's investigations and prosecutions under the Espionage and Sedition Acts. Palmer established a new antiradical division of the department's General Intelligence Bureau (the forerunner of the FBI) and appointed young J. Edgar Hoover to head it. Based on Hoover's previous experience as an employee at the Library of Congress, he quickly assembled over 200,000 index cards containing information on radical groups and individuals throughout the United States, including case histories of over 60,000 "dangerous radicals." When the nation experienced a series of strikes in the autumn of 1919, strike leaders who were aliens were deported; others were arrested under state "sedition and anarchy" laws. The Senate Committee on Education and Labor claimed, without evidence, that "anarchists, revolutionists, and Russian Soviets" were behind the steel strike. Likewise, T. T. Brewster, chief spokesman for the coal mine owners, released to the press absurd reports claiming that the coal strike had been undertaken under direct orders from Lenin and Trotsky and that Moscow gold was financing the whole project. The public was further inflamed by the establishment of both the Communist Party and Communist Labor Party in the United States in September.[66]

Based on his own fears and ambitions, as well as in response to a unanimously adopted senate resolution demanding to know why the Justice Department was not deporting a larger number of radical aliens, Attorney General Palmer authorized a series of raids on radical meetings throughout the nation on November 7, 1919, and January 2, 1920. Many of these raids occurred without proper warrants. Over 4,000 alleged radicals were rounded up in thirty-three different cities. In Lynn, Massachusetts, a meeting to discuss the formation of a cooperative bakery was dissolved, and thirty-nine participants were arrested. In New York City, a theatrical performance by a Ukrainian organization was stopped, and both the cast and the audience were arrested. Also in Manhattan, an accordion concert was halted and everyone present arrested. In Newark a man was arrested because he "looked like a radical." In New Brunswick, after a socialist club was raided, drawings of a phonograph were forwarded to demolition experts on the suspicion that they represented "the internal mechanism of various types of bombs." In Philadelphia many people were arrested when a three-story building was raided. One floor was the site of a meeting of the Russian Socialist League; the other two contained a concert hall and a vocational-technical school. Naturally, the latter two floors were the ones raided. In Chicago a vocational-technical school for Russian immigrants was raided. Algebraic formulas were termed "mysterious ciphers." In Detroit people who were attending a dance in the same building as a communist group's headquarters were arrested, along with the orchestra and a fellow who went over to see what the ruckus was about. This was surely no time to be a musician in America; it was becoming difficult to determine whether the federal officials' bias was anti-radical or anti-musical. A laconic county sheriff in Wisconsin referred to the federal agents as "a bunch of nuts," but some state and local governments carried out their own, often equally absurd, raids as well.[67]

These incidents would be comical if the consequences for some of those arrested were not so appalling. Some prisoners were subjected to various acts of violence, interrogated, and placed in overcrowded and unsanitary detention centers. Eight hundred people arrested in Detroit were imprisoned for almost a week in a dark, narrow, windowless corridor of a federal building, sleeping on the bare floor. Since there was only one toilet, some who could not wait urinated in the corridor, creating a terrible stench. The prisoners went unfed for the first twenty-four hours. To add insult to injury, photographs of these now frazzled detainees were published, accompanied by captions depicting them as "filthy Bolsheviks." A few were detained a week longer in an even worse place. The Chicago algebra students previously mentioned were placed twenty-three to an eight-man cell. The city refused to feed these prisoners, calling them a federal responsibility. As a result, a whole day passed before they were fed. Worse, throughout the country many alien prisoners were deported without trial, sometimes even without the knowledge of their families.[68]

Despite the fact that the vast majority of prisoners were ultimately released because of the complete absence of any evidence of criminality or even criminal intent, Palmer continued to insist publicly that large numbers of radicals were receiving orders directly from Lenin and Trotsky. Palmer declared, "Out of the sly and crafty eyes of many of them leap cupidity, cruelty, insanity, and crime; from their lopsided faces, sloping brows, and misshapen features may be recognized the unmistakable criminal type."[69]

Spurred on by such statements, the Red Scare spread widely. On November 10, 1919, the Supreme Court upheld the verdicts of lower courts that found four men and one woman, all Russian aliens, guilty of violating the Sedition Acts for publishing material the previous summer that called for a general strike to prevent American intervention in Russia. The immigrants received sentences that ranged from three to twenty years. Beginning on November 13, the socialist daily the *New York Call* was excluded from the mails by order of the Postmaster General. On December 21, the U.S. Army transport *Buford*, dubbed "the Soviet ark," set sail for Finland from New York, its passengers' ultimate destination the Soviet Union. The passengers consisted of 249 alleged radicals who were being deported. The U.S. government was taking no chances; 250 soldiers were assigned to guard these 249 "guests," 199 of whom were captured in Palmer's November raids. The famous anarchists Alexander Berkman and Emma Goldman, both of whom had just been released from prison for opposing conscription during the war, were aboard, along with other radicals. But so were Russians who merely desired free passage home; for small fees, labor organizers for the Union of Russian Workers had promised to "inform on them" to the government. In 1919 and 1920 thirty-two states and a few cities banned the Red flag. In April 1920 the state of New York outlawed the Socialist Party and began requiring teachers to take a loyalty oath.[70]

Journalists, who had a vested interest in selling large numbers of newspapers by recounting lurid tales, continued to do their part to stoke the Red Scare. At one point the press transformed a minor incident in which a woman broke a window on Ellis Island after discovering that her husband had been deported without her knowledge into a full-scale communist uprising. Race riots in Washington, D.C., and Chicago were blamed on Bolshevik propaganda as well.[71]

The tenor of the times was captured by Edmund Vance Cooke's poem, "Bol-she-veek":

> I mustn't call you "Miky" and you mustn't call me "wop,"
> For Uncle Sammy says it's wrong and hints we ought to stop;
> But don't you fret, there's still one name that I'm allowed to speak,
> So when I disagree with you I'll call you Bol-she-vik! veek! veek!
> It's a scream and it's a shriek;
> It's a rapid-fire response to any heresy you squeak.
> You believe in votes for women? Yah! The Bolsheviks do.

And shorter hours? And land reforms? They're Bolshevistic too.
"The Recall" and other things like that are dangerous to seek;
Don't tell me you believe 'em, or I'll call Bolshevik!
Bolshevik! veek! veek!
A reformer is a freak!
But here's a name to stop him, for it's like a lightning streak.
Bolshevik! veek! veek![72]

The Red Scare ended in the early part of 1920 when Louis F. Post, who was initially the assistant labor secretary, newly placed in charge of the matter, and then became the acting labor secretary when William B. Wilson was incapacitated by illness, refused to rubber-stamp Palmer's deportation orders, as Post's predecessor had done. When Post began reviewing the files, he was horrified to learn that most of the imprisoned aliens had received no legal counsel, that much of the evidence against them had been illegally obtained, and that many of the aliens, even those who were members of the communist parties, knew little about communism (many had been drawn into the parties through membership in organizations that had later merged with them). By April, Post had released nearly half of those apprehended in the January raids. After the House Committee on Rules, at Palmer's instigation, began hearings on the advisability of impeaching Post, the seventy-one-year-old labor secretary launched a devastating counterattack at the hearings, which led to their discontinuation. Palmer's own unconstitutional acts were then investigated, but no action was ever taken against him. Nevertheless, Palmer's presidential bid went nowhere, especially after his widely publicized warnings of radical terrorism and insurrection on May 1 (May Day) proved false. Palmer was passed over for the Democratic nomination, the socialist Eugene Debs, running for president from prison, received nearly a million votes, and the next president, Republican Warren G. Harding, released Debs from prison on Christmas Day in 1921.[73]

Not only did Wilson fail, both before his collapse from a stroke and after his recovery, to intercede in his attorney general's campaign against radical aliens, but in his December 1919 address to Congress, the president even requested, at Palmer's instigation, the passage of new peacetime sedition laws to deal with radical *citizens*. Congress balked at the request.[74]

Furthermore, Wilson's own pronouncements tended to accelerate the Red Scare. For instance, when speaking in support of the Treaty of Versailles at Kansas City on September 6, Wilson told the crowd:

And the thing we must see to is that no minority anywhere masters the majority. . . .

> The men who now are measurably in control of the affairs of Russia represent nobody but themselves. . . .
>
> There is a closer monopoly of power in Petrograd and Moscow than there ever was in Berlin, and the thing that is intolerable is not the Russian people are having their way but that another group of men more cruel than the Czar himself is controlling the destinies of that great people.
>
> And I want to say here and now that I am against the control of any minority anywhere.

At the same time that Wilson was uttering these lines, he was secretly funding a czarist regime that was hardly more representative of the Russian people than the Soviet government. On the same day Wilson told a Des Moines crowd concerning bolshevism, "It is the negation of everything that is American, but it is spreading and so long as disorder continues, so long as the world is kept waiting for the answer of the kind of peace we are going to have and what kind of guarantees there are to be behind that peace, that poison will steadily spread, more and more rapidly, until it may be that even this beloved land of ours will be distracted and distorted by it." Wilson repeated the gist of these comments in Minneapolis, where he added, "The danger to the world, my fellow citizens, against which we must absolutely lock the door in this country, is that some governments of minorities may be set up here as elsewhere." He carried the same message to St. Paul, Bismarck, Tacoma, and Seattle. At Bismarck he claimed, "Russia repudiated the Czar, who was cruel at times, and set up her present masters, who are cruel all the time and pity nobody, who seize everybody's property and feed only the soldiers that are fighting for them. And now, according to the papers, they are likely to brand every one of those soldiers so that he may not easily, at any rate, escape their clutches and desert." As elsewhere, Wilson made the statement, "We are at present helpless to assist Russia, because there are no responsible channels through which we can assist her," though he was certainly assisting the Kolchak government, however irresponsible. In Billings, Montana, Wilson noted concerning the "poison of disorder," "That poison is running through the veins of the world, and we have made the methods of communication throughout the world such that all the veins of the world are open and the poison can circulate. The wireless throws it out upon the air. The cable whispers it underneath the sea. Men talk about it in little groups, men talk about it openly in great groups, not only in Europe, but here also in the United States. There are disciples of Lenin in our own midst." In Coeur D'Alene, Idaho, he warned, "Don't think that America is immune. The poison that has spread through that pitiful nation of Russia is spreading through all Europe." He even linked a Boston police strike to the spread of bolshevism.[75]

Wilson failed to achieve senate ratification of the Treaty of Versailles, and thus American participation in his coveted League of Nations, through the use of these scare tactics. But he did help "sow dragon's teeth" that plagued the nation's foreign relations, and occasionally its domestic affairs, for decades thereafter.

Notes

1. David W. McFadden, *Alternative Paths: Soviets and Americans, 1917–1920* (Oxford: Oxford University Press, 1993), 191.

2. David Lloyd George, *Memoirs of the Peace Conference* (New Haven, Conn.: Yale University Press, 1939), Secretary's Notes of Inter-Allied Conference, vol. 1, 211–12, 216.

3. C. K. Cumming and Walter W. Pettit, eds., *Russian-American Relations, March 1917–March 1920: Documents and Papers* (New York: Harcourt, Brace, 1920; reprint, Westport, Conn.: Hyperion, 1977), 273.

4. Ibid., 280–81; U.S. Department of State, *Papers Relating to the Foreign Relations of the United States, Russia, 1919* (Washington, D.C.: Government Printing Office, 1937; reprint, New York: Kraus, 1969), Ira Nelson Morris to Frank L. Polk, December 24, 1918, 1; Colville Barclay to Frank L. Polk, January 3, 1919, 2–3; Arthur S. Link, ed., *The Papers of Woodrow Wilson* (Princeton, N.J.: Princeton University Press, 1966–1994), Maxim Litvinov to Wilson, December 24, 1918, vol. 53, 492–94.

5. U.S. Department of State, *Foreign Relations, Russia, 1919*, Notes of a Conversation Held in M. Pichon's Room, January 12, 5; Colville Barclay to Frank L. Polk, January 13, 7.

6. Ibid., Notes of a Conversation Held in M. Pichon's Room, January 16, 11–14.

7. Ibid., Leland Harrison to Joseph C. Grew, January 9, 4; Osborne to Commission to Negotiate Peace, January 18, 15–17.

8. Ibid., Notes of a Conversation Held in M. Pichon's Room, January 21, 19–25.

9. Ibid., Notes of a Conversation Held in M. Pichon's Room, January 22, 30–31; Lloyd George, *Memoirs of the Peace Conference*, vol. 1, 232; Peter Fleming, *The Fate of Admiral Kolchak* (London: Rupert Hart-Davis, 1963), 125.

10. U.S. Department of State, *Foreign Relations, Russia, 1919*, Commission to Negotiate Peace to Frank L. Polk, January 27, 35.

11. Ibid., DeWitt C. Poole to Frank L. Polk, February 4, 42–43; Commission to Negotiate Peace to Frank L. Polk, February 10, 51.

12. Ibid., Georgi V. Chicherin to the Allies, February 4, 40–42.

13. Ibid., Russian Embassy in France to Secretariat-General of Paris Peace Conference, February 12, 54; George F. Kennan, *Russia and the West under Lenin and Stalin* (Boston: Little, Brown, 1960), 127; Cumming and Pettit, eds., *Russian-American Relations*, 303–6.

14. U.S. Department of State, *Foreign Relations, Russia, 1919*, Frank L. Polk to Ernest L. Harris, February 15, 68; Link, *Papers of Woodrow Wilson*, A News Report

of a Press Conference, February 14, 1919, vol. 55, 161; Remarks to the Democratic National Committee, February 28, 1919, vol. 55, 320. For Kolchak's promise to pay the Russian debt in December 1918, see N. G. O. Pereira, *White Siberia: The Politics of Civil War* (Montreal: McGill-Queen's University Press, 1996), 112.

15. Lloyd George, *Memoirs of the Peace Conference*, vol. 1, 214–15, 242; McFadden, *Alternative Paths*, 204–5.

16. Link, *Papers of Woodrow Wilson*, Colonel Edward House to Wilson, February 19, 1919, vol. 55, 213; Ilya Somin, *Stillborn Crusade: The Tragic Failure of Western Intervention in the Russian Civil War, 1918–1920* (New Brunswick, N.J.: Transaction, 1996), 51.

17. U.S. Department of State, *Foreign Relations, Russia, 1919*, Minutes of the 14th Session of the Supreme War Council, February 14, 56–59.

18. Ibid., Notes of a Conversation Held in M. Pichon's Room, February 15, 60–67.

19. Ibid., Commission to Negotiate Peace to Frank L. Polk, February 17, 68–69; Woodrow Wilson to Commission to Negotiate Peace, February 19, 71–72; David R. Francis, *Russia from the American Embassy, April 1916–November 1918* (New York: Scribner's Sons, 1921), 309–10; Link, *Papers of Woodrow Wilson*, Wilson to Colonel Edward House, February 23, 1919, vol. 55, 229–30; David R. Francis to Robert Lansing, February 23, 1919, vol. 55, 234–35.

20. Lloyd George, *Memoirs of the Peace Conference*, vol. 1, 243–44.

21. U.S. Department of State, *Foreign Relations, Russia, 1919*, Commission to Negotiate Peace to Frank L. Polk, February 23, 73; Link, *Papers of Woodrow Wilson*, Memorandum of Winston S. Churchill, June 25, 1919, vol. 61, 164–66.

22. David S. Foglesong, *America's Secret War against Bolshevism: U.S. Intervention in the Russian Civil War, 1917–1920* (Chapel Hill: University of North Carolina Press, 1995), 254, 260; John Bradley, *Allied Intervention in Russia* (New York: Basic Books, 1968), 213; Somin, *Stillborn Crusade*, 164–65.

23. Kennan, *Russia and the West under Lenin and Stalin*, 130–31.

24. U.S. Department of State, *Foreign Relations, Russia, 1919*, Thornwell Haynes to Commission to Negotiate Peace, March 11, 76–77; William C. Bullitt to Commission to Negotiate Peace, March 16, 78–80; undated, 81–84.

25. Ibid., William C. Bullitt to Woodrow Wilson, March 25, 85–95.

26. Somin, *Stillborn Crusade*, 114.

27. Link, *Papers of Woodrow Wilson*, Diary of Colonel Edward House, March 25, 1919, vol. 56, 279; March 26, 1919, vol. 56, 309.

28. William C. Bullitt, *Testimony before the Committee on Foreign Relations, United States Senate* (New York: B. W. Huebsch, 1919), 66.

29. Ibid., 94; Link, *Papers of Woodrow Wilson*, Diary of Dr. Cary T. Grayson, April 17, 1919, vol. 57, 428n14; William C. Bullitt to Wilson, April 18, 1919, vol. 57, 459–60.

30. Lloyd George, *Memoirs of the Peace Conference*, vol. 1, 222.

31. William Appleman Williams, *American-Russian Relations, 1781–1947* (New York: Rinehart, 1952), 169; Link, *Papers of Woodrow Wilson*, Memorandum by Wil-

liam C. Bullitt, March 28, 1919, vol. 56, 387–91; Memorandum from the Russian Section of the American Commissioners to Negotiate Peace, March 31, 1919, vol. 56, 466–68; Wilson to Robert Lansing, April 1, 1919, vol. 56, 512; Robert K. Murray, *Red Scare: A Study of National Hysteria, 1919–1920* (New York: McGraw-Hill, 1955), 95–97, 276. For reference to Weinstein's diagnosis of Wilson's health problems, see Georg Schild, *Between Ideology and Realpolitik: Woodrow Wilson and the Russian Revolution, 1917–1921* (Westport, Conn.: Greenwood, 1995), 107.

32. George F. Kennan, "Russia and the Versailles Conference," *American Scholar* 30 (Winter 1960–1961): 27; McFadden, *Alternative Paths*, 256–58.

33. Leonid I. Strakhovsky, *American Opinion about Russia, 1917–1920* (Toronto: University of Toronto Press, 1961), 83, 96, 98.

34. U.S. Department of State, *Foreign Relations, Russia, 1919*, Paul S. Reinsch to William Phillips, undated, 200; William Phillips to Commission to Negotiate Peace, March 29, 200–201; Schild, *Between Ideology and Realpolitik*, 107.

35. U.S. Department of State, *Foreign Relations, Russia, 1919*, Frank L. Polk to Commission to Negotiate Peace, March 11, 99–100; Thornwell Haynes to Commission to Negotiate Peace, March 29, 96.

36. Ibid., Herbert Hoover to Woodrow Wilson, March 28, 100–101.

37. Ibid., 100.

38. Link, *Papers of Woodrow Wilson*, Wilson to Robert Lansing, January 10, 1919, vol. 53, 709.

39. Ibid., Diary of Colonel Edward House, April 19, 1919, vol. 57, 503–5; Herbert Hoover to Colonel Edward House, April 19, 1919, vol. 58, 505–8; Diary of Ray Stannard Baker, April 19, 1919, vol. 58, 508–9; Herbert Hoover to Wilson, April 23, 1919, vol. 58, 41–42; Williams, *Russian-American Relations*, 171–72; Amity Shlaes, *The Forgotten Man: A New History of the Great Depression* (New York: Harper Perennial, 2008), 30.

40. U.S. Department of State, *Foreign Relations, Russia, 1919*, Fridtjof Nansen to Woodrow Wilson, April 3, 102.

41. Kennan, "Russia and the Versailles Conference," 31.

42. U.S. Department of State, *Foreign Relations, Russia, 1919*, Big Four to Fridtjof Nansen, April 17, 108–9; Hugh C. Wallace to Frank L. Polk, May 9, 111.

43. Kennan, *Russia and the West under Lenin and Stalin*, 141–42; Lloyd George, *Memoirs of the Peace Conference*, vol. 1, 228.

44. U.S. Department of State, *Foreign Relations, Russia, 1919*, Swenson to Commission to Negotiate Peace, May 14, 112–15; Lord Robert Cecil to Sir Maurice Hankey, May 16, 115; Link, *Papers of Woodrow Wilson*, Frank L. Polk to Wilson, July 11, 1919, vol. 61, 455n1; Foglesong, *America's Secret War against Bolshevism*, 231–32; Somin, *Stillborn Crusade*, 119.

45. U.S. Department of State, *Foreign Relations, Russia, 1919*, Frank L. Polk to Roland S. Morris, May 15, 349; May 17, 349; Link, *Papers of Woodrow Wilson*, Notes of a Meeting of the Council of Four, May 10, 1919, vol. 59, 29–30; Wilson to Frank L. Polk, May 14, 1919, vol. 59, 148.

46. U.S. Department of State, *Foreign Relations, Russia, 1919*, William Phillips to Roland S. Morris, June 30, 388.

47. Ibid., Council of Four to Alexander V. Kolchak, May 26, 369; DeWitt C. Poole to Frank L. Polk, May 29, 370; Frank L. Polk to Commission to Negotiate Peace, June 11, 373; Link, *Papers of Woodrow Wilson*, Alexander V. Kolchak to Georges Clemenceau, June 4, 1919, vol. 60, 141–44; Kennan, "Russia and the Versailles Conference," 38; Pereira, *White Siberia*, 114.

48. U.S. Department of State, *Foreign Relations, Russia, 1919*, Commission to Negotiate Peace to William Phillips, June 20, 149–51.

49. Ibid., Robert Lansing to Commission to Negotiate Peace, August 2, 156–57; William Phillips to Commission to Negotiate Peace, September 9, 157; Robert Lansing to Ronald C. Lindsay, January 10, 1920, 163.

50. Ibid., Robert Lansing to Commission to Negotiate Peace, August 2, 156.

51. Strakhovsky, *American Opinion about Russia*, 85, 87; Murray, *Red Scare*, 274–75; McFadden, *Alternative Paths*, 276, 291. For reference to Martens's effort to secure recognition and supplies in exchange for Russian raw materials, see Link, *Papers of Woodrow Wilson*, Ludwig Martens to Robert Lansing, March 25, 1919, vol. 56, 548–51.

52. U.S. Department of State, *Foreign Relations, Russia, 1919*, Roland S. Morris to Robert Lansing, July 22, 394–96.

53. Ibid., Robert Lansing to Newton D. Baker, July 25, 398.

54. Ibid., Robert Lansing to Ernest L. Harris, July 26, 398–99.

55. Ibid., Roland S. Morris to Robert Lansing, July 27, 400; Robert Lansing to Ernest L. Harris, July 30, 401.

56. Ibid., Roland S. Morris to Robert Lansing, July 31, 401. For reference to the number of staff officers in Kolchak's army in comparison with the German and American armies, see Carol Willcox Melton, *Between War and Peace: Woodrow Wilson and the American Expeditionary Force in Siberia, 1918–1921* (Macon, Ga.: Mercer University Press, 2001), 95.

57. U.S. Department of State, *Foreign Relations, Russia, 1919*, Roland S. Morris to Robert Lansing, August 4, 403–5.

58. Ibid., August 8, 407–8.

59. Ibid., August 11, 409; August 16, 415.

60. Ibid., August 11, 409–10.

61. Ibid., August 12, 411; August 14, 414; August 18, 416.

62. Ibid., Robert Lansing to Ernest L. Harris, August 25, 421–22.

63. Ibid., Roland S. Morris to Robert Lansing, August 27, 422–23; William Phillips to Woodrow Wilson, September 19, 425; Woodrow Wilson to William Phillips, September 20, 426.

64. Robert J. Maddox, *The Unknown War with Russia: Wilson's Siberian Intervention* (San Rafael, Calif.: Presidio, 1977), 123.

65. Murray, *Red Scare*, 78; Robert D. Warth, "The Palmer Raids," *South Atlantic Review* 48 (January 1949): 1–2.

66. Murray, *Red Scare*, 79, 81, 83, 135, 153–55, 193–94; Warth, "Palmer Raids," 1–3; McFadden, *Alternative Paths*, 309–10.

67. Warth, "Palmer Raids," 10–12, 14–16; Murray, *Red Scare*, 195–97, 212–15.

68. Warth, "Palmer Raids," 5, 8, 10, 14; Murray, *Red Scare*, 215–16.

69. Murray, *Red Scare*, 219.

70. Ibid., 207, 224–25, 233–34, 238; Warth, "Palmer Raids," 4, 7, 11; Strak-hovsky, *American Opinion about Russia*, 89–90.

71. Murray, *Red Scare*, 83, 170–71, 178; Warth, "Palmer Raids," 8.

72. Murray, *Red Scare*, 169.

73. Warth, "Palmer Raids," 17–19, 22; Murray, *Red Scare*, 247, 249, 252–53, 262, 273; McFadden, *Alternative Paths*, 320–21.

74. Murray, *Red Scare*, 201.

75. U.S. Department of State, *Foreign Relations, Russia, 1919*, Robert Lansing to John K. Caldwell, September 9, 119–20; Link, *Papers of Woodrow Wilson*, An Address in Convention Hall in Kansas City, September 6, 1919, vol. 63, 70; An Address in the Des Moines Coliseum, September 6, 1919, vol. 63, 76–77; An Address in the Minneapolis Armory, September 9, 1919, vol. 63, 134; An Address in the St. Paul Auditorium, September 9, 1919, vol. 63, 145; An Address at Bismarck, September 10, 1919, vol. 63, 161–62; An Address in the Billings Auditorium, September 11, 1919, vol. 63, 175; An Address at Coeur D'Alene, September 12, 1919, vol. 63, 216; An Address in the Tacoma Armory, September 13, 1919, vol. 63, 244–45; An Address in the Seattle Arena, September 13, 1919, vol. 63, 263.

CHAPTER SIX

~

Hard Times, Come Again No More

And it is self-evident that in an enormous territory like Siberia, then populated by armed bands of Cossacks, bandits, Czechs, German and Austrian prisoners of war, Russians for and against their own provincial governments, and with all law and order gone with the Czarist debacle, the sending of a little handful of men like our expedition was a military crime. And the usual formula given despairing relatives inquiring about such matters—"important diplomatic considerations not understood by you"—was a poor sop to mothers whose sons were killed in that far-away land after the Armistice with no one in the United States knowing why they were there.

—U.S. Army Chief of Staff Peyton C. March[1]

Unlike President Wilson, General Graves did not spend 1919 jousting with Republican senators. His foes were far more numerous and varied. He was denounced by the Kolchak government, by the British, by the French, and by officials in the U.S. State Department. He was not disparaged by the Japanese, however, who liked to handle their problems more quietly. Rather, they attempted to drive Graves and his soldiers out of Siberia, using Ivan Kalmikov and Gregori Semenov as their proxies.

While the Japanese had no personal animosity for Graves, merely desiring complete control of northern Manchuria and eastern Siberia, the other groups had a personal dislike for the general because he insisted on interpreting his instructions not to interfere in Russian internal affairs strictly. Thus, by May 1919, at the latest, each of these groups was determined to have Graves's instructions altered to force him into supporting the Kolchak government more actively.

In fact, by May 4, relations between the American forces and Kolchak's representatives were so tense that Graves feared a physical confrontation. He wrote the War Department, "If we continue our policy here we will almost surely have conflict with Russian troops as they are determined that we cannot remain in Siberia and continue the policy of noninterference and they claim such policy is impossible under existing conditions." Secretary of War Newton Baker forwarded Graves's report to the president, writing, "Either General Graves should be directed to cooperate with the Kolchak Government, or he ought to be withdrawn." Baker preferred the latter option.[2]

Pressure from the Kolchak Government

On May 10, the Provisional Government's ambassador, Boris Bakhmetev, who continued at his post despite the nonexistence of his government, wrote to Secretary of State Lansing in Paris, warning that Graves was creating ill feeling among the officials of the Kolchak government by maintaining a neutral attitude during "Bolshevik riots" in eastern Siberia. Bakhmetev enclosed a letter from Kolchak's foreign ministry that protested the fact that Graves was treating the Bolsheviks "as a political party of ordinary character." The ministry then made the preposterous claim that Graves's attitude was the result of the fact that "the American troops in Siberia contain a considerable number of Russian immigrants, partly of Jewish extraction, favoring extremist tendencies." The ministry also suggested, in view of the growing seriousness of the situation, "that General Graves be given instructions which would determine with precision the line of conduct towards Bolshevik riots." By October 13, the ministry was requesting that Graves be recalled, writing, "His remaining at Vladivostok will lead to perpetual misunderstandings and to the growing of public discontent with Americans."[3]

In addition to these attempts to exert pressure on Graves through the State Department, Kolchak's officials also carried on shameless propaganda against American forces in Siberia. Anti-Semitic newspapers supported by the Kolchak government claimed that "Bolshevik Jews" from the East Side of New York City dominated Graves's force. This was untrue. Of the approximately 8,500 soldiers Graves commanded, more than half came from Illinois, and it is doubtful that very many were either radical or Jewish. An internal investigation by American intelligence officers found no Bolshevik sympathizers among the soldiers. In any case, two of Kolchak's corrupt generals offered to have the propaganda campaign stopped if Graves paid them $20,000 per month. Graves refused the kind offer.[4]

Pressure from the British and French

The British and French were equally vocal in their opposition to Graves. On March 3, U.S. Consul in Vladivostok John K. Caldwell reported, "General Knox criticized . . . General Graves . . . as being ignorant of real situation outside his district, unsympathetic with all efforts of Kolchak Government and of British Government (as conducted by General Knox)." On May 19, the British foreign office joined the Kolchak government in requesting that Graves's instructions be altered to allow him to cooperate with Kolchak's forces. The foreign office then reported a long list of instances in which Graves had allegedly failed to come to the support of the Japanese, the Cossacks, and even the Czechs against "bolshevik forces." The list deserved the Pulitzer prize for fiction.[5]

Criticism from the State Department

Some officials in the U.S. State Department added criticism of their own. Basil Miles, the head of the department's Russia division, wrote regarding one of Graves's reports: "I consider this report of little real value. . . . It is entirely out of perspective and written with little real knowledge of Russia and Russian ways of doing things." Safely ensconced at his desk in Washington, Miles considered himself a better judge of "Russia and Russian ways of doing things" than those stationed in Russia itself. Assistant Secretary of State Frank L. Polk was only slightly gentler in his criticism of Graves: "The American command in Siberia has always required a high degree of tact and large experience in affairs. I cannot help thinking that, in spite of the narrow limitations set by his instructions, General Graves has proved lacking in both these qualifications."[6]

Support from His Superiors

Fortunately for Graves, however, both Secretary of War Baker and U.S. Army Chief of Staff March defended him against his detractors. On May 22 Baker wrote to the president:

> I feel from all the information we have that General Graves is carefully and intelligently carrying out orders under trying circumstances, and that the efforts

made to involve him in hostile operations against some part of the Russian population are insidious and baffling. He seems to have displayed firmness and good judgment. . . . I am particularly conscious of the stringent instructions I gave him as the reasons for his unbending attitude. . . . Up to the present time he has no orders [except] to guard the railroad and preserve local order without taking sides as between the various Cossack groups, local self-governments and claimants to general jurisdiction throughout the country. Such clashes as have occurred between him and others have for the most part been caused by [anti-Bolshevik] violence toward local populations.

Baker added that Graves must not be removed because his removal "would be used to show our approval of policies with which we are not in sympathy." To Graves himself, March wrote: "Keep a stiff upper lip; I am going to stand by you until **** freezes over."[7]

While Secretary of State Lansing, who had opposed Graves's appointment because he had heard that Graves lacked the "tact and diplomacy . . . to deal with so delicate a situation where the commanding officer requires other than military ability," now offered only mild support for him, President Wilson was more forceful in praising Graves's performance of his difficult task. On March 22, 1919, after referring to Knox's criticism of Graves, Lansing wrote to Wilson, "Reports received today from the American consuls at various places in Siberia seem, however, to confirm on the whole General Graves' opinion of Japanese activities as intended to aid the reactionary party and as conducted with a view to the eventual domination of Eastern Siberia by Japan." When British Prime Minister David Lloyd George noted, at a meeting of the Big Four on May 14, that reports from British representatives in Siberia claimed that Graves was causing tension between American forces and those of Kolchak, the secretary recorded, "President Wilson said that General Graves was a man of most unprovocative character, and wherever the fault may lie, he felt sure it was not with him."[8]

Partisan Attacks on American Troops

But Graves's unpopularity with Kolchak's officials did not make him or American soldiers any more popular with the anti-Kolchak partisans in Siberia. After all, American forces were providing a valuable service for Kolchak by guarding the Trans-Siberian Railway, through which Kolchak received American and other aid, and by guarding the Suchan coal mines, which powered the trains carrying these weapons and supplies.

Thus, in the late spring and early summer of 1919, the Suchan mines were plagued by strikes of Russian miners and railway employees who were unsympathetic to the Kolchak government and by the armed attacks of anti-Kolchak partisans. From May 17 to 21, trains going to the mines were constantly strafed by snipers. Reporting on this situation, U.S. Consul Caldwell noted: "Many of these armed [partisans] are young boys and none appear to be well armed or to have much ammunition. Nevertheless, they can interfere with the railway, by destroying it at various points, for a long time to come." American soldiers at the mines were continually attacked at night by bands of partisans, who often lobbed homemade grenades that they made from the same tobacco tins that American soldiers had given them during the day, a situation eerily similar to that encountered by some American soldiers in Vietnam half a century later.[9]

On June 25, a large band of partisans attacked an American detachment at Romanovka, which was located along the railway leading to the mines. Because of a mix-up in which a sentry returned to camp at dawn (4:00 a.m. in the summertime that far north) without having been relieved, the detachment was surprised. Repeated volleys fired into the tents took their toll; one American was hit seventeen times. Fortunately, the partisans' weaponry consisted largely of single-shot rifles. Though his jaw and mouth were shattered, Lieutenant Lawrence Butler, by writing orders, pointing, and muttering, regrouped the men and held the partisans off for four hours.

American camp near Romanovka. Robert L. Eichelberger Papers, David M. Rubenstein Rare Book & Manuscript Library, courtesy of Duke University, Durham, North Carolina.

Nonetheless, the detachment was saved only when Corporal Louis Heinzman dashed through the partisan lines and brought back help, causing the partisans to flee. Nineteen Americans were killed that day, and twenty-five wounded. Discovered among the partisan dead were the village shoe repairman and a man who had occasionally sold fresh milk to the Americans. Had the American detachment been annihilated, it is likely that this event would have marked the end of American intervention in Siberia because the Wilson administration was at that very moment defending it before a congressional committee. By August the remnants of the detachment were evacuated in any case because coal was no longer being mined there due to the shortage of workers.[10]

The Kolchak Regime's Atrocities

Few of the partisans who attacked the Suchan coal mines were Bolsheviks. Most were ordinary Siberians who were outraged by the atrocities being openly committed by representatives of the Kolchak government, atrocities that the Allies were making possible by their presence in Siberia and by their aid to Kolchak. Lieutenant Colonel Robert Eichelberger, General Graves's chief intelligence officer, who had several opportunities to negotiate with various partisan bands, wrote home to his wife on April 19, "All the Allied forces here except the Americans are out against the so-called Bolsheviki. The particular band of Bolsheviki here are almost all simple peasants who have been stirred up by the murderous actions of the punitive expeditions sent out from Vladivostok." Most Siberian partisans were farmers who were deeply suspicious of all urbanites, including the Bolsheviks. Although the Soviet government belatedly financed some partisan bands because of their usefulness in distracting the Whites, Lenin wrote, "The partisan movement is to be feared like fire" because many partisans were "unwilling to subordinate themselves to the central authority," a tendency that "leads to ruin." Thus, the partisans became known as Greens, being neither White nor Red. Even after the Bolshevik victory in the civil war, when some of the partisans were integrated into the Red Army and subjected to "re-education," they rebelled against Soviet authority, especially after the Bolsheviks began seizing their grain to feed the cities.[11]

Many of the White atrocities that so enflamed the partisans were committed by order of Gregori Semenov and Ivan Kalmikov, two Cossack generals supported by Japan who were also official representatives of the Kolchak government in the Far East and who received its support and encouragement. In June 1919 Graves wrote, "The general belief is that a mere statement that a man is a Bolshevik is enough to cause him to disappear." Indeed, the Cossacks were complaining about the Americans' keeping of prisoners and granting of medical care to the wounded among them, which they likened to "feeding Bolsheviks and looking out for their sick." Graves added that the Cossacks were commandeering all of the food supplies shipped on the railways and arresting village officials when they complained. Worse, Graves later wrote that it was well known by August 1919 that Semenov "had established what were known as his 'killing stations' and he openly boasted that he could not sleep at night when he had not killed someone during the day." In the month of August alone an entire trainload of 350 Semenov prisoners were known to have been machine-gunned at one of these killing stations. In one instance Semenov murdered an entire village, sparing neither women nor children, and left their bodies to rot where they were killed. Four or five men were burned alive. Reports of these atrocities were substantiated by French and even Japanese officers. U.S. Army Intelligence estimated that Semenov was responsible for 30,000 executions in one year. Nevertheless, Kolchak promoted Semenov to the rank of major general. In fact, Kolchak's last official act was to declare Semenov his successor.[12]

It is estimated that Kalmikov executed at least 1,500 people without trial. Graves wrote of him, "It is hard to imagine a man like Kalmikoff existing in modern civilization, and there was hardly a day passed without some report of the terrible atrocities committed by him or his troops." Like Semenov, Kalmikov often disposed of victims' bodies where no one could find them. Graves wrote:

> Reports of the terrible atrocities being committed by Kalmikoff troops continued to reach American Headquarters almost daily, but as I had no means of verifying the truth of these stories I could take no action. . . .
> Under the pretext of combating bolshevism, he resorted to the unscrupulous arrest of people of some means, tortured them to secure their money and executed some on the ground of bolshevism. These arrests were so frequent that all classes of the population were terrorized and it was estimated that there were several hundred persons executed by Kalmikoff troops in the vicinity of Khabarovsk. These murders we established as best we could from peasants and depositions of local legal authorities.

Kalmikov even murdered two members of the Swedish Red Cross and stole their aid money. He boasted that killing never became monotonous to him because he varied his execution methods. Kalmikov flogged his own soldiers regularly and severely. A large body of them fled to American headquarters in Khabarovsk on January 27, 1919, and protested his conscriptions, his whippings and executions for slight offenses, his insufficient provision of food and clothing, the drunkenness and cruelty of his officers, and his mutilation and execution of civilians. Kolchak never protested Kalmikov's atrocities, though Kalmikov was another of his official representatives.[13]

If the subordination of Semenov and Kalmikov to the Japanese casts a little doubt as to Kolchak's ability to control them, there is no doubt that Generals Boris Annenkov, Pavel P. Ivanov-Rinov, and Sergei N. Rozanov were all firmly under his control and that the crimes of these men were no less great. Annenkov, leader of the Semipalatinsk Cossacks, murdered 3,000 Jews at Ekaterinburg in July 1919. In view of the location, magnitude, and perpetrator of this crime there is little doubt that it was sanctioned by the Kolchak government. In fact, when inquiries were made concerning this pogrom, the general staff at Omsk not only declined to deny their complicity in it, but even declared matter-of-factly that something had to be done "that would give the Jews something to think about." Kolchak himself was an anti-Semite and avid reader of the *Protocols of the Elders of Zion*, a highly influential but fraudulent transcript of Jewish conspirators discussing their plot to take over the world. Annenkov wore an appropriate insignia on his hat and uniform: a large skull and crossbones.[14]

Ivanov-Rinov, the commander of Kolchak's forces in the Far East, was no less brutal and no less hostile to democratic institutions. On March 2, 1919, the popularly elected vice president of the Provisional Zemstvo of Vladivostok, a local newspaper editor, and two others were arrested by order of Ivanov-Rinov. These men were placed aboard a train traveling west to one of Semenov's killing stations. Their wives protested this action to General Graves, who was impressed by their fortitude, writing, "It was remarkable to see how quiet and determined these women were." The wives asked only that Graves not aid Ivanov-Rinov in putting down the revolt against the Kolchak government that would inevitably occur as a result of the arrest of their husbands. Graves made no comment. Sir Charles Eliot, British High Commissioner in Siberia, then came to ask Graves, in an extremely agitated manner, if it was true that American troops would not interfere if a revolt occurred. Didn't Graves know that British property was at stake here? Graves told Eliot that "the United States had never been in the habit of protecting murderers, and that I did not intend doing so now and, so far as I was concerned, they could bring Ivanoff-Rinoff opposite American Headquarters and hang him to that telegraph pole until he was dead, and not an American soldier would turn his hand." Graves later wrote, "I have always believed that the British and the Japanese knew these arrests were going to be made."[15]

In fact, the British, fearing a popular uprising, had the train containing the prisoners stopped at Pogranichnaya. There the Cossacks and Japanese attempted a sleight of hand maneuver with two trains to make it appear that the prisoners were not being taken to Semenov's killing station, after all. Fortunately, the prisoners were able to smuggle out information as to their real location. Meanwhile, Graves had managed to persuade all of the Allied commanders except for the Japanese commander to draft a resolution stating that henceforth everyone arrested in Vladivostok would be tried there and that Allied commanders could send a representative to each trial to ensure fairness. The French initially objected to this resolution on the surreal ground that it represented interference in Russian internal affairs. At any rate, the zemstvo leaders were kept in prison at Nikolsk for two weeks and then released.[16]

Russian civilians of a lower status were not so fortunate. Ivanov-Rinov was brutal in his enforcement of Kolchak's conscription order of December 1918, which declared that all men of military age must report for service in his army. Ivanov-Rinov sent his troops from village to village, seeking young men. When they hid, the older men of the village were tortured and killed. Men were hung by their feet or from pins in the rafters of barns. Some were beaten so badly that their blood splattered the walls. Others had their arms broken and their teeth knocked out. One such man was already an invalid. Some were partially hanged and then let down. Others were scalded with boiling water or burned with hot irons. After being tortured in this fashion, the old men in these villages were then shot to death, generally feet first and then up along the rest of the body. Sometimes six or more bullets were used to kill one victim.[17]

One American officer who was sent to investigate Ivanov-Rinov's atrocities told Graves, "General, for God's sake, never send me on another expedition like this. I came within an ace of pulling off my uniform, joining these poor people, and helping them as best I could." Ivanov-Rinov laughed about, and boasted of, his mass slaughter. When Kolchak finally removed Ivanov-Rinov from the command of his forces in the Far East, at the insistence of the United States, he called Ivanov-Rinov to a Russian church, where he kissed him on both cheeks, proclaimed him a patriot, promoted him to lieutenant general, and gave him a gold sword.[18]

Kolchak then appointed Rozanov to replace him. Rozanov's character may be deduced from the instructions he gave his soldiers while at Krasnoyarsk prior to his promotion. He instructed them to kill every tenth person in a village that refused to reveal the location of partisan leaders and to burn any village that resisted and kill every male there. It was in recognition for services like these that Kolchak promoted Rozanov to Ivanov-Rinov's former position. Arriving in Vladivostok in September 1919, Rozanov justified Kolchak's faith in him through numerous acts of terror. In the short time between November 18, 1919, and January 31, 1920, when he was deposed, it was estimated that Rozanov murdered 500 people in the Vladivostok area alone. The figures for all of eastern Siberia, and for his entire four-month term of office, are more difficult to determine.[19]

As General Graves wrote, "Admiral Kolchak surrounded himself with former Czarist officials and because these peasants would not take up arms and offer their lives to put these people back in power, they were kicked, beaten with knouts, and murdered in cold blood by the thousands, and then the world called them 'Bolsheviks.' In Siberia, the word Bolshevik meant a human being who did not, by act or word, give encouragement to the restoration to power of representatives of Autocracy in Russia." Indeed, the Kolchak government applied the word "Bolshevik" even to moderate, popularly elected groups. Graves continued, "The zemstvos, dumas, and the cooperatives were such well known, legal, reliable, and law abiding organizations that it would have been difficult for Kolchak to have justified to the world the oppressive measures used against these people if they had been referred to by their proper names." Indeed, if Kolchak's officials were correct, 97 percent of the Siberian people were Bolsheviks, since General Graves's chief intelligence officer, Lieutenant Colonel Eichelberger, estimated that this was the percentage of Siberians who were opposed to the Kolchak government.[20]

A good illustration of the type of thinking that predominated among Kolchak's generals may be found in one of the stories Graves told in his memoirs. Upon meeting with the leaders of the Socialist Revolutionary Party, the party that had won a majority of the votes in the constituent assembly elections, Graves obtained an agreement from them to cooperate with the Kolchak government, providing it adhered to certain democratic principles. Pleased with the agreement, Graves presented it to the general who handled political affairs for the Kolchak regime. Upon hearing of the agreement, the general flew into a rage, declaring it outrageous that anyone should list conditions under which he would support the Kolchak government. Furthermore, he shouted at Graves that "before long, such characters as I had been talking to would be glad to come to the Omsk Government, put their heads on the ground, [and] beg for forgiveness and for an opportunity to support Admiral Kolchak." Clearly, Kolchak's generals belonged in the age of Ivan the Terrible.[21]

There is no question that Kolchak must be held personally responsible for the atrocities committed by his representatives. On November 22, 1919, when his government had utterly collapsed, Kolchak publicly promised to end the reign of what he himself called "the military terror" that had engulfed his regime. This demonstrates clearly that Kolchak knew about the atrocities committed on his behalf and suggests that he could have stopped them earlier had he desired.[22]

What the State Department Knew

State Department officials knew about some of these atrocities as well. They knew that Semenov was so brutal to his own men that only 3,000 of his 15,000 soldiers could be considered loyal. They knew that Semenov was periodically robbing everyone in the Chita area, Russians and Chinese alike. They knew that Semenov was engaged in prodigious acts of violence in eastern Siberia. But because they also knew that Kolchak had promoted him to the rank of major general in August 1919, they welcomed one of his representatives into the United States with open arms, while arresting a visiting representative of Russian cooperatives as a "Bolshevik." State Department officials also knew that Kalmikov was robbing, murdering, and executing without trial and that his troops were fleeing in droves to American headquarters in Vladivostok any time they saw an opportunity. They knew that a Cossack officer was swearing that it was Kalmikov who had murdered the Swedish Red Cross personnel in Siberia. They knew, as Eichelberger stated regarding Kalmikov's activities in Khabarovsk, "His actions there would have been considered shameful in the middle ages."[23]

State Department officials knew the record of Ivanov-Rinov as well. They knew that he had ordered the merciless beating with ramrods of the wives of men hiding from his conscription agents. They knew that the reason the Siberian peasantry were defenseless against his oppression was that they had largely disarmed themselves at the insistence of the Allies, who had promised to protect the people. They knew the full story of Ivanov-Rinov's arrest of the Vladivostok zemstvo leader and his three compatriots. They knew that Ivanov-Rinov had been a police officer under the czarist regime and was continuing the practices he had learned in that position. They knew that he was carrying out "arbitrary arrests of officials whose chief fault is that they are trying to build up a form of local representative government." They knew that he had eliminated all freedom of speech and freedom of the press in areas he controlled. They also knew that he was effectively controlled by Kolchak, especially after he meekly obeyed Kolchak's order relieving him of command.[24]

State Department officials knew that the Inter-Allied Railway Committee began denouncing Rozanov, Ivanov-Rinov's replacement, as another extreme reactionary and terrorist soon after he assumed command. They knew of his statements to the effect that the Russian people were incapable of self-government. They knew of the bloody executions he carried out at Krasnoyarsk, which U.S. Ambassador to Japan Roland Morris claimed were even worse than those of Semenov and Ivanov-Rinov. They knew that Rozanov's 4,000 soldiers entered Vladivostok in September 1919, shooting everything in sight. They knew that one of his officers shot and killed an American soldier in that city for no apparent reason and that Rozanov took no action to bring the guilty party to justice. They knew that Rozanov refused to remove his army from Vladivostok when called upon to do so by the Allied commanders. They knew that Kolchak wired Rozanov, ordering him to resist any Allied attempt to remove him from the city. They knew that the Kolchak government scoffed at its polite letter requesting the withdrawal of his troops from Vladivostok.[25]

There is one final fact that State Department officials knew that is worthy of mention. On June 26, 1919, Graves reported that Kolchak representatives had stopped all supplies from going into certain districts that they claimed were "Bolshevik areas." As a result, 40,000 people were left without anything to eat except wild oats. When these starving peasants sent representatives to Allied consuls to explain their grievances, Kolchak forces arrested them. As a consequence, bands of anti-Kolchak partisans were popping up in these regions, and these peasants were particularly angry at the Allies for allowing the people to be starved in this fashion.[26]

From all of these reports, two facts seem inescapable. First, dominated by murderous thugs, the Kolchak government could never have ruled Russia for any length of time without constant Allied aid in massive amounts. Second, the State Department cannot be excused from guilt on the grounds that its officials were ignorant of the Kolchak government's atrocities. Protestations aside, American aid continued to flow freely to Kolchak. The State Department's attitude was best exemplified by its cable to August Heid, the Russian Bureau's representative in Vladivostok, "You are not sending back the kind of information we want you to send."[27]

State Department Response: The Rifle Shipment

Indeed, the State Department's ability to ignore unpleasant facts was unparalleled. For instance, on September 16, 1919, Graves reported that, on September 5, Kalmikov's troops had arrested an American captain and an American corporal because they had no Russian passports. The Cossacks released the captain but brought the corporal to Khabarovsk, where they beat him severely. Fortunately, one of Graves's officers secured the corporal's release by arresting three of Kalmikov's Cossacks in retaliation. Graves reported: "I told Rozanoff that Kalmikoff Cossacks must never touch an American soldier and if they did I would arrest Kalmikoff and hold him as prisoner. Kalmikoff has called upon Cossacks [to] assemble with view to driving Americans out of Siberia. I am told by Rozanoff's assistant that Semenoff is ready to assist Kalmikoff in case of trouble with Americans." As a result, Graves stated that he was refusing to turn over the latest shipment of rifles from the United States to Kolchak representatives in Vladivostok and that he was informing the Kolchak government that "we will not give them any military supplies as long as Kolchak agents of the East are threatening to use military force against the United States." Graves added that this action had been approved by Ambassador Morris, who was then en route to Tokyo.[28]

Graves later defended his withholding of the American rifles from the Kolchak government as a necessary action, writing that he had feared that many of the rifles would fall into the hands of Semenov and Kalmikov. Graves recalled, "The American troops had no field pieces, while the Cossacks did, and the American troops were separated, by nearly two thousand miles, into detachments guarding the railroad. By the destructions of small bridges, I could not have gotten the command together, and the seven thousand men I had would have been divided into not less than four detachments, and probably many more. I can not think any American would expect me to turn these rifles over to people who wanted to use them against American troops." In fact, the Cossacks not only possessed more artillery than the Americans but also had the advantage given by Semenov's armored trains. This was the reason why, on September 17, Graves requested mountain artillery, which could pierce armored cars.[29]

Relatively secure from Cossack attacks in Washington, State Department officials did not seem anxious about the safety of American soldiers in Siberia. As a result, they were outraged neither with Kalmikov for beating an American soldier nor with Kolchak for failing to reprimand Kalmikov but instead with Graves for withholding rifles from the Kolchak government. Although Secretary of War Baker supported Graves's action, the State Department easily won President Wilson's assent to an order, issued on September 26, requiring that Graves relinquish the rifles to the Kolchak representatives. Meanwhile, State Department officials misrepresented Graves's action to the American press as an overreaction to anti-American articles printed in Vladivostok. They could not tell the press the real reason for Graves's action, that the official representatives of Kolchak in the Far East were collecting rifles for an assault on American soldiers there.[30]

On October 2, 1919, Secretary of State Lansing wired the Kolchak government, saying that he was quite sure that its failure to reprimand Kalmikov for beating an American soldier did not imply any sympathy with the action. Nevertheless, he politely requested that the Kolchak government reprimand its Far Eastern representative. This was necessary, Lansing explained, in order to prevent indignation on the part of the American public and the U.S. Army. No reprimand was ever issued by the Kolchak government, however. On October 8, Charles H. Smith, an American member of the Inter-Allied Railway Committee, reported that on October 6, Graves had ordered all American troops on the Amur railway line to concentrate at Spaskoe. Smith wrote:

> During the past two weeks both General Graves and myself have been receiving from many Russian sources, including Russian officers and members of various political parties and from members of the staff of General Rozanoff, numerous reports that there is a plot on foot to make the position of the Allies untenable in Siberia.
>
> These reports are as follows: Semenoff, Kalmikoff, and Rozanoff, all appointees of the Omsk Government, have been mobilizing some of the worst Russian elements and also enemy prisoners. This is not to go to the front but for attacking the Allies, the Americans and Czechs principally. This movement is being secretly supported by the Japanese military. . . . Their aim is to take advantage of the general discontent to use a slogan, "Away with the Allies," and to attack Americans and Czechs. . . . The idea is to make the Allies withdraw in disgust. Then the aid of the Japanese will be solicited and in payment for this the Japanese will be given commercial control of the Far East.

In his memoirs Graves listed as the sources for this information White General Dmitri Horvat, Kolchak's minister for foreign affairs Ivan Sukin, a French colonel, and the fortress commander at Vladivostok. The last official, who had access to all telegrams sent to the city, claimed that the Japanese had promised the Whites secret support in the event of such an offensive against the other Allies. Yet the State Department still insisted that the Kolchak government receive American rifles.[31]

But Graves was determined that none of the rifles should fall into the hands of the Cossacks, so he told the Kolchak government representatives in Vladivostok that he would turn the rifles over to them at Irkutsk, far west of the territories roamed by Semenov and Kalmikov. Upon hearing news of this decision, the two Cossacks were upset. They offered to help guard one of the two trains that would transport the rifles to Irkutsk, but their kind offer was rejected.[32]

The first train, containing 50,000 rifles, reached Irkutsk safely. The second train, containing another 50,000 rifles, was stopped by Semenov on the evening of October 24. Semenov demanded 15,000 rifles. Although the train was guarded only by Lieutenant Albert Ryan and fifty men of the Twenty-Seventh Infantry, the lieutenant refused to surrender the rifles. Semenov declared that if he did not surrender the rifles, they would be taken by force. Two armored trains containing a battalion of Cossacks were brought alongside the American train, but at midnight, Semenov did allow Lieutenant Ryan to cable Graves for instructions. Deeply concerned by the prospect of so many rifles coming into Semenov's possession, Graves instructed the lieutenant not to give Semenov a single rifle. Ryan barricaded the train. Once again, the Japanese intervened at the last moment. The train was released, after being detained for forty hours.[33]

Although Graves was initially relieved by the outcome of this standoff, he soon discovered that Kolchak had ordered 15,000 of the American rifles returned to his good friend Semenov as part of a deal brokered by the Japanese. None of these rifles seems to have been used by Semenov's forces on the evening in January 1920 when the *Destroyer* attacked an American platoon at Posolskaya in the Baikal sector without provocation. The armored train's portholes opened and Semenov's Cossacks fired into the boxcars in which the American soldiers were sheltered. Fortunately, villagers had warned the Americans of the attack beforehand, so that the soldiers were able to jump out and assault the train. Though outnumbered and facing a heavily armored train, the Americans, under the leadership of Lieutenant Paul Kendall, managed, with the help of reinforcements, to capture the train and forty-eight prisoners, including General Nicholas Bogomoletz. The prisoners admitted that they had robbed and murdered more than forty men and raped and killed three women. Nevertheless, Kendall was ordered to release the train and prisoners because by then American forces were evacuating Siberia. The same month Graves recovered from the Japanese 6,000 of the 15,000 American rifles that Kolchak had turned over to Semenov. They were sitting in four cars in the Vladivostok rail yard, still in their boxes. Evidently, Semenov, whose forces were dwindling from desertion by that point, had not really needed so many rifles. As for General Bogomoletz, he later fled to Japan and then to the United States. In 1941 Lieutenant Kendall saw him in Hollywood, where he owned a shoe-repair shop.[34]

The Collapse of the Kolchak Regime

Although Semenov had received the rifles he desired, there was no attack against American detachments. The reason was that the Cossacks were distracted by the imminent collapse of the Kolchak regime.

By July 1919, the Red Army had captured Perm and Ekaterinburg. A few of Kolchak's divisions were now refusing to fight. Kolchak's army was withdrawing in panic, many soldiers possessing self-inflicted wounds. By August, morale was so low that some of Kolchak's officers were abandoning their troops in order to achieve greater speed in their flight eastward. The enlisted men, also concerned with speed, were throwing down their weapons and heavy clothing. Meanwhile, Secretary of State Lansing, who had been referring to the "extreme terrorism" employed by the Bolsheviks only a year before, was now remarking that the Bolshevik treatment of conquered towns was "not as bad as expected, judging from reports as to [the Bolsheviks'] conduct in European Russia." If true, the Bolsheviks' mild treatment of the conquered probably hastened the surrender of anti-Bolsheviks.[35]

During the summer and autumn of 1919, Kolchak's situation worsened steadily. In the summer Kolchak fired his most capable general, the Czech Rudolf Gajda, when Gajda protested the Kolchak regime's reactionary policies. (Gajda's protest is especially remarkable, given that he later founded the Czech Fascist Party.)

Rudolf Gajda (seated left) and General Graves (seated center). Robert L. Eichelberger Papers, David M. Rubenstein Rare Book & Manuscript Library, courtesy of Duke University, Durham, North Carolina.

When Gajda reached Vladivostok on August 8, he told reporters: "The Kolchak Government cannot possibly stand and if the Allies support him they will make the greatest mistake in history. The Government is divided into two distinct parts: one issues proclamations and propaganda for foreign consumption stating that the Government favors and works for a Constituent Assembly; the other part secretly plans and plots for the restoration of the monarchy." White morale and troop strength dropped further in October, when the Czechs announced that they were departing for home. While it is true that Anton Denikin, aided by British tanks and aircraft, was advancing toward Moscow from southern Russia and Nicholas Yudenich was moving against Petrograd, both anti-Bolshevik offensives soon stalled. (Both were victims of the White refusal to recognize the independence of newly independent border states. But for that refusal, Yudenich might well have captured Petrograd with the help of the Finns and Baltic peoples, and the Poles would not have agreed to a cease-fire with the Bolsheviks that proved fatal to Denikin's forces. Ironically, given the Soviet Union's eventual conquest of Poland and the Baltic States under Stalin, the Poles and Baltic peoples might have been better off accepting the Whites' offer of greater autonomy within the Russian Empire.) By then, there was no westbound traffic on the Trans-Siberian Railway. Both tracks and the highway that flanked them were devoted to the mass evacuation of large numbers of soldiers and civilians, many of them suffering from typhus, frostbite, and hunger. The British and French, sensing the inevitable fall of the White governments, had already begun redirecting their money from the Whites to the states bordering Russia.[36]

On November 14, almost exactly one year after the Kolchak coup, the admiral's capital, Omsk, fell to the Red Army. In the city the Bolsheviks found enough uniforms to clothe 30,000 men, uniforms never distributed to the White soldiers by corrupt Kolchak officials, who preferred to sell them for profit. (The regime's top officers wore finely tailored British uniforms and shiny British boots while their soldiers were often reduced to rags. As much as 85 percent of some regiments' allotment of food, clothing, and other supplies was siphoned off.) More important, the Bolsheviks captured 35,000 White troops, ten generals, 1,000 officers, 2,000 machine guns, one million rifles, three million shells, and sixteen armored trains. Among the equipment seized by the Red Army were 1,000 American-made trucks.[37]

Three days later, Gajda raised the flag of rebellion against the Kolchak government, seizing the central rail yard at Vladivostok. Most of Gajda's 2,000 men were deserters from Rozanov's army. Many Vladivostok workers decided to strike in sympathy with Gajda's revolt. But Rozanov was able to suppress the rebellion, with the help of an elite corps of Russian troops trained by the British and with the assistance of British artillery. Captured deserters from Rozanov's army were immediately shot. A wounded Gajda, who had taken refuge with his fellow Czechs, was placed aboard a ship leaving the country. Had it not been for his status as a Czech and for the presence of Allied commissioners, he almost certainly would have been executed.[38]

Even while the Kolchak government was on the verge of collapse, Lansing was urging the British not to engage in even the most informal discussions with the Bolsheviks, claiming that the Soviet government was about to fall. The British foreign office assured him via the American ambassador, on November 28, that he had nothing to fear in that regard. On November 30, the U.S. minister to Denmark, Norman Hapgood, informed Lansing that everyone returning from Russia was reporting that the White situation was hopeless, but that "they have gone so crazy over Bolshevism in the United States that there is small hope of their seeing the situation." Hapgood was clearly speaking to the wrong person. On December 2, the minister reported that the Soviet government was again willing to negotiate through Maxim Litvinov. Lansing made no reply. On December 3, Lansing learned that Yudenich's army no longer existed, while Denikin's and Kolchak's forces continued to retreat in disorder. Again, the anti-Bolshevik official who reported these facts noted that the Bolsheviks were committing no atrocities and seemed to be treating the Siberian people well. They were even offering Kolchak's former officers and soldiers civilian and military positions and were holding discussions with the Socialist Revolutionaries of Siberia, something the Kolchak government had steadfastly refused to do.[39]

Yet when Lansing learned that Lloyd George had declared that he would give no further aid to the Whites and would see if some agreement could be reached with the Bolsheviks, he responded: "The uselessness of reaching a satisfactory understanding with the Bolsheviki has been demonstrated by past experience. The ultimate aims of the Bolsheviks are hostile to all existing governments and any apparent compromise which they may make with these governments is vitiated by their avowed opportunism."[40]

On December 23, 1919, Lansing was forced to ask President Wilson to withdraw U.S. troops from Siberia. Lansing wrote, "The truth of the matter is the simple fact that the Kolchak Government has utterly collapsed. The armies of the Bolsheviks have advanced into Eastern Siberia, where they are reported to be acting with moderation. The people seem to prefer them to the officers of the Kolchak regime. Further, the Bolshevik army is approaching the region where our soldiers are, and contact with them will lead to open hostilities and to many complications. In other words, if we do not withdraw we shall have to wage war against the Bolsheviks."[41]

Kolchak's situation was so hopeless by then that he was ordering Semenov to stop the Czechs from leaving Siberia by blowing up bridges and tunnels if necessary, an order that made no sense because it would have blocked his own evacuation as well. Semenov then cabled the Czech commanders, boasting that he would force them to support Kolchak. Ernest L. Harris, the U.S. Consul-General in Irkutsk and one of Kolchak's most ardent supporters, wrote, "It is felt by Allied representatives here that Kolchak's mentality is breaking up under the tremendous strain of the past two months. The tone of the telegrams which he has forwarded to the Czechs and the foreign representatives here would almost indicate this." French General Maurice Janin even expressed the belief that Kolchak had become a cocaine addict. By the final day of 1919, the Red Army had reached Lake Baikal.[42]

In early January 1920, Kolchak submitted himself and the remainder of the imperial gold reserve, worth 200 million rubles (roughly $100 million), to the protection of the Czechs. But the Czechs, who had helped capture this reserve from the Bolsheviks at Kazan (at which point it had consisted of 650 million rubles), felt little loyalty to Kolchak, who had just been attempting to detain them against their will—and who had, in fact, ruined their previous year. Thus, when it became apparent that they could not evacuate their large force from Siberia in time to avoid conflict with the Bolsheviks, the Czechs surrendered Kolchak and his gold to them in exchange for the promise of a safe evacuation.[43]

Kolchak was tried by a Soviet court and executed by firing squad on February 7, 1920. He was killed on the very spot outside Irkutsk where his own security forces had killed many prisoners. The gold was dispatched to Moscow.[44]

Kalmikov and Semenov escaped to the protection of the Japanese. After the Japanese left Siberia, Kalmikov foolishly fled to China, a poor choice in view of the brutal raids he had carried out against the Chinese, who killed him. After spending most of the interwar period in Europe, Semenov commanded troops for the Japanese in Manchuria in World War II but was captured by the Soviets in 1945 and hanged the following year.[45]

Evacuations

Meanwhile, the American chaplain was busy marrying eighty American soldiers to Russian women, as the American force prepared to leave Siberia. The first contingent of American soldiers departed on January 17. On April 1, the last contingent, led by General Graves, departed Siberia, while the Japanese remained. Was this the April Fools' joke that the Japanese had been preparing for a year and a half? In any case, as a token of goodwill, the Japanese did send an army band down to the docks to serenade the departing Americans. The band played Stephen Foster's apt melody, "Hard Times, Come Again No More." The Bolsheviks had succeeded in doing what the Japanese had failed to do; they had driven the Americans out of Siberia.[46]

With American and British assistance, approximately 57,000 Czechs were evacuated from Siberia between February and September 1920. Roughly 13,000 of their compatriots had died in Siberia. In the late summer a final contingent of 100 Czech amputees reached the United States, where they were fitted with artificial limbs paid for by the American Red Cross. The Czech Corps' Russian nightmare was finally over—but only in a manner of speaking. The Soviets backed a communist overthrow of the democratic government of Czechoslovakia in 1948, thereby bringing the nation into the Soviet camp. Twenty years later Soviet forces crushed a Czech revolt. That year, the only Czech legionnaire to return to Russia, Czech President Ludovik Svoboda, journeyed to Moscow to plead for the release of Alexander Dubcek, whom the Russians had imprisoned for declaring Czechoslovakia's independence.[47]

Seeing the handwriting on the wall, Lloyd George, who had ordered the withdrawal of the remaining British troops from Siberia on November 1, 1919, ended British participation in the Allied blockade of Soviet Russia in January 1920, effectively ending it. Infuriated by what he viewed as British abandonment of principle for selfish gain, Wilson refused to lift trade restrictions on the Soviet Union for another six months, and then only because it became apparent that an economic blockade lacking British support was futile. But Wilson still discouraged commerce with the Soviet Union, telling American businessmen that the Bolsheviks were unreliable trade partners and warning them that the U.S. government would not help them if the Bolsheviks failed to meet their financial obligations. Nevertheless, despite the absence of any official recognition of the Soviet government, the Republican administrations of the 1920s permitted the development of a substantial Soviet-American trade.[48]

In October 1920 Poland made peace with the Soviet Union, causing the last remaining sizable anti-Bolshevik army, under Peter Wrangle, to evacuate 100,000 soldiers and almost 50,000 civilians from the Crimea to Turkey on Russian and French ships. In July of the following year the very last anti-Bolshevik army, a small force in Mongolia, surrendered, thus ending the Russian Civil War.[49]

Though the Japanese contracted their zone of occupation to the coastal area surrounding Vladivostok (while simultaneously expanding it in the

island of Sakhalin), they did not withdraw from Siberia completely until October 25, 1922. The Japanese government's decision to withdraw was based
on domestic opposition, fear of a protracted war with the Soviet Union,
which was now stronger and more united, and diplomatic pressure from the
United States. In fact, when the Japanese finally withdrew from Siberia, the
Far Eastern Republic, a communist buffer state controlled by the Soviet government, publicly thanked the United States for its efforts to secure Japanese
withdrawal. What are friends for?[50]

Notes

1. Peyton C. March, *The Nation at War* (Garden City, N.Y.: Doubleday, 1932),
131–32.

2. U.S. Department of State, *Papers Relating to the Foreign Relations of the United
States, Russia, 1919* (Washington, D.C.: Government Printing Office, 1937; reprint,
New York: Kraus, 1969), William S. Graves to Adjutant General Peter Harris, May
4, 492–93; Arthur S. Link, ed., *The Papers of Woodrow Wilson* (Princeton, N.J.: Princ-
eton University Press, 1966–1994), William S. Graves to Adjutant General Peter
Harris, May 4, 1919, vol. 58, 570.

3. U.S. Department of State, *Foreign Relations, Russia, 1919*, Boris Bakhmetev to
Robert Lansing, May 10, 495–96; Henri de Bach to DeWitt C. Poole, October 13,
531.

4. William S. Graves, *America's Siberian Adventure, 1918–1920* (New York:
Cape and Smith, 1931), 110, 112; Link, *Papers of Woodrow Wilson*, Fred McAver
and Others to Wilson, August 20, 1919, vol. 62, 433–34; Norman E. Saul, *War and
Revolution: The United States and Russia, 1914–1921* (Lawrence: University Press of
Kansas, 2001), 326. According to Secretary of War Newton Baker, 8,477 American
soldiers, including support personnel, were stationed in Siberia in September 1919.
See Robert K. Murray, *Red Scare: A Study of National Hysteria, 1919–1920* (New
York: McGraw-Hill, 1955), 45.

5. U.S. Department of State, *Foreign Relations, Russia, 1919*, John K. Caldwell to
Robert Lansing, March 3, 473; William S. Graves to Adjutant General Peter Harris,
May 4, 492; Clerk to Robert Lansing, May 19, 499–500.

6. Ibid., Frank L. Polk to Commission to Negotiate Peace, May 9, 494; Robert J.
Maddox, *The Unknown War with Russia: Wilson's Siberian Intervention* (San Rafael,
Calif.: Presidio, 1977), 125.

7. Link, *Papers of Woodrow Wilson*, Newton D. Baker to Wilson, May 21, 1919,
vol. 59, 409–10; Graves, *America's Siberian Adventure*, 159–60.

8. Link, *Papers of Woodrow Wilson*, Robert Lansing to Wilson, March 22, 1919,
vol. 56, 184; Carol Willcox Melton, *Between War and Peace: Woodrow Wilson and
the American Expeditionary Force in Siberia, 1918–1921* (Macon, Ga.: Mercer University Press, 2001), 47; Graves, *America's Siberian Adventure*, 160; U.S. Department of

State, *Foreign Relations, Russia, 1919*, Notes of a Meeting Held at President Wilson's House, Place des Etats-Unis, Paris, May 14, 496–97.

9. U.S. Department of State, *Foreign Relations, Russia, 1919*, John K. Caldwell to Robert Lansing, May 29, 504; Maddox, *Unknown War with Russia*, 100; Graves, *America's Siberian Adventure*, 188.

10. Maddox, *Unknown War with Russia*, 101–3; Robert L. Willett, *Russian Sideshow: America's Undeclared War, 1918–1920* (Washington, D.C.: Brassey's, 2003), 227–29, 237.

11. Melton, *Between War and Peace*, 177; N. G. O. Pereira, *White Siberia: The Politics of Civil War* (Montreal: McGill-Queen's University Press, 1996), 157–68.

12. Graves, *America's Siberian Adventure*, 241–42, 246; Roy MacLaren, *Canadians in Russia, 1918–1919* (Toronto: Macmillan of Canada, 1976), 277; Link, *Papers of Woodrow Wilson*, William S. Graves to Adjutant General Peter Harris, June 21, 1919, vol. 62, 84–86.

13. Graves, *America's Siberian Adventure*, 127–29; Willett, *Russian Sideshow*, 182–83; R. Ernest Dupuy, *Perish by the Sword: The Czechoslovakian Anabasis and Our Supporting Campaigns in North Russia and Siberia, 1918–1920* (Harrisburg, Pa.: Military Service Publishing, 1939), 236.

14. Graves, *America's Siberian Adventure*, 266; Ilya Somin, *Stillborn Crusade: The Tragic Failure of Western Intervention in the Russian Civil War, 1918–1920* (New Brunswick, N.J.: Transaction, 1996), 149.

15. Graves, *America's Siberian Adventure*, 169–71.

16. Ibid., 171–73.

17. Ibid., 147, 153–55.

18. Ibid., 156, 238.

19. Ibid., 214, 248, 317, 325.

20. Ibid., 103, 110.

21. Ibid., 117–18.

22. Ibid., 287.

23. Ibid., 104–5; U.S. Department of State, *Papers Relating to the Foreign Relations of the United States, Russia, 1918* (Washington, D.C.: Government Printing Office, 1931–1932; reprint, New York: Kraus, 1969), Alfred Thomson to Robert Lansing, December 9, vol. 2, 457; U.S. Department of State, *Foreign Relations, Russia, 1919*, Colonel Robert Eichelberger to Director of Military Intelligence, March 31, 486; Paul S. Reinsch to Robert Lansing, May 18, 499; August 8, 514.

24. U.S. Department of State, *Foreign Relations, Russia, 1919*, William S. Graves to Adjutant General Peter Harris, February 25, 469–72; Roland S. Morris to Frank L. Polk, March 8, 475–78; Frank L. Polk to John K. Caldwell, March 8, 478; Frank L. Polk to Commission to Negotiate Peace, March 18, 482; May 14, 497.

25. Ibid., Charles H. Smith to Frank L. Polk, July 15, 511; Paul S. Reinsch to Robert Lansing, August 8, 513; Roland S. Morris to Robert Lansing, August 14, 514; William S. Graves to Adjutant General Peter Harris, September 27, 521; John K. Caldwell to Robert Lansing, September 30, 522–23; Robert Lansing to Ernest L. Harris, October 3, 526; Henri de Bach to DeWitt C. Poole, October 13, 530.

26. Ibid., William S. Graves to Adjutant General Peter Harris, June 26, 508–9.

27. Graves, *America's Siberian Adventure*, 255.

28. U.S. Department of State, *Foreign Relations, Russia, 1919*, William S. Graves to Adjutant General Peter Harris, September 16, 515.

29. Graves, *America's Siberian Adventure*, 259–61.

30. U.S. Department of State, *Foreign Relations, Russia, 1919*, Adjutant General Peter Harris to William S. Graves, September 26, 519; Maddox, *Unknown War with Russia*, 108–9; Graves, *America's Siberian Adventure*, 257–58.

31. U.S. Department of State, *Foreign Relations, Russia, 1919*, Robert Lansing to Ernest L. Harris, October 2, 525; Charles H. Smith to Robert Lansing, October 8, 527–28; Graves, *America's Siberian Adventure*, 251.

32. Graves, *America's Siberian Adventure*, 260–61.

33. Ibid., 261–62; U.S. Department of State, *Foreign Relations, Russia, 1919*, Charles H. Smith to Robert Lansing, October 26, 539; Charles D. Tenney to Robert Lansing, October 29, 541.

34. Graves, *America's Siberian Adventure*, 263–65; Willett, *Russian Sideshow*, 259–60, 268.

35. U.S. Department of State, *Foreign Relations, Russia, 1919*, William S. Graves to Adjutant General Peter Harris, July 10, 206–7; Paul S. Reinsch to Frank L. Polk, July 19, 209; Robert Lansing to Commission to Negotiate Peace, August 29, 212–13.

36. Richard Goldhurst, *The Midnight War: The American Intervention in Russia, 1918–1920* (New York: McGraw-Hill, 1978), 231, 264–65; Maddox, *Unknown War with Russia*, 110, 125; Richard Luckett, *The White Generals: An Account of the White Movement and the Russian Civil War* (New York: Viking, 1971), 322; Peter Fleming, *The Fate of Admiral Kolchak* (London: Rupert Hart-Davis, 1963), 166; Somin, *Stillborn Crusade*, 64–65, 165.

37. Goldhurst, *Midnight War*, 234; Melton, *Between War and Peace*, 200; Pereira, *White Siberia*, 130.

38. U.S. Department of State, *Foreign Relations, Russia, 1919*, Charles D. Tenney to Robert Lansing, November 17, 545; David Macgowan to Robert Lansing, November 17, 546–47; November 18, 547; Goldhurst, *Midnight War*, 239, 241; Luckett, *White Generals*, 310; Dupuy, *Perish by the Sword*, 253.

39. U.S. Department of State, *Foreign Relations, Russia, 1919*, Robert Lansing to Norman H. Davis, November 24, 124–25; John W. Davis to Robert Lansing, November 28, 125; Norman Hapgood to Robert Lansing, November 30, 126–27; December 2, 127; Charles D. Tenney to Robert Lansing, December 3, 229.

40. Ibid., Commission to Negotiate Peace to Robert Lansing, November 29, 126; Robert Lansing to John W. Davis, December 4, 129.

41. Link, *Papers of Woodrow Wilson*, Robert Lansing to Woodrow Wilson, December 23, 1919, vol. 64, 219.

42. U.S. Department of State, *Foreign Relations, Russia, 1919*, John F. Stevens to Robert Lansing, December 24, 232; Charles D. Tenney to Robert Lansing, December 28, 235; December 30, 235; Luckett, *White Generals*, 311.

43. U.S. Department of State, *Foreign Relations, Russia, 1919*, Paul S. Reinsch to Robert Lansing, August 29, 214; Fleming, *Fate of Admiral Kolchak*, 88.

44. Goldhurst, *Midnight War*, 264; Fleming, *Fate of Admiral Kolchak*, 217.

45. Graves, *America's Siberian Adventure*, 91, 317; MacLaren, *Canadians in Russia*, 278.

46. Maddox, *Unknown War with Russia*, 130–31; Graves, *America's Siberian Adventure*, 338; Melton, *Between War and Peace*, 205; Willett, *Russian Sideshow*, 258, 262.

47. Goldhurst, *Midnight War*, 257–58; MacLaren, *Canadians in Russia, 1918–1919*, 212; Dupuy, *Perish by the Sword*, 270.

48. MacLaren, *Canadians in Russia*, 211; Link, *Papers of Woodrow Wilson*, Wilson to Norman H. Davis, July 3, 1920, vol. 65, 492; Linda Killen, *The Russian Bureau: A Case Study in Wilsonian Diplomacy* (Lexington: University Press of Kentucky, 1983), 140, 147; David W. McFadden, *Alternative Paths: Soviets and Americans, 1917–1920* (Oxford: Oxford University Press, 1993), 337.

49. Luckett, *White Generals*, 384, 389; Fleming, *Fate of Admiral Kolchak*, 218.

50. George F. Kennan, *Russia and the West under Lenin and Stalin* (Boston: Little, Brown, 1960), 112; James William Morley, *The Japanese Thrust into Siberia, 1918* (New York: Columbia University Press, 1957), 309; Maddox, *Unknown War with Russia*, 135; Fleming, *Fate of Admiral Kolchak*, 232; MacLaren, *Canadians in Russia*, 212.

Conclusion

There isn't a nation on earth that would not resent foreigners sending troops into their country for the purpose of putting this or that faction in charge of their Governmental machinery. The result is not only an injury to the prestige of the foreigners intervening, but is a great handicap to the faction the foreigner is trying to assist. The moment that the United States took sides in the Russian conflict, which was at variance with the solemn assurance made to the Russian people by President Wilson, her reputation for honesty of purpose and fair dealing was discredited.

—General William S. Graves, Commander of the
American Expeditionary Force in Siberia.[1]

President Woodrow Wilson ordered U.S. intervention in Siberia at a time when the Allied situation on the Western Front was desperate in order to help anti-Bolshevik Russians overthrow the Soviet government and re-create the Eastern Front. As the situation became less desperate and the demise of the Central Powers more certain, Wilson began to see the Bolsheviks and the Japanese as the two greatest threats to the new world order he envisioned. The function of American soldiers in Siberia then became that of ensuring that the Whites received Allied aid and that the Japanese did not absorb eastern Siberia and northern Manchuria. Thus, the Siberian intervention is a prime example of what some have termed "mission creep," the tendency of interventions toward self-perpetuation through the alteration of initial goals.

The Siberian intervention was a complete failure. In the beginning it failed to lead to the formation of a new Eastern Front; later it failed to cause the destruction of the Soviet government and to thwart Japanese schemes in Siberia and Manchuria. Wilson dispatched American soldiers to Siberia based on what he himself dubbed "the shadow of a plan," rather than on a fully formed, rational plan. His semi-mystical, ethnocentric belief that Russians would rally around a foreign force merely because it contained fellow Slavs held little promise of validation even before the British and Japanese rendered intervention hopeless, the former by helping to overthrow a democratically inclined government and replacing it with a regime led by unpopular czarists, the latter by sending massive numbers of troops to eastern Siberia for clearly imperialistic purposes.

If Wilson had set out to do so, it would have been difficult for him to have fashioned for ordinary Russians a more unpopular regime than one dominated by czarist officers backed by the hated Japanese, victors in the recent Russo-Japanese War. The Japanese even went out of their way to increase the Russian humiliation by sending to Vladivostok as part of their intervention force a battleship captured from the Russians in that previous war.[2]

Although Wilson was unfortunate in having such allies as the British and Japanese as his intervention partners, their actions were far from unforeseeable. As noted earlier, British Prime Minister David Lloyd George believed that Wilson was apprehensive about intervening in Russia because he feared that the British desired to replace the Soviet government with a friendly czarist regime; indeed, Wilson was so suspicious that he failed to include the British and French in his intervention plan, though he should have known that such an exclusion would not stop them from sending troops. As also noted earlier, Wilson's army chief of staff warned him that the Japanese would use American intervention as a cloak for their own imperialist schemes. This is precisely what occurred. Without the American invitation to intervene, it is virtually certain that the influential liberal faction in the Japanese government, whose members were rightly suspicious of the intentions of the Japanese military, would have continued to oppose intervention successfully. Once the liberal faction agreed to the intervention in order to please Wilson, the Japanese army was able to use the opening to implement its own preexisting plan for large-scale intervention and absorption of eastern Siberia. Wilson had no one but himself to blame for disregarding the warnings of his own advisers.[3]

The only positive aspect of the entire affair was the behavior of the American military authorities involved in the intervention. Secretary of War Newton D. Baker and U.S. Army Chief of Staff Peyton C. March unceasingly opposed the intervention as both improper and impractical and defended General Graves and his officers against the attacks of the Allies and of the anti-Bolshevik zealots who dominated the State Department. On November 27, 1918, Baker wrote to the president:

> I do not know if I rightly understand Bolshevism. So much of it as I do understand I don't like, but I have a feeling that if the Russians do like it, they are entitled to have it and that it does not lie with us to say that only ten percent of the Russian people are Bolsheviks and that therefore we will assist the other ninety percent in resisting it. . . . I have always believed that if we compelled the withdrawal of the Germans and Austrians we ought then to let the Russians work out their own problem. Neither the method nor the result may be to our liking, but I am not very sure that the Russians may not be able to work it out better if left to themselves, and more speedily, than if their primitive deliberations are confused by the imposition of ideas from the outside.

Wilson's decision to send American soldiers to Russia marked the only significant instance during the war in which he disregarded the advice of his military advisers, and the consequences of that disregard were disastrous.[4]

General Graves and his soldiers reacted to the atrocities of Kolchak's Siberian representatives in the same manner as the Czechs, Canadians, and all other objective observers. They acted according to the best traditions of the U.S. Army. Indeed, Graves's insistence on interpreting the *aide memoire* strictly to forbid interference in Russian internal affairs was probably the chief reason that American casualties in Siberia were relatively low: 170 killed, 52 wounded, which was only about 40 percent of the number of American casualties in North Russia under a much more interventionist British command, though approximately 60 percent more Americans served in Siberia than in North Russia and though they stayed almost a year longer.[5]

The relatively low casualty count in Siberia does not change the fact that extended troop deployments to a distant nation always exact great hardship on soldiers and their families. This is especially the case when troops are deployed to a harsh climate like that of Siberia, plagued by bitter cold in the winter and by disease-carrying mosquitoes in the summer. On August 20, 1919, a committee selected by the families of over 4,000 Illinois soldiers in Siberia handed President Wilson this rather poignant petition:

> The organization which delegates us as a committee consists of fathers, mothers, wives, brothers and sisters of these men in service in Siberia. Our people are poor in purse but patriotic and loyal to this government and have voluntarily taxed themselves to send this committee to Washington to present this petition to you in person.

We further represent to you that everyone in our organization is a patriotic American citizen, that their sons and husbands were ready to make any sacrifice during the war even to the extent of losing their lives, without questioning either the wisdom or policy of sending these troops to Siberia. Since the signing of the armistice and the army of the enemy has been demobilized, we have for the past nine months been hoping and praying daily that our boys in Siberia would be returned to the states.

Our boys in Siberia have made piteous appeals to us to do something to hasten their return home to their loved ones and the land they love. In answer to their appeals, we herewith present to you petitions containing over one hundred thousand names attesting to the sincerity of purpose in which this petition was circulated for this appeal. We have written and petitioned the War Department. We do not intend in this petition to raise or discuss the question as to the motives for sending our troops to Siberia, nor the reason for keeping them there—we come only as human beings with the natural affection for our boys and husbands, and beg and implore you as Commander-in-Chief to return our boys to their homes immediately.

We place our complete confidence in you and feel that we will be able to return to Chicago with a message of good cheer from you to the relatives of the boys in Siberia who are broken in spirit, shattered of health, and those who need their loved ones.

To his credit, the president responded sympathetically, promising to replace roughly half of the draftees serving in Siberia with volunteers before winter. He seems to have kept his word, if the complaints of American commanders regarding the departure of experienced soldiers and their replacement by raw recruits are any indication.[6]

President Wilson's Russian policy did not merely fail to achieve the purposes for which he intended it. As George F. Kennan has pointed out, it was the Allies' unwillingness to accept the Soviet government, combined with their unwillingness to treat Germany fairly, that prevented any kind of stable postwar settlement. World War II essentially began with the Nonaggression Pact between the Soviet Union and Germany, the two powers most mistreated at the Paris Peace Conference. Without this pact, there would have been no German invasion of Poland, which was the official start of the war.[7]

In January 1917 Wilson had declared that World War I must conclude with a "peace without victory" since a punitive settlement with Germany would "leave a sting, a resentment, a bitter memory upon which the terms of the peace would rest, not permanently, but only as upon quicksand." Wilson failed to follow the logic of this prophetic statement for the same reason he ignored his own highly touted principle of self-determination where the colonies of the Allies were concerned, for the same reason that he gave the British and French the Middle East as a spoil of war via the notorious League of Nations mandate system, and for the same reason that he legitimated Japanese control over the Chinese province of Shantung: because he was obsessed with the fear that one of the Allies would refuse to sign the peace treaty or join the League of Nations, the institution on which he rested his dreams of a peaceful world. The irony was that even after all of these compromises, the U.S. Senate refused to ratify the treaty or join the league because Republicans feared that ratification would undermine the nation's sovereignty, an objection the president might have overcome had he been willing to compromise on key provisions of the league's charter. Wilson compromised where he should not have, in allowing the Allies to despoil Germany, and refused to compromise where he should have, with his own nation's senate. Had Wilson held to his principles concerning the treatment of Germany in the treaty, there is little evidence to suggest that the Allies would have carried through on their threats not to sign it or join the league, especially since the United States held billions of dollars of Allied debt and was pouring $100 million worth of food into Europe.[8]

Adolf Hitler would never have won widespread popular support in Germany if the Germans had been treated fairly at the peace conference. There is also reason to believe that the U.S. return to isolationism in the 1920s and 1930s, a development that allowed the fascist dictators an open field for aggression, was partly the result of the disillusionment of the American people with the nature of the peace negotiated in Paris and with the intervention in Russia, especially when contrasted with Wilson's soaring, utopian rhetoric. It was widely asked whether the United States had not fought the Central Powers, entangling itself in European alliances for the first time at the cost of so much blood and treasure, merely to aid the Allies in despoiling the world. Senator Henry Cabot Lodge's chief objection to Article 10 of the League Covenant, which mandated that members defend one another's territory against aggressors, was that it would compel the United States to go to war repeatedly to "guarantee the integrity of the far-flung British empire." Similarly, Senator Hiram Johnson was quite effective in combating Wilson's argument that the League of Nations was necessary to the prevention of future wars by retorting that at the very moment Wilson made this claim, "American youths . . . were being slain . . . in Siberia, in a war not declared by the American people or the American Congress, but directed in secrecy in Paris by what now constitutes the League of Nations." Surely, U.S. membership in a formal league would only result in American involvement in additional interventions around the world to support the British and French empires.[9]

Wilson's policy had equally disastrous effects in Russia. R. H. Bruce Lock-hart, British envoy to the Bolsheviks, wrote regarding Allied intervention, "It was a blunder. It raised hopes which could not be fulfilled. It intensi-fied the civil war and sent tens of thousands of Russians to their deaths. Indirectly, it was responsible for the [Red] Terror. Its direct effect was to provide the Bolsheviks with a cheap victory, to give them new confidence, and to galvanize them into a strong and ruthless organism." Lockhart was no Bolshevik, but his intimate acquaintance with their leaders enabled him to see the folly of those "experts" who wrote them off as a weak rabble: "For months I had lived cheek by jowl with men who worked eighteen hours a day and who were obviously inspired by the same spirit of self-sacrifice and abnegation of worldly pleasure which animated the Puritans and the early Jesuits." The Bolsheviks' ideology, while wrongheaded, furnished them with a religious zeal that made them a formidable foe, especially when presented with evidence that seemed to validate that ideology. The intervention of the Western capitalist powers on behalf of reactionary forces in what seemed a transparent attempt to squelch the Revolution and return Russia to a czarist system certainly seemed to them to qualify as such evidence.[10]

George F. Kennan, a diplomat in the Soviet Union in several different postings, not to mention the architect of the doctrine of containment that eventually won the Cold War, wrote:

> Until I read the accounts of what transpired during these episodes, I never fully realized the reasons for the contempt and resentment borne by the early Bol-sheviki toward the Western powers. Never, surely, have countries contrived to show themselves so much at their worst as did the Allies in Russia from 1917 to 1920. Among other things, their efforts served everywhere to compromise the enemies of the Bolsheviki and to strengthen the Communists themselves. So important was this factor that I think it may well be questioned whether Bolshevism would ever have prevailed throughout Russia had the Western governments not aided its progress to power by this ill-conceived interference.

Wilson himself seemed to acknowledge the truth of this theory as early as November 1920, only seven months after American soldiers left Siberia. Wilson wrote, "As to Russia, I cannot but feel that Bolshevism would have burned out long ago if let alone." Nevertheless, Wilson continued to deny any responsibility for the result, claiming that the real culprit was not his sound policy of sending a small number of troops to protect vital railways, but his blundering allies, who had provoked Russian resentment by their open meddling in Russian politics, ignoring the fact that his decision to intervene opened the door to their highly predictable behavior.[11]

It was not just lower-class supporters of the Bolsheviks who were indignant over Allied support for Kolchak and his cutthroats. General Graves once reported that a representative of the democratic zemstvos told him, "The middle class are bitter against the newly formed Russian troops as they are whipping and otherwise maltreating the people and this resentment may extend to the Allies, as the people believe this condition could not exist if Allied troops were not in Siberia." When combined with the Russian resentment against the Allies for pressuring the nation into continuing its involvement in a devastating world war, this bitterness was profound.[12]

General Graves could see that this appraisal of Russian middle-class sentiment could be applied to the other classes in Siberia as well. He later wrote: "The Siberian people were sure to reason that the presence of foreign soldiers made it possible for the Cossacks to murder, beat, and rob men, women, and children. They are sure to come to this conclusion because the stubborn facts justify it. These facts have been, and may continue to be, hidden from the American people, but they are not hidden from the Russian people. The acts of these Cossacks and other Kolchak leaders under the protection of foreign troops, were the greatest asset to bolshevism that could have been devised by man. The atrocities were of such a nature that they are to be remembered by, and recounted to, the Russian people for fifty years after they were committed."[13]

It is impossible to determine with any degree of certainty whether the Allies might have been successful in overthrowing the Soviet government had they exerted serious pressure on Kolchak to reform his government, since this tactic was never seriously employed. The Allies seemed satisfied with Kolchak's empty pronouncements that reforms would come "when conditions will allow them," conditions that never seem to have arrived. The reward for such promises, which cost Kolchak nothing, was generally more aid. But it must be observed that democratic reforms were wholly repugnant to Kolchak and his czarist clique, as shown by their treatment of constituent assembly members and zemstvo leaders, so that there is no reason to believe that any amount of pressure would have converted Kolchak into Pericles.

Another option would have been for the Allies to have sent large armies to aid Kolchak. The optimum time for such an expedition to have attempted to overthrow the Soviet government would have been in the first half of 1918, before Trotsky organized and improved the Red Army; in fact, some historians have suggested that an Allied force of as little as 30,000 soldiers landing at Archangel and Murmansk might have taken Petrograd and Moscow at that time. But with the Germans threatening to capture Paris and win the war, the Allies were understandably reluctant to release even that number of troops from the Western Front in order to accomplish what for them was at best a lesser goal. By the time the armistice with the Central Powers ended the German threat, the Red Army was much more powerful and could no longer be defeated by a limited intervention. No nation was prepared to pay the vast sums required of a large-scale invasion of Soviet Russia, and few Allied soldiers were willing to fight to restore autocratic rule there. Even if a large expeditionary force could have been organized and financed by the Allies, and even if this force had been successful in overthrowing the Soviet government, there is still no evidence to suggest that the hugely unpopular Kolchak government would have lasted two weeks beyond the departure of the expeditionary force from Russia. In the areas where it operated the Kolchak government was detested, and all the more so because it was being foisted on the Russian people by foreigners. As General Tasker Bliss, the U.S. representative to the Supreme War Council, wrote, "The real trouble in Russia will begin after the Kolchak Government wins out."[14]

Although the triumph of the Bolsheviks in the Russian Civil War was not solely the result of Allied intervention in Russia, there is little doubt that the intervention strengthened the Soviet regime it was intended to topple. Ironically, this outcome was tragic precisely because the Allies were correct in suspecting that the Red Terror was but the tip of an iceberg of brutality of which the Soviet regime was capable. The Marxist-Leninist ideology of its leaders justified absolute ruthlessness in the prosecution of class warfare, which it depicted as the inexorable engine of history, a ruthlessness that culminated in the reign of Joseph Stalin, who slaughtered tens of millions of his nation's own citizens. The outcome was also tragic because it led to the Cold War, forty-five years in which the world held its collective breath over the possibility of nuclear annihilation.[15]

From the study of this and other interventions, it would seem that interventions are impractical when they involve giving aid to autocratic factions. With good reason, such groups are seldom popular and become even more unpopular by virtue of the foreign aid.

Whether it is more practical to aid democratically inclined factions depends on the situation. The Allies had been aiding the democratically inclined Siberian government for months before the Kolchak coup but could not seem to gain much ground from the Bolsheviks. This was due partly to the weak leadership of that government, which seems to have been a common characteristic of the pro-democratic forces of Russia, and due partly to the fact that the Allies' reputation in Russia had already suffered great losses due to their insistence that Russia continue its calamitous war against the

Central Powers, a war that seemed to serve the interests of the Allies rather than those of Russia.

Furthermore, the anti-Bolsheviks in Russia were incredibly disunited. On September 25, 1918, U.S. Consul-General in Irkutsk Ernest L. Harris wrote regarding this disunity: "Time wasted in petty politics. No large grasp of whole situation or ability, even among intelligent classes, to view procedure from an all-Russian standpoint. Their horizon bounded by what they can see from their village church steeples." On November 1, he added: "Dissension and strife exist everywhere among the political and military leaders and the disposition to intrigue and mutual distrust of one another keeps them from organizing under one leadership, and working out a definite course of action. . . . Not even the presence of the Japanese, whom they fear and hate, is sufficient to serve as a factor to spur them to unity." Similarly, after touring Siberia in 1918–1919, *New York Times* correspondent Carl Ackerman wrote, "My own opinion is, after traveling in both Europe and Asia since the first revolution in Russia, that at least seventy-five percent of the people are, or would be, against the Bolsheviki if there were an election held where every one could vote, but this three-fourths majority is not united." In 1917–1920 the Whites shared a common political hatred without sharing a common political ideology. The Reds were fewer in number than the Whites but much more united and disciplined. As one of Kolchak's ministers put it, "There [among the Reds] all elements are subordinated to one dominant idea, one will. Here everyone acts on the basis of his own desire at his own risk."[16]

An excellent illustration of the disunity that plagued the Whites concerns the disputes between the various anti-Bolshevik factions of northern Russia. After the Whites gained control of Archangel in August 1918, their government was paralyzed by bitter disputes between the Socialist Revolutionaries, led by Nicholas Tchaikovsky, and the czarists, led by a Russian naval officer then using the assumed name George E. Chaplin. These two men could not agree on the manner in which their military forces would be organized, who was to command them, or who should be responsible for law and order in Archangel. They even argued about what color should be featured on the government's flag. Once, trying to be helpful, Tchaikovsky suggested that Alexander Kerensky, the former leader of the Provisional Government, might be persuaded to come to Archangel. In response Chaplin declared that if Kerensky did so, Chaplin would arrest him immediately. Chaplin still considered the overthrow of the czar a reprehensible crime. At one point Chaplin kidnapped the Socialist Revolutionary leaders and deported them to a frigid island, from which the Allies retrieved them. By that time, the people of northern Russia were disgusted with this farcical situation and with the chaos that resulted from it.[17]

It would seem unlikely that factions so bitterly divided on fundamental principles of government could have coexisted in a democratic society, much less forged one. If there ever was a golden opportunity for a democratic Russia, a legitimate question in itself, it was not lost in 1918 or 1919 but in 1917 when the Allies pressured Russia's infant democracy into continuing a devastating war. Partly as a result of this Allied interference, by 1918 Russia was an ideologically fragmented society whose sole democratic government in all of its history had failed miserably to secure "peace, land, and bread" for its citizens. In such a context the prospects for a lasting democracy were poor at best.

In retrospect, it seems that perhaps the best that the Allies could have salvaged from the disastrous situation in Russia by 1918 or 1919 was cordial relations with each of Russia's political factions, including the Bolsheviks. Most of the Bolshevik leaders recognized that their regime had serious needs and were prepared to be conciliatory in order to meet them. To be sure, this accommodating attitude may have died once the regime's immediate needs had been met. The ideology of Lenin and Trotsky was fundamentally undemocratic and saw accommodation to capitalist powers as a mere matter of expedience. But it is also true that the results of a cordial relationship between the United States and the Soviet government could hardly have been worse than those of the policy enacted in its place. At any rate, the Soviet government was not any more undemocratic or untrustworthy than the Kolchak regime, to which the United States gave millions of dollars and which tortured and killed Siberian peasants, or for that matter, the old czarist regime, which the United States had recognized for over a century.

From an American point of view, what was particularly tragic was the loss of an opportunity to establish a special relationship with Russia. All classes of Russians, except for the nobility, had long preferred Americans to Europeans. As a result, the Bolsheviks were more favorably inclined to the United States than to the European nations. As late as September 2, 1918, after American troops had already landed at Archangel and Vladivostok, Soviet Commissar for Foreign Affairs Georgi Chicherin, reporting to the Central Executive Committee on the state of Soviet foreign relations, declared, "We have adopted a different attitude with regard to the Americans to whom measures of retaliation do not apply. Although the government of the United States has been obliged to consent to intervention, this consent is merely formal." The committee agreed with Chicherin's policy. In fact, over a month after American forces landed on Russian soil, U.S. Consul-General in Moscow DeWitt C. Poole was still at liberty. He left Soviet Russia of his own will. The envoys of the Allies, on the other hand, were detained and watched closely. The property of a number of American companies, such as Singer, International Harvester, and Westinghouse, was exempted from Soviet nationalization decrees. American diplomats in Soviet Russia were allowed to send coded messages to their embassies. While the world war continued, the Soviet government sold large quantities of platinum, copper, lead, and even guns and ammunition to the United States, sales that kept these precious commodities out of German hands. As late as October 5, 1919, in reply to questions posed to him by the *Chicago Daily News*, Lenin declared, "We are decidedly for an economic understanding with America—with all countries, but *especially* with America" (emphasis in original). A few months later he explained to another American reporter, "We shall need American manufactures—locomotives, automobiles, etc.—more than those of any other country."[18]

Should the United States have sided with the Bolsheviks against the Whites? Certainly not, unless as part of a cunning plan to destroy the Bolsheviks, because this policy would have been as objectionable to the Russian people as the one adopted. By 1918, the only course that offered the slightest hope of a successful outcome was to have remained on speaking terms, if possible, with all Russian factions and to have allowed Russia to determine its own form of government. This is what Russia eventually did in any case, but that determination was greatly influenced by the blockade and invasion of its soil by foreign powers, and these policies greatly antagonized the government that prevailed.

The United States then repeated the same mistake in China, offering $1 billion in financial support to the corrupt and reactionary regime of Chiang Kai-Shek between 1945 and 1949, which contributed to the triumph of Mao, and providing even greater financial and military support to various corrupt, incompetent, and autocratic governments in South Vietnam, which contributed to the victory of Ho Chi Minh. The Vietnam War was a case study in the inept prosecution of a counterinsurgency campaign. General William Westmoreland's conventional "search and destroy" tactics produced heavy American casualties, thereby undermining popular support for the war without achieving meaningful results, and the massive bombing of South Vietnam, including the use of napalm, antagonized the South Vietnamese populace by causing civilian deaths and devastating the countryside. Westmoreland rejected proposals to deploy American soldiers in villages throughout the country, where they might have gotten to know the people, might have provided them with protection from the Vietcong that was essential to securing their support, and might have received invaluable intelligence from them. American support for the Shah of Iran and Anastasio Somoza in Nicaragua helped produce the Khomeini and Sandinista regimes respectively. The fear of communism repeatedly caused the nation that gave birth to modern democracy in opposition to European autocracy to support autocracies the world over.[19]

Yet not all American counterinsurgency efforts have ended in failure. Although the United States lost 4,234 soldiers in the Filipino insurrection of 1898–1902, the United States defeated the insurgents by granting the Filipinos greater political autonomy than they had enjoyed under the Spanish and by rewarding the Filipino elites who cooperated with the American occupation with political posts and business opportunities, the peasants with peace and security. The U.S. Army also acquired goodwill by building schools and hospitals and establishing sanitation programs, which reduced disease. The army's garrisoning of the countryside forced American soldiers to get to know the people, which led to better intelligence. The U.S. Navy helped with fire support, supplies, and the blockade of insurgents. All of these factors helped make this one of the most successful counterinsurgency campaigns in modern times. (Based on this success and others in Latin America, in the 1930s the Marines even published a *Small Wars* manual that suggested measures for winning crucial popular support in counterinsurgency campaigns, while warning of the dangers inherent in them. Westmoreland ignored this volume, which is why its warnings of ambushes by cunning insurgents able to acquire superior intelligence leading to long wars without a clear outcome now read like a dark prophecy of the Vietnam War.) Another success, though admittedly achieved against a much smaller insurgency, was the Allied defeat of the Nazi "Werewolves" who plagued the Allied occupiers of Germany in the months after the German surrender. Allied success against this insurgency, which claimed forty-two American lives between June and December 1945 but only three in 1946, was undoubtedly aided by German war weariness, disgust with the Nazis, and, in West Germany, fear of the Russians. In the 1940s and 1950s U.S. military advisers also successfully helped train government forces from Greece to the Philippines in the suppression of communist insurgencies, though such training notably involved the deployment of only a relatively small number of American military personnel.[20]

Furthermore, in the last decade, the United States seems to have finally learned at least part of the historical lesson offered by events in Russia and Vietnam—not the part about avoiding interventions altogether, but the part about at least attempting to form governments in the nation in question that enjoy some popular support. A real effort has been made in both Iraq and

Afghanistan to hold elections in order to form governments that the indigenous population can consider their legitimate representatives. This does not remove the stigma that is often attached to domestic governments that are defended by foreign troops, nor does it deal with the serious challenge of forming democratic institutions in nations that lack democratic traditions and may even possess cultures that are resistant to democracy, or with the equally serious challenge of uniting nations torn by sectarian and ethnic strife, but it is an element that is absolutely essential to have any chance of success at all.

Notes

1. William S. Graves, *America's Siberian Adventure, 1918–1920* (New York: Cape and Smith, 1931), 82.

2. Carl W. Ackerman, *Trailing the Bolsheviki: Twelve Thousand Miles with the Allies in Siberia* (New York: Charles Scribner's Sons, 1919), 229.

3. For reference to the crucial role Wilson's invitation played in breaking the deadlock within the Japanese Government concerning intervention, see James William Morley, *The Japanese Thrust into Siberia, 1918* (New York: Columbia University Press, 1957), 312.

4. Arthur S. Link, ed., *The Papers of Woodrow Wilson* (Princeton, N.J.: Princeton University Press, 1966–1994), Newton D. Baker to Wilson, November 27, 1918, vol. 53, 227–28; March 3, 1919, vol. 55, 399; Betty M. Unterberger, *The United States, Revolutionary Russia, and the Rise of Czechoslovakia*, 2nd ed. (College Station: Texas A & M University Press, 2000), 260.

5. Richard Goldhurst, *The Midnight War: The American Intervention in Russia 1918–1920* (New York: McGraw-Hill, 1978), 210, 220.

6. Link, *Papers of Woodrow Wilson*, Frank McAver and Others to Wilson, August 20, 1919, vol. 62, 433–34; Wilson to McAver, August 26, 1919, vol. 62, 515; Robert L. Willett, *Russian Sideshow: America's Undeclared War, 1918–1920* (Washington, D.C.: Brassey's, 2003), 175, 193, 238.

7. George F. Kennan, *Russia and the West under Lenin and Stalin* (Boston: Little, Brown, 1960), 121.

8. Ibid., 122; Robert Lansing, *The Peace Negotiations: A Personal Narrative* (Boston: Houghton-Mifflin, 1921), 244–45, 255–56, 261, 267; Georg Schild, *Between Ideology and Realpolitik: Woodrow Wilson and the Russian Revolution, 1917–1921* (Westport, Conn.: Greenwood, 1995), 13, 114; Frank Ninkovich, *The Wilsonian Century: U.S. Foreign Policy since 1900* (Chicago: University of Chicago Press, 1999), 73, 75.

9. Schild, *Between Ideology and Realpolitik*, 114; Ninkovich, *Wilsonian Century*, 74; David S. Foglesong, *America's Secret War against Bolshevism: U.S. Intervention in the Russian Civil War, 1917–1920* (Chapel Hill: University of North Carolina Press, 1995), 297.

10. R. H. Bruce Lockhart, *British Agent* (New York: G. P. Putnam's Sons, 1933), 285, 308.

11. Kennan, *Russia and the West under Lenin and Stalin*, 117; Linda Killen, *The Russian Bureau: A Case Study in Wilsonian Diplomacy* (Lexington: University Press of Kentucky, 1983), 130.

12. Graves, *America's Siberian Adventure*, 158.

13. Ibid., 341–42.

14. Ilya Somin, *Stillborn Crusade: The Tragic Failure of Western Intervention in the Russian Civil War, 1918–1920* (New Brunswick, N.J.: Transaction, 1996), 40; Betty M. Unterberger, *America's Siberian Expedition, 1918–1920* (Durham, N.C.: Duke University Press, 1956; reprint, New York: Greenwood, 1969), 164.

15. For a compelling account of Stalin's reign of terror, see Anton Antonov-Ovseyenko, *The Time of Stalin: Portrait of a Tyranny* (New York: Harper and Row, 1981).

16. U.S. Department of State, *Papers Relating to the Foreign Relations of the United States, Russia, 1918* (Washington, D.C.: Government Printing Office, 1931–1932; reprint, New York: Kraus, 1969), Ernest L. Harris to Robert Lansing, September 25, vol. 2, 387; November 1, vol. 2, 420; Ackerman, *Trailing the Bolsheviki*, 33; N. G. O. Pereira, *White Siberia: The Politics of Civil War* (Montreal: McGill-Queen's University Press, 1996), 174.

17. Kennan, *Russia and the West under Lenin and Stalin*, 85.

18. Leonid I. Strakhovsky, *American Opinion about Russia, 1917–1920* (Toronto: University of Toronto Press, 1961), 78–79; David W. McFadden, *Alternative Paths: Soviets and Americans, 1917–1920* (Oxford: Oxford University Press, 1993), 4–5, 130; C. Leiteizen, ed., *Lenin on the United States: Selected Writings by V. I. Lenin* (New York: International Publishers, 1970), Answers to Questions Put by a *Chicago Daily News* Correspondent, October 5, 1919, 417; Talk with Lincoln Eyre, Correspondent of *The World* (USA), 447.

19. Barbara W. Tuchman, *Stilwell and the American Experience in China, 1911–1945* (New York: Macmillan, 1971), 653, 676–77; Max Boot, *The Savage Wars of Peace: Small Wars and the Rise of American Power* (New York: Basic Books, 2002), 289, 294, 299, 307–8, 316.

20. Boot, *Savage Wars of Peace*, 125–28, 282–85. See also Charles Whiting, *Werewolf: The Story of the Nazi Resistance Movement, 1944–1945* (Barnsley, UK: Pen and Sword, 1996).

~

Selected Bibliography

Primary Sources

Ackerman, Carl W. *Trailing the Bolsheviki: Twelve Thousand Miles with the Allies in Siberia*. New York: Charles Scribner's Sons, 1919.

Baker, Ray Stannard, ed. *Woodrow Wilson: Life and Letters*. New York: Doubleday, 1927–1939.

Baker, Ray Stannard, and William E. Dodd, eds. *The Public Papers of Woodrow Wilson*. New York: Harper, 1925–1927.

Beneš, Eduard. *My War Memoirs*. Translated by Paul Selver. Boston: Houghton-Mifflin, 1928.

Bourne, Kenneth, and D. Cameron Watt, eds. *British Documents on Foreign Affairs*. Washington, D.C.: University Publications of America, 1984.

Bunyan, James, and H. H. Fisher, eds. *The Bolshevik Revolution, 1917–1918: Documents and Materials*. Baltimore: Johns Hopkins University Press, 1936.

Cumming, C. K., and Walter W. Pettit, eds. *Russian-American Relations, March 1917–March 1920: Documents and Papers*. New York: Harcourt, Brace, 1920; reprint, Westport, Conn.: Hyperion, 1977.

Daglish, Robert, ed. *Collected Works of Lenin*. Translated by Clemens Dutt. Moscow: Progress Publishers, 1960–1965.

Degras, Jane, ed. *Soviet Documents on Foreign Policy, 1917–1945*. Oxford: Oxford University Press, 1951–1954.

Fisher, H. H., and Elena Varneck, eds. *The Testimony of Kolchak and Other Siberian Materials*. Translated by Elena Varneck. Stanford: Stanford University Press, 1935.

Foch, Ferdinand. *The Memoirs of Marshal Foch*. Translated by T. Bentley Mott. Garden City, N.Y.: Doubleday, 1931.

Gardner, Lloyd C., ed. *Wilson and Revolutions, 1913–1921.* New York: J. B. Lippincott, 1976.

Golder, Frank Alfred, ed. *Documents of Russian History, 1914–1917.* Gloucester, Mass.: Peter Smith, 1927.

Graves, William S. *America's Siberian Adventure, 1918–1920.* New York: Cape and Smith, 1931.

Hindenburg, Paul von. *Out of My Life.* Translated by P. A. Holt. New York: Harper, 1921.

Ishii, Kikujiro. *Diplomatic Commentaries.* Translated and edited by William R. Langdon. Baltimore: Johns Hopkins University Press, 1936.

Lansing, Robert. *The Peace Negotiations: A Personal Narrative.* Boston: Houghton-Mifflin, 1921.

———. *War Memoirs of Robert Lansing, Secretary of State.* Indianapolis, Ind.: Bobbs-Merrill, 1935.

Leiteizen, C., ed. *Lenin on the United States: Selected Writings by V. I. Lenin.* New York: International Publishers, 1970.

Link, Arthur S., ed. *The Papers of Woodrow Wilson.* Princeton, N.J.: Princeton University Press, 1966–1994.

Lloyd George, David. *Memoirs of the Peace Conference.* New Haven, Conn.: Yale University Press, 1939.

———. *War Memoirs of David Lloyd George.* Boston: Little, Brown, 1935–1937.

Lockhart, R. H. Bruce. *British Agent.* New York: G. P. Putnam's Sons, 1933.

Ludendorff, Erich. *My War Memories.* London: Hutchinson, 1919.

March, Peyton C. *The Nation at War.* Garden City, N.Y.: Doubleday, 1932.

Masaryk, Thomas G. *The Making of a State: Memories and Observations, 1914–1918.* Translated and introduced by Henry Wickham Steed. New York: Frederick A. Stokes, 1927.

Palmer, Frederick, ed. *Bliss, Peacemaker: The Life and Letters of General Tasker Howard Bliss.* New York: Dodd, Mead, 1934.

Seymour, Charles, ed. *The Intimate Papers of Colonel House Arranged as a Narrative.* Boston: Houghton-Mifflin, 1926–1928.

Sisson, Edgar. *One Hundred Red Days.* New Haven, Conn.: Yale University Press, 1931.

Trotsky, Leon. *The History of the Russian Revolution.* Translated by Max Eastman. New York: Simon and Schuster, 1937.

Unterberger, Betty M., ed. *American Intervention in the Russian Civil War.* Lexington, Mass.: D. C. Heath, 1969.

U.S. Department of State. *Papers Relating to the Foreign Relations of the United States: The Lansing Papers, 1914–1920.* Washington, D.C.: Government Printing Office, 1939–1940.

———. *Papers Relating to the Foreign Relations of the United States, Russia, 1918.* Washington, D.C.: Government Printing Office, 1931–1932; reprint, New York: Kraus, 1969.

————. *Papers Relating to the Foreign Relations of the United States, Russia, 1919.* Washington, D.C.: Government Printing Office, 1937; reprint, New York: Kraus, 1969.

Secondary Sources

Bailey, Thomas A. *America Faces Russia: Russian-American Relations from Early Times to Our Day.* Ithaca, N.Y.: Cornell University Press, 1950.

Boot, Max. *The Savage Wars of Peace: Small Wars and the Rise of American Power.* New York: Basic Books, 2002.

Bradley, John. *Allied Intervention in Russia.* New York: Basic Books, 1968.

Coffman, Edward M. *The War to End All Wars: The American Military Experience in World War I.* Oxford: Oxford University Press, 1968.

Davis, Donald E., and Eugene P. Trani. "The American YMCA and the Russian Revolution." *Slavic Review* 33 (Fall 1974): 469–91.

Debo, Richard K. *Revolution and Survival: The Foreign Policy of Soviet Russia, 1917–1918.* Toronto: University of Toronto Press, 1979.

Dupuy, R. Ernest. *Perish by the Sword: The Czechoslovakian Anabasis and Our Supporting Campaigns in North Russia and Siberia, 1918–1920.* Harrisburg, Pa.: Military Service Publishing, 1939.

Ellis, John. *Eye-Deep in Hell: Trench Warfare in World War I.* New York: Pantheon, 1976.

Fike, Claude E. "The United States and Russian Territorial Problems, 1917–1920." *Historian* 24 (Fall 1962): 331–46.

Fleming, Peter. *The Fate of Admiral Kolchak.* London: Rupert Hart-Davis, 1963.

Foglesong, David S. *America's Secret War against Bolshevism: U.S. Intervention in the Russian Civil War, 1917–1920.* Chapel Hill: University of North Carolina Press, 1995.

Fowler, W. B. *British-American Relations, 1917–1918: The Role of Sir William Wiseman.* Princeton, N.J.: Princeton University Press, 1969.

Goldhurst, Richard. *The Midnight War: The American Intervention in Russia, 1918–1920.* New York: McGraw-Hill, 1978.

Guins, George C. "The Siberian Intervention, 1917–1919." *Russian Review* 28 (October 1969): 428–40.

Hanna, William. "American Intervention into Siberia." *American History Illustrated* 19 (April 1984): 8–11, 44–47.

Keegan, John. *The First World War.* New York: Alfred A. Knopf, 1999.

Kennan, George F. "Russia and the Versailles Conference." *American Scholar* 30 (Winter 1960–1961): 13–42.

————. *Russia and the West under Lenin and Stalin.* Boston: Little, Brown, 1960.

————. "The Sisson Documents." *Journal of Modern History* 28 (June 1956): 130–54.

————. *Soviet-American Relations, 1917–1920.* Princeton, N.J.: Princeton University Press, 1968.

———. "Soviet Historiography and America's Role in the Intervention." *American Historical Review* 65 (January 1960): 302–22.

Killen, Linda. *The Russian Bureau: A Case Study in Wilsonian Diplomacy.* Lexington: University Press of Kentucky, 1983.

———. "The Search for a Democratic Russia: Bakhmetev and the United States." *Diplomatic History* 2 (Summer 1978): 237–56.

Lasch, Christopher. "American Intervention in Siberia: Reinterpretation." *Political Science Quarterly* 77 (June 1962): 205–23.

Levin, N. Gordon. *Woodrow Wilson and World Politics.* Oxford: Oxford University Press, 1968.

Liddell Hart, B. H. *The War in Outline, 1914–1918.* New York: Random House, 1936.

Luckett, Richard. *The White Generals: An Account of the White Movement and the Russian Civil War.* New York: Viking, 1971.

Lyandres, Semion. "The 1918 Attempt on the Life of Lenin: A New Look at the Evidence." *Slavic Review* 48 (Fall 1989): 432–48.

Maddox, Robert J. *The Unknown War with Russia: Wilson's Siberian Intervention.* San Rafael, Calif.: Presidio, 1977.

———. "Woodrow Wilson, The Russian Embassy, and Siberian Intervention." *Pacific Historical Review* 36 (November 1967): 435–48.

Mayer, Arno J. *Political Origins of the New Diplomacy, 1917–1918.* New Haven, Conn.: Yale University Press, 1959.

McFadden, David W. *Alternative Paths: Soviets and Americans, 1917–1920.* Oxford: Oxford University Press, 1993.

Melton, Carol Willcox. *Between War and Peace: Woodrow Wilson and the American Expeditionary Force in Siberia, 1918–1921.* Macon, Ga.: Mercer University Press, 2001.

Morley, James William. *The Japanese Thrust into Siberia, 1918.* New York: Columbia University Press, 1957.

Murray, Robert K. *Red Scare: A Study of National Hysteria, 1919–1920.* New York: McGraw-Hill, 1955.

Ninkovich, Frank. *The Wilsonian Century: U.S. Foreign Policy since 1900.* Chicago: University of Chicago Press, 1999.

Pereira, N. G. O. *White Siberia: The Politics of Civil War.* Montreal: McGill-Queen's University Press, 1996.

Saul, Norman E. *War and Revolution: The United States and Russia, 1914–1921.* Lawrence: University Press of Kansas, 2001.

Schild, Georg. *Between Ideology and Realpolitik: Woodrow Wilson and the Russian Revolution, 1917–1921.* Westport, Conn.: Greenwood, 1995.

Sivachev, Nikolai. *Russia and the United States.* Translated by Olga Adler Titelbaum. Chicago: University of Chicago Press, 1979.

Somin, Ilya. *Stillborn Crusade: The Tragic Failure of Western Intervention in the Russian Civil War, 1918–1920.* New Brunswick, N.J.: Transaction, 1996.

Strakhovsky, Leonid I. *American Opinion about Russia, 1917–1920*. Toronto: University of Toronto Press, 1961.

Thompson, John M. *Russia, Bolshevism, and the Versailles Peace*. Princeton, N.J.: Princeton University Press, 1966.

Trani, Eugene P. "Woodrow Wilson and the Decision to Intervene in Russia: A Reconsideration." *Journal of Modern History* 48 (September 1976): 440–61.

Ullman, Richard H. *Anglo-Soviet Relations, 1917–1921*. Princeton, N.J.: Princeton University Press, 1961–1973.

Unterberger, Betty M. *America's Siberian Expedition, 1918–1920*. Durham, N.C.: Duke University Press, 1956; reprint, New York: Greenwood, 1969.

———. "President Wilson and the Decision to Send American Troops to Siberia." *Pacific Historical Review* 24 (February 1955): 63–74.

———. *The United States, Revolutionary Russia, and the Rise of Czechoslovakia*. 2nd ed. College Station: Texas A & M University Press, 2000.

———. "Woodrow Wilson and the Bolsheviks: The 'Acid Test' of Soviet-American Relations." *Diplomatic History* 11 (Spring 1987): 71–90.

Warth, Robert D. "The Palmer Raids." *South Atlantic Review* 48 (January 1949): 1–23.

White, John Albert. *The Siberian Intervention*. Princeton, N.J.: Princeton University Press, 1950.

Willett, Robert L. *Russian Sideshow: America's Undeclared War, 1918–1920*. Washington, D.C.: Brassey's, 2003.

Williams, William Appleman. "The American Intervention in Russia, 1917–1920." *Studies on the Left* 3 (Fall 1963) and 4 (Winter 1964): 24–48 and 39–57 respectively.

———. *American-Russian Relations, 1781–1947*. New York: Rinehart, 1952.

Woodward, David R. "The British Government and Japanese Intervention in Russia during World War One." *Journal of Modern History* 46 (December 1974): 663–85.

Index

~

About the Author

Carl J. Richard is professor of history at the University of Louisiana at Lafayette. He is the author of several noted books, including *Greeks and Romans Bearing Gifts* and *Why We're All Romans*.